XSL Essentials

XSL Essentials

Michael Fitzgerald

Wiley Computer Publishing

John Wiley & Sons, Inc.

NEW YORK · CHICHESTER · WEINHEIM · BRISBANE · SINGAPORE · TORONTO

Publisher: Robert Ipsen
Editor: Cary Sullivan
Assistant Editor: Christina Berry
Managing Editor: Marnie Wielage
Associate New Media Editor: Brian Snapp
Text Design & Composition: Publishers' Design and Production Services, Inc.

Designations used by companies to distinguish their products are often claimed as trademarks. In all instances where John Wiley & Sons, Inc., is aware of a claim, the product names appear in initial capital or ALL CAPITAL LETTERS. Readers, however, should contact the appropriate companies for more complete information regarding trademarks and registration.

This book is printed on acid-free paper. ∞

Published by John Wiley & Sons, Inc.

Published simultaneously in Canada.

This publication is designed to provide accurate and authoritative information in regard to the subject matter covered. It is sold with the understanding that the publisher is not engaged in professional services. If professional advice or other expert assistance is required, the services of a competent professional person should be sought.

Library of Congress Cataloging-in-Publication Data:

   ISBN 0-471-41620-7

Printed in the United States of America.

10 9 8 7 6 5 4 3 2 1

For Robert G. Fitzgerald—*filius est pars patris*

Contents

Acknowledgments

I want to thank the editors at Wiley who have helped make this book a reality. I appreciate very much Cary Sullivan's vision of XML and her perseverance even when the going was tough. Christina Berry was a tremendous help in dealing with day-to-day manuscript issues, and I could always count on her cheerfulness, frayed nerves notwithstanding. Marnie Wielage handled the last details so well, and did an excellent job transforming the manuscript into its final book form. And thanks to my wife Cristi for hanging on and supporting me through a very trying time.

Introduction

Extensible Stylesheet Language or XSL is a member of the World Wide Web Consortium's family of Extensible Markup Language (XML) specifications. It is divided into two parts. The first part, XSL Transformations (XSLT), transforms XML documents into new XML, XHTML, HTML, or text documents. XSLT also depends on the XML Path Language or XPath to locate and help process the various parts of XML documents.

The second part is referred to as XSL alone or, more commonly, XSLFO, short for XSL formatting objects. XSLFO is a language for formatting or styling documents for presentation in a variety of output formats, including Portable Document Format (PDF).

How This Book Is Organized

This book is driven by working, hands-on examples, and it is based on the assumption that, just as you don't need to know everything about a car to drive one, you don't need to know everything about XSL before you can do something useful with it. I also assume that you are like most people, anxious to move forward quickly without getting bogged down in the details.

The book is divided into two parts. Part One, "Transforming XML Documents," explores the transformation part of XSL and comprises Chapters 1 through 9. Part Two, "Formatting XML Documents," provides an overview of the formatting part of XSL and includes Chapters 10 through 12.

Chapter 1, "A Simple Transformation," steps through the transformation of a small XML document with a very simple transformation stylesheet and introduces you to a variety of readily available XSLT processors.

Chapter 2, "XML Output," walks you through the details of producing XML output using the output instruction element.

Chapter 3, "HTML and XHTML Output," guides you through the process of producing HTML and XHTML results, even round-tripping from XML to XHTML and back to the original XML.

Chapter 4, "Getting More Results," explains a number of topics including nodes, patterns, expressions, embedded stylesheets, and calling named templates.

Chapter 5, "Sorting and Numbering Lists," teaches you how to use the sort and number instruction elements, as well as the format-number() function and its partner element, decimal-format.

Chapter 6, "Conditional Processing," shows you how to process nodes conditionally using the if and choose instructions.

Chapter 7, "Variables and Parameters," explores how to create global and local variables and parameters.

Chapter 8, "Multiple Documents," demonstrates how to include or import multiple stylesheets and work with multiple XML documents using the document() function.

Chapter 9, "More XSLT," wraps up our discussion of XSLT with a wide array of topics, including a demonstration of keys and a review of XPath axes, plus an overview of both XSLT and XPath functions.

Chapter 10, "A Simple Formatted Document," introduces you to XSLFO and teaches you how to set up page masters and do some other basics, such as defining headings and paragraphs as blocks.

Chapter 11, "XSLFO Tables, Lists, and More," of course, helps you create tables and lists. This chapter also summarizes formatting properties (there are about 250 total) and briefly explains the XSLFO area model, an extension of the Cascading Style Sheet (CSS) box model.

Chapter 12, the final chapter, is called "XSL Technology Review" and is a rapid-paced review of the terminology and features of XSLT and XSLFO. Glossary terms are highlighted in bold and are explained in a narrative context.

Who Should Read This Book

This book is a learn-by-doing book. It is for anybody who needs to start using XSL today. From the first pages of the first chapter, you will be asked to exercise example after example. As you do so, I think you will find a number of stylesheets that you can adapt to your own needs and purposes. The examples in this book are focused on transforming and formatting B2B-related XML documents.

If you have a background in HTML, XHTML, or XML, that will help move you along faster. If you don't have a markup language background, however, don't worry: The introductory material in Chapter 1 will give you a good enough start with XML that you should have little problem following this book or using its examples.

My aim in presenting many examples is to get you on your own feet as quickly as possible. In doing so, I have left some of the picky little details of XSL until later in the book or have pointed to them in the XSLT, XSLFO, and XPath recommendations.

If you are impatient about getting up and running on XSLT and XSLFO, I think this book will help you get where you want to go in a hurry.

Tools You Will Need

You can run the examples in this book from the command line on either a Windows or Linux platform. The XSLT examples in this book have been tested using the Saxon, XT, MSXSL, and Xalan C++ (or TestXSLT) XSLT processors, which all may be run from a Windows command prompt. You can also use TestXSLT on a Linux command line. All these processors are available for free download. Instructions on where to find these processors and how to get started using them are in Chapter 1. Table 1.1 lists a number of XSLT processors beside the four I just mentioned along with download information. If you are a Java programmer, you can find instructions on using a Java implementation of XSLT near the end of Chapter 9.

There are a handful of XSLFO formatters available at the time of this writing. I have decided to use only Apache's FOP processor because it is free, runs on both Windows and Linux (and other platforms), and generally produces good results. It is not yet a full implementation of XSLFO, but I think it is the best bet overall at the current time.

What's on the Companion Web Site and CD-ROM

You can find the companion site for this book at www.wiley.com/compbooks/fitzgerald. There you will find an archive of the examples files in this book (about 100 of them) and a number of other resources, including links for downloading processors, reference materials, and other useful material. If necessary, it is here that I will post updates to the book and any errata information that comes to light after the book is in print. The accompanying CD-ROM contains all the example files from the book and several XSLT processors.

Let's Get to Work

I must confess that one of the reasons I wrote this book is because XSL is a lot of fun. I know not everyone will reach that same conclusion, but because I have spent my career working with text in many forms, I find that XSL is an irresistible tool for transforming and formatting that text. If you read this book from cover to cover, I think you will agree with me.

I don't know about you, but I believe it's time to stop yacking and get something done. Chapter 1 is the place to start.

XSL Essentials

PART

One

Transforming
XML Documents

Part One explains how to transform an XML document into a new document, including XML, XHTML, HTML, or plain text documents. Chapter 1, "A Simple Transformation," walks through the simple steps of transforming a document, provides a brief review of both an XML document and an XSLT stylesheet, and lists XSLT processors. Chapter 2, "XML Output," considers the particulars of XML output while Chapter 3, "HTML and XHTML," details how to produce HTML and XHTML output. Chapter 4, "Getting More Results," discusses nodes, patterns, expressions, and a variety of other topics including modes and embedded stylesheets. Chapter 5, "Sorting and Numbering Lists," demonstrates how to sort nodes, generate lists, and format numbers. Chapter 6, "Conditional Processing," shows you how to process nodes with if and choose. Chapter 7, "Variables and Parameters," examines how to use variable, param, and with-param. Chapter 8, "Multiple Documents," explores how to include and import additional stylesheets and process more than one XML document at a time. Chapter 9, "More XSLT," wraps up Part One with demonstrations of keys and functions, among many other topics.

CHAPTER
1

A Simple
Transformation

Extensible Markup Language (XML) doesn't stand alone. Additional specifications such as Extensible Stylesheet Language or XSL support the mission of XML. XSL allows you to both transform and format XML documents.

XSL has two parts or specifications:

- XSL Transformations (XSLT) for transforming XML documents
- XSLFO for formatting or applying styles to XML documents

These recommendations are produced by the World Wide Web Consortium or W3C. You can find the XSLT recommendation at www.w3.org/tr/xslt/ and the XSLFO draft recommendation at www.w3.org/tr/xsl.XSLFO is not an official name for the formatting part of XSL, but a commonly used one that I'll adopt in this book to distinguish it from its peer, XSLT. Document Style Semantics and Specification Language or DSSSL (ISO/IEC 10179:1996) is a transformation and formatting language for Standard Generalized Markup Language (SGML) that was a key influence on the development of XSL.

> **NOTE** This part of the book—that is, Part One, "Transforming XML Documents"—covers XSLT. The next part, Part Two, "Formatting XML Documents," covers XSLFO.

XSLT relies on yet another W3C recommendation called the XML Path Language, or XPath. XPath identifies and addresses the parts or nodes of an XML document that you want to transform. It does so by means of what are called location paths. You can find the XPath specification—which became a W3C recommendation on the same day as XSLT—at www.w3 .org/tr/xpath.

What Can You Do with XSLT?

XSLT is a powerful language that allows you to change, reuse, and repurpose XML documents. Here are some examples of what you can do:

- Transform an XML document into a new XML document
- Transform an XHTML document into a new XML or XHTML document
- Transform an XML document into an HTML document
- Transform an XML document into a text document
- From an XML document that stores text in several languages, extract only the parts of the document that contain the text that is in a given language
- Extract many documents from a single XML source file, for example, one ready for print, one for the Web, one for a Unix man page, and yet another for an online help system
- Transform an XML document written in one B2B vocabulary to another B2B vocabulary

These are some of the ways you can use XSLT, but they by no means make up a comprehensive list. I think that's enough of an introduction to XSLT. Let's launch into a working example.

A Simple XSLT Example

First, we need something to transform, namely, an XML document. Here is an example of a well-formed XML document called `order.xml`, a simple purchase order document that is suitable for a business-to-business (B2B) transaction:

```
<?xml version="1.0" encoding="utf-8"?>

<Order partner="06-853-2535">
```

```
<Date>2001-06-01</Date>
<Item type="ISBN">0471416207</Item>
<Quantity>40</Quantity>
<Comments>First order this month.</Comments>
<ShippingMethod class="4th">USPS</ShippingMethod>
</Order>
```

Now we have an XML document; we need something to transform it. The following XSLT stylesheet (`order.xsl`) extracts a bit of information from `order.xml`, namely the content of the `Item` element:

```
<stylesheet version="1.0" xmlns="http://www.w3.org/1999/XSL/Transform">
<output method="text" encoding="utf-8"/>

<template match="Order">
 ISBN: <apply-templates select="Item"/>
</template>

</stylesheet>
```

The resulting output that this XSLT stylesheet produces when applied to the XML document will look like this:

```
ISBN: 0471416207
```

What Just Happened?

We have taken an uncomplicated XML document and applied an equally uncomplicated XSLT stylesheet to it. The stylesheet looked for the `Item` element in the XML source, grabbed its contents, and kicked out those contents as a result. That content is the International Standard Book Number (ISBN) for this book, as the `type` attribute of `Item` hinted.

The big deal here is that you can take an existing document and easily morph or repurpose its content, creating a new document from it. With XSLT, you can, in effect, recycle content, redesigning it for use in new documents or shaping it to fit countless purposes.

From a single source, you can create documents in XML, XHTML, HTML, or plain text. With XSLFO, you can also create Portable Document Format (PDF) documents for the Web and for printing, as well as other output formats. XSLT is a welcome tool for folks who have to manage and reuse information—documents and data—when reuse can save a bunch of time and money.

Now that you have an inkling of how XSLT works and why it's good for the world, I'll launch into the details about the XML document and the XSLT stylesheet.

The XML Document

I assume that you are already familiar with XML, but I'll offer a few words of explanation as a refresher. If you are familiar enough with XML to be able to grasp what is going on in the document just by looking at it, you can skip this section and move on to the next, *The XSLT Stylesheet*.

The XML Declaration

The first line of the document is an XML declaration:

```
<?xml version="1.0" encoding="utf-8" ?>
```

Though it is not mandatory, the XML declaration is commonly used, and it usually is a good idea. It tells the XML processor that is reading the document that it is, in fact, an XML document. An XML declaration is part of what is called the *prolog* of the XML document.

The XML declaration also provides information about what version of XML you are using. If it is present, the XML declaration must include a `version` attribute. XML is currently at version 1.0, as it has been since it appeared on the scene in early 1998.

The XML declaration has two other attributes: `encoding` and `stand-alone`. Sometimes the attributes in an XML declaration are called *pseudo-attributes* because even though they look like them, they are not the same as element attributes.

Character Encoding

The optional `encoding` attribute declares the character set for the document; in this case, it's UTF-8. Values for `encoding` are not case sensitive: `UTF-8` works just as well as `utf-8`. So what is UTF-8?

UTF-8

UTF is short for *Universal Character Set Transformation Format*, and UTF-8 character set corresponds to the UCS-2 (16-bit) and UCS-4 (32-bit) characters sets defined jointly by the Unicode and ISO/IEC 10646 standards. These character sets represent characters in most of the writing systems in the world.

The first 128 characters of Unicode match the US-ASCII character set. Each Unicode character is assigned a hexadecimal value, with 0000 through 007F matching the decimal values 0 through 127 for US-ASCII.

UTF-8 can represent the relatively small US-ASCII set, plus thousands more characters.

In fact, UTF-8 maps each Unicode character from one to six octets (8-bit bytes), whereas US-ASCII characters are defined by only one 7-bit byte each. This means that it is possible for UTF-8 to encode up to 2^{31} characters. If you do the math, that's a lot of characters.

The standalone Attribute

The XML declaration has another optional attribute, `standalone`, which is not shown. This attribute allows you to directly specify that the document has external markup declarations, such as in an external document type definition or DTD, that are not included in the current document. If you leave the `standalone` attribute out, and if you have external declarations anyway, an XML processor will default to `standalone="no"` so you can't get too worried about skipping the `standalone` attribute. That's all I'll say about it for now.

The PI

You can readily pick out a PI by its use of angle brackets and questions marks in its syntax (`<?` and `?>`). A PI is an instruction intended for consumption by a processing application. An example of a PI, not shown in `order.xml`, is called the XML stylesheet processing instruction. (An XML declaration is not considered a PI.)

An XML Stylesheet PI

The stylesheet PI, which, like the XML declaration, is also part of the document prolog, takes this form:

```
<?xml-stylesheet href="order.xsl" type="text/xsl"?>
```

The `href` attribute points to the stylesheet that is to be applied to the XML document. This instance refers to a local stylesheet in the current directory. You could just as well use a URI for a remote resource on the Web, such as the following:

```
<?xml-stylesheet href="http://www.testb2b.org/B2B/order.xsl"
    type="text/xsl"?>
```

A `type` of `text/xsl` indicates the content type, commonly called a MIME type. This alerts the processor as to what kind of content to expect.

If the content of order.xsl does not match the content type, the processor should bark at you.

If you are familiar with HTML and Cascading Style Sheets (CSS), you are likely familiar with this HTML element:

```
<link href="order.css" type="text/css">
```

This element will apply an external CSS stylesheet to the HTML document that links to it. You can learn more about the XML stylesheet PI—and its relationship to link—from the W3C recommendation, "Associating Style Sheets with XML," available at www.w3.org/tr/xml-stylesheet/.

By the way, you can also use the XML stylesheet PI to link an XML document to a CSS stylesheet shown here:

```
<?xml-stylesheet href="order.css" type="text/css"?>
```

We won't be discussing CSS much in this book; however, it is important to know that you can format and style XML documents with CSS as well as XSL.

Order, the Root Element

The first actual element in the document is the Order element. The first element of an XML document is the root element. This root element—also known as the document element—is an ancestor of all other elements in the document.

Order's partner Attribute

You may recognize the value in Order's partner attribute. It's a DUNS number, which is short for Data Universal Numbering System. DUNS numbers were developed by Dun & Bradstreet (www.dnb.com) and have been adopted by B2B frameworks and vocabularies as a convenient way to identify a business entity. Dun & Bradstreet stores information on more than 57 million businesses worldwide.

A Gang of Siblings

All other elements in the document besides Order are children of the root element. This parent-child or ancestor-descendant structure is inherent in XML and is important to understanding how XSLT works. These remaining elements are all children of Order and have a sibling relationship to each other. Figure 1.1 shows you the parent-child relationships of all these elements.

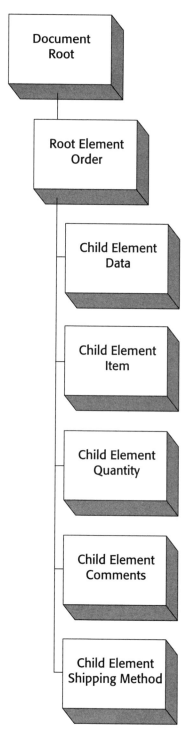

Figure 1.1 Parent-child relationships of elements in order.xml.

At the top of Figure 1.1 is the document root or node. This is the conceptual root of the entire document and is not the same thing as the root element. The first element, Order, is the root or document element. The other elements, Date, Item, Quantity, Comments, and ShippingMethod, are all children of Order and siblings of each other. A sibling has a peer relationship with other elements that are on the same level or that have the same parent.

Elements are also said to have ancestor-descendant relationships as well. These relationships apply when there are intervening element generations, as shown in the following fragment example:

```
<ancestor>
 <parent>
  <child>
   <descendant></descendant>
  </child>
 </parent>
</ancestor>
```

The child element is both a direct child of parent and a descendant of parent. The ancestor element is both a parent to the parent element and an ancestor of parent. On the other hand, ancestor is only an ancestor of child and descendant is only a descendant of parent. These concepts will be useful as we apply XPath location paths and axes in succeeding examples.

Self-Describing Data

The name of each element in this document fortunately gives a hint as to its purpose. This is one of the nice things about XML—that is, that you can name an element or attribute suitably, so that a human reader, as well as a machine, can identify its purpose from its name. It's a sort of built-in metadata.

This, however, is by no means mandatory. You can name elements and attributes whatever you want—as long as you use characters that are legal for XML names—but if you need to communicate and share information with other human beings, it's a good idea to use meaningful names.

OK. That about covers the XML source document. Now on to the stylesheet that transforms it.

The XSLT Stylesheet

An XSLT processor applies an XSLT stylesheet to an XML document. This is one way to apply a stylesheet, but not the only way. Some XSLT processors allow you to submit the names of the documents by using an XML stylesheet PI. You'll learn more about these processors in the section *A List of XSLT Processors*, later in this chapter. Let's have a closer look at our little stylesheet before we go there.

The stylesheet and transform Elements

An XSLT stylesheet is an XML document, complete with elements, attributes, and so forth. The root element of an XSLT stylesheet can be either a stylesheet or a transform element. They are synonymous with one another and have the exact same attributes. You can use either one, whichever suits your fancy.

Top-Level and Instruction Elements

XSLT has two kinds of elements: top-level elements and instruction elements. Top-level elements are direct or immediate children of the stylesheet (or transform) element. Instruction elements represent instructions to be given to an XSLT processor from within a template. Such a processor will know what to do when it encounters these instruction elements. By the time you get done reading this book, you should know them pretty well, too. I'll mention distinctions between top-level and instruction elements throughout this book. A few XSLT elements may be used both at the top-level and as instructions.

The stylesheet I presented earlier in the chapter used the stylesheet element as the root element. You could just as well use transform. Your new stylesheet (order-transform.xsl) would be functionally equivalent if it looked like the following:

```
<transform version="1.0" xmlns="http://www.w3.org/1999/XSL/Transform">
<output method="text" encoding="utf-8"/>

<template match="Order">
 ISBN: <apply-templates select="Item"/>
</template>

</transform>
```

You choose. Either will do. But in my experience, for whatever the reason, I see stylesheet more often than transform. I'll stick with stylesheet throughout this book.

The version Attribute

The version attribute is mandatory in a stylesheet or transform element. You have to use it in the stylesheet or transform elements. The current version is 1.0, but work on version 2.0 of XSLT is underway and will have a different feature set (at this writing, version 1.1, though planned, is on hold; see Chapter 12, "XSL Technology Review," for details). Any good XSLT processor will reject a document that does not contain a version attribute in its root element, along with a valid attribute value.

The stylesheet element and likewise transform have two additional attributes, extension-element-prefixes and exclude-result-prefixes. They both deal with namespace prefixes; you'll learn about exclude-result-prefixes in Chapter 3, "HTML and XHTML Output," and about extension-element-prefixes in Chapter 9, "More XSLT."

The XSLT Namespace

The stylesheet root element has what looks like an attribute but really isn't. The following includes a default namespace declaration, not just an xmlns attribute:

```
<stylesheet version="1.0" xmlns="http://www.w3.org/1999/XSL/Transform">
```

What this declaration is saying is that this element (stylesheet) and all its children fall within the XSLT namespace, namely http://www.w3 .org/1999/XSL/Transform. This is a Uniform Resource Identifier (URI) that acts as a unique namespace identifier. I know, it looks like a Uniform Resource Locator (URL) that should be able to dereference a resource on the W3C Web site, but it's not. You can try it. This is the response you'll get from the W3C Web server:

```
This is the XSLT namespace.
```

Not much of a resource. The use of URL for namespace IDs is confusing, I know, and has been a bone of contention since the namespaces recommendation came out in January 1999 (see www.w3.org/tr/rec-xml-names/) because we are used to seeing URLs being tied to real resources. Perhaps a little more background on URIs will help us.

URIs

A URI is really a superset that encompasses the URL as well as the URN (Uniform Resource Name) syntax (see www.ietf.org/rfc/rfc2396.txt). You probably already know about the syntax of a URL: If you are on the Web much, you use them all the time. You may not be aware, though, of URN syntax.

URNs

URNs provide a syntax to form resource identifiers that can be independent of a resource or a scheme or protocol name. A URN is a unique name that uses the following syntax:

```
urn:namespace-identifier:namespace-specific-string
```

The leading `urn:` prefix with a colon (`:`) can be either uppercase or lowercase. The next part is the namespace identifier (NID). The NID is supposed to establish the syntactic (not semantic) interpretation of the string that follows after the next colon. NIDs, like the `urn:` prefix, can be uppercase or lowercase. The last part is called the namespace specific string (NSS). Here is an example of a URN namespace identifier:

```
urn:testb2b-org:order
```

Now that you understand the basics of URNs, let's get back to the general question of namespaces.

Why Are URLs Used in Namespaces?

One of the main ideas behind why URLs are used in namespace IDs is that a URI can be unique by virtue of its being ascribed to the owner of a domain, such as a Web domain (www.w3.org, for example). The owners of a domain can assign a unique ID, so, theoretically, unique namespaces won't be undermined by a collision with other names.

But, if it is just a unique name, then why use a scheme name, such as, `http://`, which suggests the use of the HTTP protocol? One reason is that the namespaces recommendation from W3C does not forbid having a resource at the other end of a URL; it just does not mandate it, so the URLs in namespaces could legally go either way. The next version of the namespace recommendation, whenever it appears, will clear things up a bit, I hope.

A Namespace Prefix

You can add a prefix to your namespace declaration. The common, conventional prefix for the XLST namespace is `xsl:`, as shown in the following fragment:

```
xmlns:xsl="http://www.w3.org/1999/XSL/Transfrom
```

You are not forced to use the `xsl:` prefix; you can come up with about any prefix you want, but `xsl:` is the common, conventional prefix you'll see in this book and most often elsewhere.

Once you declare a prefix for the XSLT namespace, you have to use it for all elements in that namespace, or the XSLT processor won't know what namespace those elements and attributes are from. Let me clarify this a bit more.

Because a prefix is not specified, this declaration is considered a default namespace.

```
<stylesheet version="1.0" xmlns="http://www.w3.org/1999/XSL/Transform">
```

In a default namespace, the element containing the declaration, plus all of its child elements, are within the designated namespace. When you use a default namespace, the attributes are considered not within that namespace or any other namespace for that matter. One reason is that their scope remains only within the elements that use them.

When you use a prefix, you have to add the prefix to all elements within that namespace. In this case, our next little stylesheet (`order-ns-prefix.xsl`) will look like this:

```
<xsl:stylesheet version="1.0"
xmlns:xsl="http://www.w3.org/1999/XSL/Transform">
<xsl:output method="text" encoding="utf-8"/>

<xsl:template match="Order">
 ISBN: <xsl:apply-templates select="Item"/>
</xsl:template>

</xsl:stylesheet>
```

You can apply the prefix to attributes as well, but that usually is not necessary. You can declare more than one namespace in a given `stylesheet` element (or other elements as well). Sometimes a prefixed attribute from one namespace will be used in an element from another namespace. This is permissible, as long as the namespaces are properly used and applied.

The output Element

The stylesheet in this example uses an `output` element. This element determines how to output the result tree. You don't have to use this element, but it permits you, the programmer, to be precise about what the output of the XSLT stylesheet will be.

In our example, the output is `text`, as specified in the `method` attribute. You can also use `xml` and `html` as values for `method`. Your XSLT processor may be able to recognize some other format; the recommendation allows for it to recognize other names for this attribute beyond text, `xml`, and `html`.

You can also specify the output character encoding for the resulting document with the `encoding` attribute. The example shows UTF-8, but other encoding is possible, such as ISO-8859-1 (Latin-1), UTF-16, or even US-ASCII. Not all XSLT processors support all these character encodings, but you are on safe ground with UTF-8.

The `output` element has 10 attributes; we have discussed only the two shown in the example. You will learn more about the `output` element in the section *Output Methods*, later in this chapter. The other attributes will be discussed in the next chapter.

The Template

I have done a little bit of woodworking in my day. Sometimes, when you want to cut a pattern out of a piece of wood, you can clamp a template onto the wood and then use the template as a cutting guide for a saw or router. This woodworking example helps me understand how XSLT uses templates as well.

The `template` element in XSLT defines rules that are applied to an XML document when the XSLT processor discovers the pattern that the template specifies. The rules usually impose some sort of change to the document, whether a simple plain-text conversion, the addition of new XML elements, a conversion to HTML, or any other change, when the template matches a given pattern.

The pattern is defined in the element's `match` attribute. This attribute, shown in the `template` start-tag, contains an abbreviated XPath location path, which amounts to the name of the root element in the document:

```
<template match="Order">
```

When the XSLT stylesheet is applied to the document, the `template` element instructs the XSLT processor to find the `Order` element in the document and then to process it and all of its children.

The template in our example has a child element called `apply-templates`, as shown here:

```
ISBN: <apply-templates select="Item"/>
```

The `apply-templates` element is an empty element in this instance, meaning that it has no character content. This example shows it with one attribute, `select`. The `select` attribute contains a location path, too: an abbreviated XPath location path for the `Item` element. Because of this, instead of processing all the children of `Order`, the XSLT processor will select only the child of `Order` named `Item` and then process its content:

```
ISBN: 0471416207
```

When you select the `Item` element with `apply-templates`, it resolves to something known as a node-set. A node-set is a list of nodes and can contain a list of one or more nodes. An element is an example of a node. The example stylesheet `order.xsl` returns a node-set with the `Item` element and its text content. The text content is a text node and is a child node of `Item`. Too much jargon? Don't worry: Chapter 4, "Getting More Results," discusses nodes in more detail. You know all you need to know about nodes for the moment.

The value-of Element

Here is another version of our simple stylesheet (`order-value-of.xsl`) that will produce the same result even though it uses a different instruction element called `value-of`:

```
<stylesheet version="1.0" xmlns="http://www.w3.org/1999/XSL/Transform">
<output method="text" encoding="utf-8"/>

<template match="Order">
 ISBN: <value-of select="Item"/>
</template>

</stylesheet>
```

The `value-of` element simply extracts the string value of the child or children of the selected node, in this case, the text node child of `Item`. As you progress through the book, you will learn more about `value-of`.

The Source Tree and the Result Tree

The XML document is referred to as the source tree and the XSLT output is referred to as the result tree. The source and result of a transformation can be documents stored in files, but they can also be some other input or output stream, and they are generally called *trees* rather than files. This tree structure is a well-known data model from computer science. For more information, see the section called *The Tree Data Model* in Chapter 12.

I think that by now you understand the rudiments of how an XSLT processor can transform a document from one form to another. Let's have a look at what XSLT processors are available to you to start transforming documents on your own today.

Transforming order.xml with MSXSL on Windows

MSXSL is a command-line XSLT processor for the Windows platform from MSXML 3.0 that calls the msxml3.dll (see Table 1.1 for details and download information). It is fast and claims 100 percent W3C XSLT recommendation compliance. At the time of this writing, a preview release of MSXML 4.0 is also available.

Assuming that you have downloaded, installed, and placed it within your path environment variable, this is how you would transform order.xml with MSXSL (msxsl.exe):

```
msxsl order.xml order.xsl
```

Given the source files, this transform yields the following result:

```
ISBN: 0471416207
```

If you want to direct output to a file, you can also invoke MSXSL in the following way:

```
msxsl order.xml order.xsl -o order.out
```

You have just created a file named order.out. Have a look at it with this command:

```
type order.out

ISBN: 0471416207
```

These brief examples show you just a few ways to use MSXSL. What if you are on a Unix platform, such as Linux? You can use the Xalan XSLT processor on the Linux platform as well.

Transforming order.xml with Xalan on Linux

Now let's have a go at the C++ version of Xalan on a Linux platform (see Table 1.1 for details and download information). The command-line interface to Xalan C++ is called TestXSLT (testxslt.exe). Assuming, again, that you have downloaded and installed the C++ version of Xalan on Linux and placed it in the path, all as instructed on the Apache Web site (http://xml.apache.org), a command line would appear as follows:

```
testXSLT -in order.xml -xsl order.xsl
```

When you issue the command in this way, you will see the following output:

```
========= Parsing order.xsl ==========
Parse of order.xsl took 0 milliseconds
========= Parsing order.xml ==========
Parse of order.xml took 10 milliseconds
=============================
Transforming...
 ISBN: 0471416207
transform took 10 milliseconds

Total time took 20 milliseconds
```

As you saw in the MSXSL example, you can also direct the output of this command to a file using this syntax:

```
testXSLT -in order.xml -xsl order.xsl -out order.out
```

You created a file named order.out with this command. Use cat to look at it:

```
cat order.out

ISBN: 0471416207
```

You can quiet down the output of TestXSLT with the –q command-line option:

```
testxslt -q -in order.xml -xsl order.xsl
```

With this option, you will see only output like the following:

```
ISBN: 0471416207
```

Now have a look at the command-line processor called Instant Saxon.

Transforming order.xml with Instant Saxon on Windows

Instant Saxon is another command-line XSLT processor for Windows (see Table 1.1 for details and download information). It is written in Java by Michael Kay and can run as Java on other platforms, but the most convenient way to use it on Windows is as a command line executable, that is, as `saxon.exe`. Again, as I show this command line, I am assuming that you have downloaded Instant Saxon, installed it according to the instructions provided, and placed it within your path environment variable. This is how to transform `order.xml` with it:

```
saxon order.xml order.xsl
```

Just as you have seen before, this transform will yield the following:

```
ISBN: 0471416207
```

If you want to direct your output to a file, you can also invoke Instant Saxon in the following way:

```
saxon -o order.out order.xml order.xsl
```

Command-line options such as –o come first when you use Instant Saxon. Again, you can have a look at `order.out` with the type command:

```
type order.out

ISBN: 0-71416207
```

You can do one other thing with Instant Saxon: If you add an XML stylesheet PI to `order.xml` that references `order.xsl`, Instant Saxon can call `order.xsl` with the -a option, without specifying the stylesheet on the command line, as in this example:

```
saxon -a order.xml
```

The prolog in the source would look like this:

```
<?xml version="1.0" encoding="utf-8"?>
<?xml-stylesheet href="order.xsl" type="text/xsl"?>
```

Transforming order.xml with XT

The last processor I'll mention is XT, an XSLT processor written in Java by James Clark, the editor of the XSLT recommendation. It also has a version that runs as a simple executable on the Windows platform (see Table 1.1 for details and download information). It is one of the faster implementations, but it is not 100 percent compatible with the final W3C XSLT recommendation.

Assuming that you have downloaded, installed, and placed it within your path environment variable, this is how you would transform `order.xml` with XT (`xt.exe`):

```
xt order.xml order.xsl
```

The transform produces the following familiar result:

```
ISBN: 0471416207
```

If you want to direct output to a file, use:

```
xt order.xml order.xsl order.out
```

Have a look at order.out with:

```
type order.out

ISBN: 0471416207
```

So far you have seen just a sampling of XSLT processors. There are more where they came from, but these processors—MSXSL, TestXSLT, Saxon, and XT—should be all the tools you need to run the XSLT examples in this book on a Windows platform—or in the case of TestXSLT, on Linux as well.

A List of XSLT Processors

Every day the number of XSLT processors seems to be growing. A list of these processors, along with the URLs from which you can download them, may be found in Table 1.1. I won't be using all these XSLT processors in the book, but I will be using the small variety already mentioned—MSXSL, TestXSLT, Saxon, and XT.

> **NOTE** This not a complete list of XSLT processors. By the time you read this list, it is possible that several other processors may have appeared on the scene. If you are shopping around, it would be a good idea to check the W3C's XSL activity page under the *Software* heading for other offerings, available at www.w3.org/Style/XSL/#software.

Table 1.1 XSLT Processors

NAME	DESCRIPTION
4XSLT	4XSLT is part of Fourthought's 4Suite, a suite of open-source XML and database tools written in Python (see www.python.org). 4XSLT also provides an XSLT API. Both source and binary distributions are available for Windows and Linux at http://4suite.org/download.epy. You can find out more about Fourthought XML Consultants at www.fourthought.com.

Table 1.1   (*Continued*)

NAME	DESCRIPTION
eXcelon Stylus	Stylus is a visual editor for XSLT that also includes a debugger. You can get it from www.exceloncorp.com/products/excelon_stylus.html. (A version is available for free download; however, there is a charge for the production version.)
iXSLT	Infoteria's iXSLT is a Windows C++ implementation of the XSLT specification. You can get it from www.infoteria.com. (Free download; license fee.)
jd.xslt	This is a Java implementation of XSLT by Johannes Döbler, available for free download from www.aztecrider.com/xslt/.
libxslt	Developed by Daniel Veillard, libxslt is a C implementation of XSLT. It is available under an open-source license (GNOME/GNU) and will be included in future Linux distributions such as Red Hat (www.redhat.com). The libxslt library also requires libxml, which is available for download at the same location, namely, http://xmlsoft.org/XSLT/.
MSXSL	Microsoft's MSXSL is, of course, a Windows-only processor. It is small (16 KB) and fast (written in C++). It actually calls Microsoft's XML Parser MSXML 3.0 (`msxml3.dll`). In order to use `msxsl.exe`, you need to install `msxml3.dll` as well. You can download `msxml3.dll` from http://msdn.microsoft.com/xml/c-frame.htm?/xml/general/xmlparser.asp. You can download the `msxsl.exe` processor, plus a few pages of documentation, from http://msdn.microsoft.com/code/sample.asp?url=/msdn-files/027/001/485/msdncompositedoc.xml. (Keep your eyes open for the upgrade to MSXML 4.0 at http://msdn.microsoft.com/xml/.)
Napa	Napa is a high-performance XSLT processor written by Kevin Jones. It has a command-line interface and runs on Windows, Linux, and FreeBSD. You can download it from www.tfi-technology.com/xml/napa.html.
Oracle XDK	Oracle's XML Developer's Kit offers an XSLT processor in Java, C, C++, and PL/SQL. You'll find more information at http://technet.oracle.com/tech/xml/.
Sabletron	Sabletron is Ginger Alliance's validating XSLT processor written in C++ for the Windows NT, Linux, and Solaris platforms. It is under an open source license. You can find it at www.gingerall.com/charlie-bin/get/webGA/act/sablotron.act.
Saxon	Michael Kay has written a highly regarded XSLT processor called Saxon. It is written in Java, so it can run on either Windows or Unix. The Instant Saxon version comes as a Windows executable only. You will find the downloads at http://saxon.sourceforge.net.

continues

Table 1.1   XSLT Processors (*Continued*)

NAME	DESCRIPTION
Unicorn XSLT	Swiss-based Unicorn Enterprises SA produces a standard, database, and professional edition of their XSLT processor, available at www.unicorn-enterprises.com/download.html.
Xalan	Xalan is an XSLT processor, available in Java and C++ versions, for both Windows and Unix platforms. This programming activity is sponsored by the Apache XML Project, which, among other things, also produces the Xerces XML parser. You will find both Xalan and Xerces downloads at http://xml.apache.org. Xalan, by the way, depends on the Xerces processor, so you will get Xerces with your Xalan download.
XML Spy	Altova, an Austrian company, produces the popular XML Spy WYSIWYG XML editor, which also includes Infoteria's iXSLT processor (version 3.5 and later). The download is available from www.xmlspy.com/download.html. (Free download; license fee.)
XMLwriter	Wattle Software's XMLwriter includes an XSLT processor. You can find it at www.xmlwriter.net/index.shtml. (Free download; license fee.)
XT	James Clark, the editor of the W3C XSLT specification, also wrote a Java-based processor to demonstrate how XSLT worked. Just about anyone who has produced an XSLT processor since then has probably consulted Clark's source code, if only to pay homage to the pioneer of XSLT. (Clark, by the way, invented the moniker *XML*). You can download XT from www.jclark.com/xml/xt.html.

NOTE   **XSLT processor performance varies. Before adopting an XSLT processor for wide use, it's a good idea to run some sort of testing or benchmarking to compare performance and robustness. For some help, have a look at Kevin Jones' benchmarking test called XSLBench (www.tfi-technology.com/xml/xslbench.html) or Datapower's XSLTMark (www.datapower.com/XSLTMark/).**

Output Methods

You can use XSLT to transform an XML source into a plain text, XML, or HTML. If well formed, XHTML is legally XML, so you can use XHTML as source and result as well. Did you catch all that? If not, the following list covers the possible type-to-type transformations with XSLT:

- XML to XML
- XHTML to XML

- XML to XHTML
- XML to HTML
- XHTML to HTML
- XML to text
- XHTML to text

What about transforming good old HTML to XML? That won't work satisfactorily unless you first turn your HTML into XHTML so that it conforms to the XML 1.0 recommendation. Then it will work fine.

> **NOTE** Some people say you can transform HTML with XSLT, but I didn't have a thrilling experience with it. If you want to give it go, by all means don't let me stop you from trying.

The method Attribute

Remember what the `output` element looks like? A fragment showing it follows:

```
<xsl:output method="text" encoding="utf-8"/>
```

The `output` element is an empty element, that is, it holds no content. It passes along information to the XSLT processor in its attributes. In this sample, the `method` attribute indicates plain `text` output, and the `encoding` attribute stipulates UTF-8 encoding in the output.

The XSLT 1.0 recommendation offers two other values for the `method` attribute besides `text`: `xml` and `html`. In addition to these three options, you can also supply a qualified name (QName) that will indicate a method that is specific to a given XSLT processor and namespace. By qualified I mean that the name falls within a declared namespace and is preceded by a prefix that is associated with that prefix. A QName has a little broader definition that that, but this definition suits our present purpose. (You can read more about qualified names in Section 2.4 of the XSLT 1.0 recommendation and in Section 3 of the XML namespaces recommendation, available at www.w3.org/tr/REC-xml-names#NT-QName.)

To illustrate, let's say that an XSLT processor such as Saxon supports the Rich Text Format (RTF) output method. RTF is a common format for writing word-processing files such as from Microsoft Word, Corel WordPerfect, or Adobe FrameMaker. Saxon doesn't currently support RTF output, nor does any other processor I know of, but let's just pretend it does. In the following fragment, the `stylesheet` element includes a declaration to the

Saxon namespace, with a prefix, and then the `output` element uses a qualified name (`saxon:rtf`) as a value of the `method` attribute:

```
<xsl:stylesheet version="1.0"
xmlns:xsl="http://www.w3.org/1999/XSL/Transform"
xmlns:saxon="http://icl.com/saxon"/>
...
<xsl:output method="saxon:rtf" encoding="utf-8"/>
```

Again, using `saxon:rtf` is not available at this time, but wouldn't it be nice if it were possible in the future? I suspect such an implementation is not trivial.

A recap of the possible values for the `method` attribute is given in Table 1.2.

NOTE It is best to use lowercase for `method` values. Some processors accept uppercase, such as XT and TestXSLT, but others do not—Saxon and MSXSL, for example. All these processors accept lowercase.

Output Defaults

Using the `output` element in a stylesheet is optional. If you choose not to use the `output` element, the XSLT processor will default to XML or HTML output. The trigger for default HTML output is when the first element in the result tree—that is, the root or document element—is the `html` element, the XSLT processor knows that HTML is the default output method.

The Default HTML Method

There are a few more particular conditions that must be met in order to trigger the HTML default method. The `html` element in the result tree must not only be the root element but also can be in any combination of

Table 1.2   Values of the method Attribute

VALUE	DESCRIPTION
xml	Sets the output method to XML.
html	Sets the output method to HTML.
text	Sets the output method to plain text.
QName	Sets the output method to a namespace-qualified method specific to a given XLST processor. A fictitious example would might look like this: `saxon:rtf`.

uppercase or lowercase, such as HTML, Html, html, or even htML. It must not contain a namespace declaration; if it does, the declaration must be empty or null. In addition, if any text node precedes the html element, it must contain only whitespace. If your result tree meets all these conditions, you don't need to use the output element to output HTML. (You can learn more about the HTML output method in Chapter 3, "HTML and XHTML Output.")

The Default XML Method

To activate XML default output, you don't need to do anything outright. You don't need to use the output element or write a special element to the result tree. By default, the XSLT processor will automatically output an XML declaration, like the following:

```
<?xml version="1.0" encoding="UTF-8"?>
```

As you know, an XML declaration, if used, must contain a version attribute (or what is sometimes called a pseudo-attribute in a PI) with a value of 1.0 (for right now, anyway). The encoding attribute is optional, but XSLT processors normally give you a default encoding, which varies. Saxon, Xalan, and XT default to UTF-8, but MSXSL uses UTF-16.

When you output UTF-16 to an MS-DOS or Windows command prompt window, the output doesn't look very good because of the way the default code page interprets the UTF-16 multibyte characters. On the screen, it looks like there is extra space between characters. If you redirect UTF-16 output to text file, however, it will look OK.

> **NOTE** To view attractive output on the screen with MSXSL, you will have to use the output element with the encoding attribute set to something beside UTF-16, such as UTF-8 or US-ASCII.

Next Stop: XML Output

After reading this chapter, you should have a basic idea of how XSLT works. You just learned how to produce default output as either HTML or XML. In the next chapter, you will learn more about how the XML output method works.

XML Output

We'll zero in on XML-to-XML output in this chapter. First, let's have a look at the XML document that we transformed in Chapter 1, "A Simple Transformation," —`order.xml`, a purchase order suitable for a B2B transaction:

```xml
<?xml version="1.0" encoding="utf-8" ?>

<Order partner="06-853-2535">
 <Date>2001-06-01</Date>
 <Item type="ISBN">0471416207</Item>
 <Quantity>40</Quantity>
 <Comments>First order this month.</Comments>
 <ShippingMethod class="4th">USPS</ShippingMethod>
</Order>
```

We transformed it with the following XSLT stylesheet (`order.xsl`), which extracted some text from the XML document, that is, the ISBN that was the content of the `Item` element:

```xml
<stylesheet version="1.0" xmlns="http://www.w3.org/1999/XSL/Transform">
<output method="text" encoding="utf-8"/>

<template match="Order">
 ISBN: <apply-templates select="Item"/>
</template>

</stylesheet>
```

Applying the Default XML Output Method

As mentioned earlier, to get an XSLT processor to output XML by default, you don't need the output element. Its absence indicates that you want to generate XML output by default.

In the following example (order-default-xml.xsl), let's simply drop the output element and see what happens:

```
<stylesheet version="1.0" xmlns="http://www.w3.org/1999/XSL/Transform">

<template match="Order">
 ISBN: <apply-templates select="Item"/>
</template>

</stylesheet>
```

If you apply this stylesheet to order.xml, you will get a result similar to the following:

```
<?xml version="1.0" encoding="UTF-8"?>
 ISBN: 0471416207
```

The XML declaration looks familiar, but the ISBN below it does not look like well-formed XML. It's just text. Where are the tags? We need to do a few more things with the stylesheet to transform order.xml to a real XML document. We'll start by adding a few literal result elements.

Literal Result Elements

A literal result element in XSLT is created by adding literal text directly to your template in the form of XML elements. If you follow a few rules, this is a simple, abbreviated way to add content to a result tree. I'll show you how.

Following is a new edition of our stylesheet (order-literal.xsl) that adds two literal result elements, shown in bold:

```
<xsl:stylesheet version="1.0"
xmlns:xsl="http://www.w3.org/1999/XSL/Transform">

<xsl:template match="Order">
<newOrder>
 <ISBN>
  <xsl:apply-templates select="Item"/>
 </ISBN>
</newOrder>
</xsl:template>

</xsl:stylesheet>
```

I've also added the namespace prefix `xsl:` to the XSLT elements to distinguish them from the literal result elements `newOrder` and `ISBN`. The result should look something like the following:

```
<?xml version="1.0" encoding="utf-8"?>
<newOrder><ISBN>0471416207</ISBN></newOrder>
```

Now that looks more like real XML, complete with an XML declaration, a root element, `newOrder`, and its child, `ISBN`.

Adding a Namespace Declaration

You can also add namespace information to these literal result elements in several ways, such as adding a namespace declaration to the `stylesheet` start-tag, as shown in `order-ns-order.xsl`:

```
<xsl:stylesheet version="1.0"
xmlns:xsl="http://www.w3.org/1999/XSL/Transform"
xmlns="http://www.testb2b.org/order">

<xsl:template match="Order">
<newOrder>
 <ISBN>
  <xsl:apply-templates select="Item"/>
 </ISBN>
</newOrder>
</xsl:template>

</xsl:stylesheet>
```

When you perform that transformation with this stylesheet, a default namespace declaration will be added to the root element, as follows:

```
<?xml version="1.0" encoding="utf-8"?>
<newOrder xmlns="http://www.testb2b.org/order">
<ISBN>0471416207</ISBN></newOrder>
```

Another option is adding the declaration directly to the literal result element, as shown in this fragment:

```
<newOrder xmlns="http://www.testb2b.org/order">
```

The output would look the same as when you declared the namespace in the `stylesheet` start-tag. You could add a prefix to the declaration, as in `order-ns-order-prefix.xsl`:

```
<xsl:stylesheet version="1.0"
xmlns:xsl="http://www.w3.org/1999/XSL/Transform"
```

```
xmlns:order="http://www.testb2b.org/order">

<xsl:template match="Order">
 <order:newOrder>
  <order:ISBN>
   <xsl:apply-templates select="Item"/>
  </order:ISBN>
 </order:newOrder>
</xsl:template>


</xsl:stylesheet>
```

Your result would then look like this:

```
<?xml version="1.0" encoding="utf-8"?>
<order:newOrder xmlns:order="http://www.testb2b.org/order">
<order:ISBN>0471416207</order:ISBN></order:newOrder>
```

You could add the prefix to a declaration in a literal result element newOrder in the stylesheet and get the same thing, as in:

```
<xsl:template match="Order">
 <order:newOrder xmlns:order="http://www.testb2b.org/order">
  <order:ISBN>
   <xsl:apply-templates select="Item"/>
  </order:ISBN>
 </order:newOrder>
</xsl:template>
```

These few examples should give you an idea of how to produce default XML output. If you use the output element, you can turn out even better results.

More output Element Options

You can produce XML results by default without it, but if you include the output element, you can have much more control over your results. This element offers a number of other attributes to help you. A complete, alphabetized list of the attributes of output is provided in Table 2.1.

Multiple output Elements

It is possible to have multiple instances of the output element in a stylesheet, whether in a single stylesheet or through imported or included stylesheets (see Chapter 8, "Multiple Documents," for more information on importing or including stylesheets). No matter the number, the attributes of

Table 2.1   output Element Attributes

ATTRIBUTE	DESCRIPTION
cdata-section-elements	Specifies a list of whitespace-separated element names that will contain CDATA sections in the result tree. A CDATA escapes characters that are normally interpreted as markup, such as a less-than sign (<) or an ampersand (&).
doctype-public	Places a public identifier in a document type declaration in a result tree.
doctype-system	Places a system identifier in a document type declaration in a result tree.
encoding	Sets the preferred encoding type, such as UTF-8, UTF-16, ISO-8859-1 through ISO-8859-9, and US-ASCII. These values are not case sensitive, meaning that UTF-8 is equivalent to utf-8.
indent	Indicates that the XSLT processor may indent content in the result tree. Possible values are yes or no. The default is no when method="xml".
media-type	Sets the media type (MIME type) for the content of the result tree.
method	Specifies the type of output. Legal values are xml, html, text, or another qualified name. An example of a QName (fictitious) is saxon:rtf.
omit-xml-declaration	Tells the XSLT processor to include or not include an XML declaration in the result tree. Value must be either yes or no. The default, used in absence of this attribute, is no.
standalone	Tells the XSLT processor to include a standalone pseudo-attribute in the XML declaration (if not omitted) with a value of either yes or no. This indicates whether the document depends on external markup declarations, such as those in an external DTD.
version	Sets the version number for the output method such as the version of XML used for output (default is 1.0).

multiple instances of output are merged by the XSLT processor. For example, if you had three output elements in a single stylesheet, such as:

```
<xsl:output method="xml"/>
<xsl:output encoding="us-ascii"/>
<xsl:output indent="yes"/>
```

all three attributes would be interpreted as if they were in the same out-put element. Conflicting attributes are resolved according to the rules of import precedence (see Chapter 8). If there is a conflict in the value of an output attribute and the XSLT processor fails to report an error, it is oblig-ated to use the last value in a stylesheet, based on import precedence. I am simplifying the rules to make them easier to grasp. You'll get more on how the rules work later, but for now, if you had two conflicting attributes in a stylesheet, as in:

```
<xsl:output omit-xml-declaration="no"/>
<xsl:output omit-xml-declaration="yes"/>
```

the last instance (yes) wins out. This is the basic idea. I won't bore you with the intricacies (not yet, anyway).

Controlling the XML Declaration

Several attributes help you control the XML declaration, namely omit-xml-declaration, version, encoding, and standalone. Each of these is explained in the sections that follow.

Omitting the XML Declaration

If your output method is XML, whether by default or by an explicit method type (method="xml"), the XSLT processor will output an XML declaration at the top of your result tree. The XML declaration is not a requirement, so you can drop it if you wish.

You can turn this behavior off with the omit-xml-declaration attribute, as shown in this fragment:

```
<xsl:output method="xml" omit-xml-declaration="yes"/>
```

A value of yes means that no XML declaration will be written to the result tree. An omit-xml-declaration with a value of no has the same effect as not using the attribute at all; that is, the XML declaration is not omitted. This is the default behavior.

The version Attribute

When the output method is XML, the version attribute determines what version is used to output XML to the result tree. By default, the version is 1.0, which lines up nicely with the current XML recommendation. It is not unlikely that this will change in the future, so the version attribute helps you handle that.

The version used to output the XML should be reflected as the XML version number in an XML declaration (if the output method is xml, it is not omitted), but an XSLT processor is not required to do this. In the future, when more than one version of XML may be available, if an XSLT processor does not understand or support the version specified, it should use an earlier version of XML that it does recognize.

If XML version 2.0 were available now (it's not as of this writing), you could use the version attribute to set what version to use when outputting XML to the result tree. Though not required, some XSLT processors reflect this in the version pseudo-attribute of the XML declaration. For example, given the following use of the version attribute:

```
<xsl:output method="xml" version="2.0" encoding="utf-8"/>
```

the XML declaration would show up with this version like this, if you use the Saxon or TestXSLT processors:

```
<?xml version="2.0" encoding="utf-8"?>
```

Again, this behavior is not required, so your XSLT processor may or may not support it.

Character Encoding and the encoding Attribute

The value of the encoding attribute in the output element signals to the XSLT processor the preferred character encoding for the result tree output, values such as UTF-8, UTF-16, ISO-8859-1, or even US-ASCII. Not all character sets are available with all XSLT processors, but processors are required to at least respect the values UTF-8 and UTF-16. The official, recognized set of names for character sets is maintained by the Internet Assigned Numbers Authority (IANA) in a document available at ftp://ftp.isi.edu/in-notes/iana/assignments/character-sets. Many character set names are defined in this document, but only a few of them are available for practical purposes in XSLT processors.

It is all a matter of what you want to do. Most processors support UTF-8 by default, which is a pretty good all-around encoding scheme (see the section titled *UTF-8* in Chapter 1). Both MSXSL and TestXSLT support UTF-16 and US-ASCII, but Saxon and XT do not support either of them. MSXSL, TestXSLT, and Saxon appear to support Japanese character sets such as

ISO-2022-JP and Shift_JP, but XT does not. If your XML is marked up with a Western European language, you will likely be perfectly satisfied with UTF-8.

As you can probably guess, and have already seen, you specify the `encoding` attribute as shown in the following fragment:

```
<xsl:output method="xml" encoding="ISO-2022-JP"/>
```

producing the following output to an XML declaration as the result:

```
<?xml version="1.0" encoding="ISO-2022-JP"?>
```

Adding the standalone Pseudo-Attribute

As you read in Chapter 1, the `standalone` pseudo-attribute in an XML declaration lets you state explicitly whether the document depends on external markup declarations—such as those found in an external document type definition (DTD) pointed to by a document type declaration (such as `<!DOCTYPE Order SYSTEM "Order.dtd">`). The value `yes` is the default, meaning that the document is standalone and does not depend on external markup. The absence of `standalone` in an XML declaration indicates the default setting (`yes`).

If you include the `standalone` attribute in the `output` element, as shown here:

```
<xsl:output method="xml" standalone="no"/>
```

then the XML declaration will appear in the result tree as follows:

```
<?xml version="1.0" standalone="no"?>
```

If the XML document is not standalone, then it is more than likely that your result tree will include a document type declaration, such as this one:

```
<!DOCTYPE order SYSTEM "order.dtd">
```

Several `output` attributes give you some control over the document type declaration that winds up in your result tree.

Controlling the Document Type Declaration

Two attributes of `output` specify either a system or public identifier for a DTD. A system identifier (`doctype-system`) points to a document type definition or DTD that is either a remote or a local file. A public identifier (doctype-public) is a general ID mechanism that identifies a broad and often formally accepted standard.

For example, if the output element has a doctype-system attribute as shown in the following fragment:

```
<xsl:output method="xml" doctype-system="order.dtd" />
```

the result tree will reflect this with the following document type declaration:

```
<!DOCTYPE Order SYSTEM "order.dtd">
```

The document element Order is represented just as it is in the result tree. If it is qualified with a namespace prefix, then it will appear with a prefix in the document type declaration, like so:

```
<!DOCTYPE order:Order SYSTEM "order.dtd">
```

You might also use a remote DTD, as this fragment shows:

```
<xsl:output method="xml"
doctype-system="http://www.testb2b.org/B2B/order.dtd"/>
```

which would yield the following:

```
<!DOCTYPE Order SYSTEM "http://www.testb2b.org/B2B/order.dtd">
```

XHTML, for example, may be identified with a public identifier. The following is a public identifier for the transitional DTD that is associated with XHTML 1.0:

```
-//W3C/DTD XHTML 1.0 Transitional//EN
```

I offer a few lines here to explain a breakdown of this public identifier, moving from left to right:

- The minus sign (–) indicates that this identifier is not registered with the International Standards Organization (ISO). If this identifier were registered with ISO, you would use a plus sign (+). Otherwise, you use a minus sign.

- Two slashes (//) follow and then the name of the owner of the DTD—in this case, it's the World Wide Web Consortium (W3C).

- Following the owner name is a slash followed by a description, as in "DTD XHTML 1.0 Transitional." This can include spaces, as you can see, but it should be brief.

■ Finally come another pair of slashes and the language identifier EN for English, an ISO 639 two-letter language code.

This should give you the basic idea. An XML processor that recognizes a public identifier like this will know how to find the DTD, though the resource path, whether local or remote, may be hidden from the view of users. To see how this works, you could add a `doctype-public` attribute to the `output` element, as shown here, with a public identifier:

```
<xsl:output method="xml" doctype-public="-//TestB2B/DTD Order 1.0//EN"/>
```

This attribute/value pair would produce a document type declaration that looks something like this:

```
<!DOCTYPE Order PUBLIC "-//TestB2B/DTD Order 1.0//EN">
```

If your stylesheet includes both the `doctype-public` and `doctype-system` attributes, such as this:

```
<xsl:output method="xml"
doctype-public="-//TestB2B/DTD Order 1.0//EN"
doctype-system="http://www.testb2b.org/B2B/order.dtd" />
```

you can expect output like the following (which includes both IDs):

```
<!DOCTYPE Order PUBLIC "-//TestB2B/DTD Order 1.0//EN"
"http://www.testb2b.org/B2B/order.dtd">
```

Indenting Output

You no doubt noticed earlier this XML result tree, produced by applying `order-literal.xsl` to `order.xml`:

```
<?xml version="1.0" encoding="utf-8"?>
<newOrder><ISBN>0471416207</ISBN></newOrder>
```

You can produce a more shapely result by adding the `indent` attribute to your `output` element. XSLT processors are not required to add white-space or indentation to a result tree, even if `indent` is set to `yes`, but all the processors tested with the examples in this book do make the XML output more attractive when you use `indent` with the value `yes`. For example, if your stylesheet includes the following:

```
<xsl:output method="xml" encoding="utf-8" indent="yes"/>
```

and you use Saxon to transform `order.xml`, you will get this more attractive result:

```
<?xml version="1.0" encoding="utf-8"?>
<newOrder>
   <ISBN>0471416207</ISBN>
</newOrder>
```

Other processors will give you slightly different output, but all those tested—XT, TestXSLT, Saxon, and MSXSL—break up the result tree nicely with line breaks.

> **NOTE** If you are transforming mixed content—element content that mixes parsed character data and elements freely—from a source tree, using `indent` with a `yes` value may produce unreliable results.

CDATA Sections

In an XML document, a CDATA section protects text from the XML processor so that the section may contain characters that might otherwise be interpreted as markup (such as < and &). XML processors ignore the content within CDATA sections, which start with `<![CDATA[` and end with `]]>`.

The `cdata-section-elements` attribute has as a value a list of whitespace-separated element names from among the elements in the result tree. These elements (one or more) are simply permitted to allow their content to be escaped by a CDATA section. Without this designation, any CDATA sections in the content of an element—in an element's text node—are dropped. For example, given this instance of `output`:

```
<xsl:output method="xml" cdata-section-elements="order:Publisher" />
```

the transformation would permit a CDATA section to be passed from source to result, such as this:

```
<order:Publisher>The book is published by <![CDATA[John Wiley &
Sons]]></order:Publisher>
```

Media Type

By default, XSLT assigns a media type to an XML result tree of the type `text/xml`. You can control the media type for a result tree with the `media-type` attribute of `output`. You do so by the following markup:

```
<xsl:output method="xml" media-type="application/xml"/>
```

You will not see the value of the `media-type` attribute in the result tree, but the value is made available to the XSLT processor.

An Example Using the output Element

Now that you have got acquainted with the attributes of output, let's apply the following stylesheet (order-output.xsl), which uses a number of output's attributes to order.xml:

```
<xsl:stylesheet version="1.0"
xmlns:xsl="http://www.w3.org/1999/XSL/Transform"
xmlns:order="http://www.testb2b.org/order">
<xsl:output method="xml" encoding="utf-8" indent="yes" standalone="no"
omit-xml-declaration="no" doctype-system="neworder.dtd" />

<xsl:template match="Order">
 <order:newOrder>
  <order:ISBN>
   <xsl:apply-templates select="Item"/>
  </order:ISBN>
 </order:newOrder>
</xsl:template>

</xsl:stylesheet>
```

The result tree should look close to the following:

```
<?xml version="1.0" encoding="utf-8" standalone="no"?>
<!DOCTYPE order:newOrder SYSTEM "neworder.dtd">

<order:newOrder xmlns:order="http://www.testb2b.org/order">
 <order:ISBN>0471416207</order:ISBN>
</order:newOrder>
```

Creating Content in the Result Tree

XSLT sets forth several elements that are intended to help create XML and other content in a result tree. In this section, I'll discuss several of the simpler elements. They are listed in Table 2.2. Other related elements will be explained in later chapters of this book.

I'll discuss each of the elements from Table 2.2 in the following sections. You'll get an introduction to them here. Most of them will appear from time to time throughout the rest of the book. At the end of this section, you will find an example that uses all the elements mentioned.

Table 2.2   Elements That Create XML Results

ELEMENT	TYPE	DESCRIPTION
attribute	Instruction	Creates an attribute node within an element node in a result tree.
attribute-set	Top-level	Creates a set of attributes that can be associated with an element in a result tree.
comment	Instruction	Adds a comment node to a result tree.
element	Instruction	Creates an element node in a result tree.
processing-instruction	Instruction	Creates a processing instruction (PI) node in a result tree.
text	Instruction	Creates a text node in the result tree.

The processing-instruction Element

You are already familiar with the XML stylesheet PI, as it was described in a previous section. You can add a PI to your result tree with the process-ing-instruction element. The following element placed in a template:

```
<xsl:processing-instruction name="xml-stylesheet">href="new.css"
type="text/css"</xsl:processing-instruction>
```

will produce the following output in a result tree:

```
<?xml-stylesheet href="new.css" type="text/css"?>
```

> **NOTE** You can't output an XML declaration with processing-instruction. You should use the output element to do that.

The comment Element

You no doubt remember what an XML comment looks like, don't you? It looks just like the comments you find in SGML and HTML documents. You can place comments in an XML result tree with the XSLT instruction element comment. For example, the following:

```
<xsl:comment> XSL Essentials by John Wiley &amp; Sons </xsl:comment>
```

will create a comment like this in the result tree:

```
<!-- XSL Essentials by John Wiley & Sons -->
```

The ampersand (&) in the result is produced by the entity reference
& in the source. An XML processor will ignore characters such as &
and <, which are normally associated with markup, if they occur in comment. An XSLT processor, however, will interpret them as markup in a
comment element, so they must be escaped with an entity reference.

The hyphen character (-) alone or in a sequence of two or more hyphens
(--) is illegal in comments, so if it happens to appear within comment tags,
an XSLT processor will add spaces around the hyphens. An XSLT processor should take the following quite useless comment definition:

```
<xsl:comment>--</xsl:comment>
```

and produce a mitigated output:

```
<!--- - -->
```

to keep a downstream XML processor from overheating.

The element Element

In Chapter 1, I introduced you to the literal result element, which is an
abbreviated way to introduce element content into your result tree. You
can also take a more formal approach in adding elements with an XSLT
instruction element called element. Rather than using the following literal result elements—newOrder and ISBN—in a template, as you did
before:

```
<xsl:template match="Order">
<newOrder>
 <ISBN>
  <xsl:apply-templates select="Item"/>
 </ISBN>
</newOrder>
</xsl:template>
```

you can use element instead, as shown here:

```
<xsl:template match="Order">
 <xsl:element name="newOrder">
  <xsl:element name="ISBN">
   <xsl:apply-templates select="Item"/>
```

```
     </xsl:element>
     <xsl:element name="Title">XSL Essentials<xsl:element>
     </xsl:element>
   </xsl:template>
```

and produce the following result tree:

```
<?xml version="1.0" encoding="utf-8"?>
<newOrder>
 <ISBN>0471416207</ISBN>
 <Title>XSL Essentials</Title>
</newOrder>
```

You can see that these elements, as any XML element, can hold character data or other elements as content. You could have mixed content or define an empty element as well.

The name attribute of element has as a value the name of the element being defined; element also has several other attributes, namely namespace and use-attribute-sets. The namespace attribute allows you to include a namespace declaration in the result. If the element name includes a prefix, this prefix will be associated with the declared namespace. To show how this works, given the following instance of the element start-tag:

```
<xsl:element name="order:newOrder"
namespace="http://www.testb2b.org/order">
```

you would see this fragment in your result tree:

```
<order:newOrder xmlns:order="http://www.testb2b.org/order">
```

If you plan to include all elements computed with element in a single namespace, it is best to declare the namespace in the stylesheet start-tag. Any element created with element will be associated with that namespace in the result tree if its name attribute value has a matching prefix.

I'll make this a little more concrete. Given the following namespace declaration and element definition:

```
<xsl:stylesheet version="1.0"
xmlns:xsl="http://www.w3.org/1999/XSL/Transform"
xmlns:order="http://www.testb2b.org/order">

<xsl:template match="Order">
 <xsl:element name="order:newOrder">
  <xsl:element name="order:ISBN">
   <xsl:apply-templates select="Item"/>
...
```

the result tree, shown here in part, will reflect the namespace declaration like this:

```
<order:newOrder xmlns:order="http://www.testb2b.org/order">
 <order:ISBN>0471416207</order:ISBN>
 . . .
```

One more attribute applies to element: `use-attribute-sets`. I will explain this in the following sections.

The attribute Element

Using the `attribute` element, you can add an attribute to an element that is created in the result tree. Let's say that you wanted to recreate from the source tree the `partner` attribute of `Order` in the `newOrder` element in the result tree. Here is a fragment of a template that would do this:

```
<xsl:template match="Order">
 <xsl:element name="order:newOrder">
  <xsl:attribute name="order:partner">
   <xsl:value-of select="@partner"/>
  </xsl:attribute>
  <xsl:element name="order:ISBN">
 . . .
```

The QName for the attribute is `order:partner`; a value for this attribute is computed by returning the string value of the `partner` attribute with the `@partner` location path. The `partner` attribute in the source holds a DUNS number, a value that you want to reuse. The resulting output will look something like the following:

```
<order:newOrder order:partner="06-853-2535"
xmlns:order="http://www.testb2b.org/order">
```

You can add more than one attribute to an element by defining multiple instances of the `attribute` element as children of the element to which you want to add attributes. You can also define a set of attributes that you can reuse with as many elements as you wish. You do this with the `attribute-set` element.

Using the attribute-set Element

Another way to define attributes is with the `attribute-set` element. This element allows you to create a group of attributes and then enables you to refer to that group by name. You can then add these groups of attributes to as many elements as you want.

The `attribute-set` attribute is a top-level element, that is, a direct child of `stylesheet` (`transform`). Imagine that you plan to use a pair of attributes consistently throughout a stylesheet. You would define this group as shown in the following stylesheet (`attribute-set.xsl`):

```
<xsl:stylesheet version="1.0"
xmlns:xsl="http://www.w3.org/1999/XSL/Transform">
<xsl:output method="xml" encoding="utf-8" indent="yes"/>
<xsl:attribute-set name="date">
 <xsl:attribute name="year">2001</xsl:attribute>
 <xsl:attribute name="month">06</xsl:attribute>
 <xsl:attribute name="day">01</xsl:attribute>
</xsl:attribute-set>

<xsl:template match="Order">
 <xsl:element name="newOrder" use-attribute-sets="date">
  <xsl:element name="ISBN">
   <xsl:apply-templates select="Item"/>
  </xsl:element>
 </xsl:element>
</xsl:template>

</xsl:stylesheet>
```

The `use-attribute-sets` attribute of `element` allows you to use one or more attribute sets with an element. The `attribute-set` element also has a `use-attribute-sets` attribute, making it possible to chain attribute sets together. (The `copy` element, the only other element that makes use of the `use-attribute-sets` attribute, is described in Chapter 3, "HTML and XHTML Output.")

The stylesheet `attribute-set.xsl`, if applied to `order.xml`, would produce the output shown here:

```
<?xml version="1.0" encoding="utf-8"?>
<newOrder year="2001" month="06" day="01">
 <ISBN>0471416207</ISBN>
</newOrder>
```

The text Element

A `text` instruction element simply adds a text node to the result tree, similar to literal text added (without using an element). Given a template that produces literal text, such as that highlighted in bold text in the following snippet:

```
<xsl:template match="Order">
 ISBN: <xsl:apply-templates select="Item"/>
```

```
   </xsl:template>
```

you could likewise use the `text` element to create text in the result tree:

```
<xsl:template match="Order">
 <xsl:text>ISBN: </xsl:text><xsl:apply-templates select="Item"/>
</xsl:template>
```

Both the literal result and `text` element templates would produce something along these lines:

```
<?xml version="1.0" encoding="utf-8"?>
ISBN: 0471416207
```

Disabling Output Escaping

The `text` element has an optional attribute, `disable-output-escaping`, that directs the XSLT processor to turn off output escaping. In other words, with output escaping off, an escaped character, such as `&lt;`, will appear in the output as the literal character `<`, rather than just as an entity reference. For example, the following instance of `text`:

```
<xsl:text disable-output-escaping="yes">John Wiley &amp; Sons</xsl:text>
```

produces this text in the result tree:

```
John Wiley & Sons
```

> **NOTE** The `value-of` element is the only other element in XSLT 1.0 that has the `disable-output-escaping` attribute.

One Last Example

Applying the next example, `order-all.xsl`, to `order.xml` exercises a variety of XSLT elements that you have learned in this chapter.

```
<xsl:stylesheet version="1.0"
xmlns:xsl="http://www.w3.org/1999/XSL/Transform"
xmlns:order="http://www.testb2b.org/order">
<xsl:output method="xml" encoding="utf-8" indent="yes"/>
<xsl:output doctype-system="neworder.dtd" standalone="no" />

<xsl:template match="Order">
 <xsl:processing-instruction name="xsl-stylesheet">href="new.css"
type="text/css"</xsl:processing-instruction>
 <xsl:element name="order:newOrder">
  <xsl:attribute name="order:partner">
```

```
  <xsl:value-of select="@partner"/>
 </xsl:attribute>
 <xsl:comment> International Standard Book Number </xsl:comment>
 <xsl:element name="order:ISBN">
  <xsl:apply-templates select="Item"/>
 </xsl:element>
 <xsl:comment> Book Title </xsl:comment>
 <xsl:element name="order:Title">XSL Essentials</xsl:element>
 </xsl:element>
</xsl:template>

</xsl:stylesheet>
```

The stylesheet produces the following result tree:

```
<?xml version="1.0" encoding="utf-8" standalone="no"?>
<?xsl-stylesheet href="new.css" type="text/css"?>
<!DOCTYPE order:newOrder SYSTEM "neworder.dtd">

<order:newOrder xmlns:order="http://www.testb2b.org/order"
order:partner="06-853-2535">
<!-- International Standard Book Number -->
<order:ISBN>0471416207</order:ISBN>
<!-- Book Title -->
<order:Title>XSL Essentials</order:Title>
</order:newOrder>
```

On to HTML Output

This chapter has given you the basics of transforming XML to XML. There's a lot more to learn about this, and be assured that important information will be coming your way as you continue reading. But before I do that, I'll cover the basics of transforming XML to HTML and XHTML in the next chapter.

HTML and XHTML Output

HTML and Hypertext Transfer Protocol (HTTP) are foundational technologies of the World Wide Web. The simplicity and ready availability of HTML and HTTP made it possible for the Web to grow at a phenomenal rate in the 1990s. The idea of replacing HTML with XML is ill founded because it does not take into account how widespread the use of HTML is.

When television appeared in the 1950s, it may have seemed to some that it was poised to take over radio's preeminence, but it did not. In the early twenty-first century, radio is as strong and pervasive, worldwide, as it ever has been, though television, likewise, captures the imaginations of hundreds of millions of people around the globe. Will the electronic book overtake the bound, paper book? Will cellular phone systems crush the plain old telephone system (POTS)? Will Microsoft Word replace Adobe FrameMaker? Based on my experience, the answer is no. Technology advances seem inevitable in our age, but advances do not always mean immediate replacement of earlier technology. Granted, not too many of us use the telegraph to communicate any longer, but email isn't going to replace ground or snail mail anytime soon.

So HTML is probably going to be with us for a long time. It is very widely supported, not only by Web browsers, but also by other applications. If you need to throw something together quickly for the Web, doing so in HTML is about the simplest of solutions. That's why it's mighty handy that XSLT has built-in support for outputting HTML.

It's also a good thing that HTML is merging with XML in the form of Extensible HyperText Markup Language or XHTML. You will learn how to output both to a result tree in this chapter. I'll even show you how to make the round trip from XML to HTML to XHTML and back to XML.

Default HTML Output

In Chapter 1, "A Simple Transformation," I mentioned a few conditions under which you can use the default HTML output method with XSLT, that is, without specifying `method="html"` in the `output` element. I'll run them past you here again:

- The `html` element must be the root element in the result tree.

- The `html` element can be expressed in any combination of uppercase or lowercase, such as HTML, Html, html, or even htML.

- The `html` element should not contain a namespace declaration; if it does, the declaration must be empty or null.

- If any text nodes precede the `html` element, the node must contain only whitespace.

If your result tree meets all these conditions, you will invoke the default HTML output method. The following stylesheet (`order-default-html.xsl`), which invokes the default HTML method, may be applied to `order.xml`. The HTML literal result elements are highlighted in bold:

```
<xsl:stylesheet version="1.0"
xmlns:xsl="http://www.w3.org/1999/XSL/Transform">

<xsl:template match="Order">
<html>
<head>
<title>Order from: <xsl:apply-templates select="@partner"/></title>
</head>
<body>

<h1>Order from: <xsl:apply-templates select="@partner"/></h1>
<p><b>Date: </b><xsl:apply-templates select="Date"/></p>
<p><b>Item: </b><xsl:apply-templates select="Item"/></p>
<p><b>Quantity: </b><xsl:apply-templates select="Quantity"/></p>
<p><b>Comment: </b><xsl:apply-templates select="Comments"/></p>
<p><b>Ship By: </b><xsl:apply-templates select="ShippingMethod"/></p>
</body>
</html>
```

```
</xsl:template>
</xsl:stylesheet>
```

You are already familiar with the `stylesheet` and `template` elements. You also probably know something of HTML, so the literal result elements, such as `html`, `head`, and so forth, shown in bold type, are already in your bag.

The `html` element is, of course, the root element of the document. The `head` element commonly contains a `title` element, plus information that is often hidden from normal view, such as `META` tags or `script` and `style` elements. The content of the `title` element is usually displayed by a browser in its window title bar (at the top of the window). The `match` attribute in the `template` element is looking for the `Order` element in the source document (`order.xml`). The location path `@partner` in the `select` attribute of `apply-templates` means that you want to select the contents of the attribute `partner` in the start-tag of `Order`.

The `h1` element is a level-1 heading that also selects the `partner` attribute. Following that are p, or paragraph, elements. Each p element also contains an inline b element that specifies bold text. A bit of bold text identifies the content of each of the child elements of `Order`, each of which is selected by an instance of `apply-templates`.

The HTML method, whether using the default method or the `output` element, expects that the elements in your stylesheet be well formed, just as with XML. For example, in HTML, it is not uncommon to use a p start-tag alone, without an end-tag. An XSLT processor won't let you get away with that. When you begin an element with a start-tag, it must close with an end-tag.

Likewise, you cannot use the HTML br (break) start-tag alone in a stylesheet, as in `<br>`. Breaks must be specified with an end-tag, as in either `<br/>` or `<br></br>`. Breaks, however, are output to the result tree only as `<br>`. That seems a little tricky, but it will keep your processor from bothering you about it.

The br element is an empty element. An empty element carries no content between tags, but it may have attributes. No end-tags are output for empty elements in HTML output, though they must have end-tags in the stylesheet. In other words, an `img` literal result element, or any other empty element in HTML, must be represented in the stylesheet as:

```
<img src="cover.jpg"></img>
```

or as an empty element:

```
<img src="cover.jpg"/>
```

but the HTML output will drop the end-tag or empty element syntax so that it looks like this:

```
<img src="cover.jpg">
```

Output from `order-default-html.xsl` to a result tree will vary slightly, depending on what XSLT processor you use, but the output will look similar to this attractive result from Saxon:

```
<html>
 <head>
  <meta http-equiv="Content-Type" content="text/html; charset=utf-8">
  <title>Order from: 06-853-2535</title>
 </head>
 <body>
  <h1>Order from: 06-853-2535</h1>
  <p><b>Date: </b>2001-06-01
  </p>
  <p><b>Item: </b>0471416207
  </p>
  <p><b>Quantity: </b>40
  </p>
  <p><b>Comment: </b>First order this month.
  </p>
  <p><b>Ship By: </b>USPS
  </p>
 </body>
</html>
```

The HTML META tag, which was not specified in the stylesheet, is a gift from the XSLT processor. It is output only if there is a head element in your stylesheet, whether by literal result element or with XSLT's element. (MSXSL, Saxon, and TestXSLT output the META tag with default HTML, but XT does not.) The media type of text/html is the default HTML media type, as specified by the XSLT recommendation (Section 16.2), and Saxon's default character encoding (charset) is UTF-8. This media type and character set information in the META tag may be used in an HTTP header field and by a browser in transporting or rendering the HTML document.

As mentioned in Chapter 1, you can use an XSLT command-line processor to direct your output to a file in several ways. For example, let's say that you wanted to send output to a file with any of the four processors I am using in the book. Examples for each follow:

```
saxon -o c:\orders\06-853-2535\2001-06-01-0001-order.html order.xml
order-default-html.xsl

msxsl order.xml order-default-html.xsl -o c:\orders\06-853-2535\2001-06-
```

```
01-0001-order.html
```

```
xt order.xml order-default-html.xsl c:\orders\06-853-2535\2001-06-01-
0001-order.html
```

```
testxslt -in order.xml -xsl order-default-html.xsl -out c:\orders\06-
853-2535\2001-06-01-0001-order.html
```

There is also another simple way to redirect output, just using the redirect switch (>) from the operating system, as these examples show (superfluous with XT):

```
saxon order.xml order-default-html.xsl > c:\orders\06-853-2535\2001-06-
01-0001-order.html
```

```
msxsl order.xml order-default-html.xsl > c:\orders\06-853-2535\2001-06-
01-0001-order.html
```

```
xt order.xml order-default-html.xsl > c:\orders\06-853-2535\2001-06-01-
0001-order.html
```

```
testxslt -in order.xml -xsl order-default-html.xsl > c:\orders\06-853-
2535\2001-06-01-0001-order.html
```

If you were to look at the HTML document as is with a browser (`c:\orders\06-853-2535\2001-06-01-0001-order.html`) you would see something that looks like Figure 3.1.

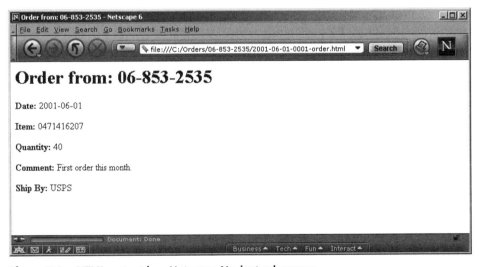

Figure 3.1   HTML output in a Netscape Navigator browser.

Adding Style to HTML with CSS

The output shown in Figure 3.1 does not separate the content and presentation of the document very well. In the beginning, back in the simpler days of the Web, Tim Berners-Lee lumped content and presentation elements together in HTML (such as p with b or i), which is an adequate approach in many instances. XML, in and of itself, has essentially no concept of presentation. It provides a way to describe documents and data, but for the most part, format and style are left to Cascading Style Sheets (CSS) or XSLFO.

Netscape Navigator and other browsers have internal stylesheets that help to render HTML documents. For example, the document in Figure 3.1 shows evidence of that with its use of a serif font and different font sizes, even though the HTML document indicates nothing directly about fonts.

You can improve the appearance of this document by adding some CSS to it. The next example stylesheet (`order-default-html-style.xsl`) adds a `script` element to the `head` element. The `script` element contains a few CSS style rules for the HTML elements h1, p, and b:

```
<xsl:stylesheet version="1.0"
xmlns:xsl="http://www.w3.org/1999/XSL/Transform">

<xsl:template match="Order">
<html>
<head>
<title>Order from: <xsl:apply-templates select="@partner"/></title>
<style>
h1 {font-family:Verdana,Arial,Helvetica,sans-serif;font-size:18pt;text-
align:center}
p {font-family:Verdana,Arial,Helvetica,sans-serif;font-size:12pt}
b {font-size:14pt;font-weight:bold}
</style>
</head>
<body>

<h1>Order from: <xsl:apply-templates select="@partner"/></h1>
<p><b>Date: </b><xsl:apply-templates select="Date"/></p>
<p><b>Item: </b><xsl:apply-templates select="Item"/></p>
<p><b>Quantity: </b><xsl:apply-templates select="Quantity"/></p>
<p><b>Comment: </b><xsl:apply-templates select="Comments"/></p>
<p><b>Ship By: </b><xsl:apply-templates select="ShippingMethod"/></p>
</body>
</html>

</xsl:template>
</xsl:stylesheet>
```

The `script` element, embodied in `head`, contains CSS style rules that instruct a CSS-compliant browser how to render HTML elements with a bit of flair. If you are not already acquainted with CSS, here is a breakdown of the `h1` style rule so that you can get a picture of what is going on:

```
h1 {font-family:Verdana,Arial,Helvetica,sans-serif;font-size:18pt;text-
    align:center}
```

The `h1` is a selector. It selects the element to which you are to apply a style. The information enclosed in the braces ({   }) tells the browser (or some other HTML processor) what properties to apply to `h1` and what values are associated with those properties.

The `font-family` property indicates that the browser should use the Verdana font to render the content of `h1`. If the browser is on a Windows NT machine that has recently had an operating system upgrade (since 1996 at least), it will have no trouble finding this font (such as in the directory `c:\winnt\fonts`). If the browser can't find the Verdana font, it will look for the Arial font, an old Windows standby. If you are not on a Windows box, the first font the browser may find is the Helvetica font, which is commonly available on Unix systems as well as Windows. If it can't find any of these fonts, the browser is instructed just to find the first available sans-serif font on its system and use that font.

The `h1` rule also contains the `font-size` property, specifying a size of 18 points (there are 72 points to the inch), and the `text-align` property with a value of `center`, which will center the element on the canvas (in the browser).

The style rule for p (paragraph) includes the `font-family` property and `font-size` property as well:

```
p {font-family:Verdana,Arial,Helvetica,sans-serif;font-size:12pt}
```

The rule for b (bold) includes a `font-size` plus, for good measure, a `font-weight` property:

```
b {font-size:14pt;font-weight:bold}
```

The built-in stylesheet for the browser will render b tags in bold without it, but the `font-weight` property gives you more finely tuned control. Other values beside `bold` include `normal`, `bolder`, and `lighter`.

If you want to read more about CSS, check out the recommendation at www.w3.org/tr/rec-css2/. Figure 3.2 shows this HTML output enhanced by CSS in Microsoft Internet Explorer (IE).

With all this, we haven't moved beyond the default HTML output method. It's time to move forward.

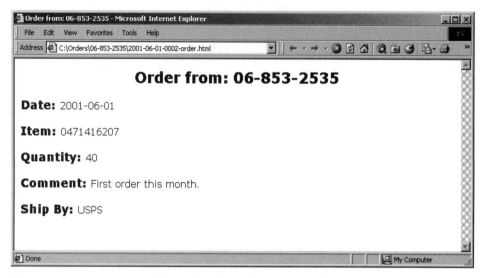

Figure 3.2   HTML output with CSS in Microsoft Internet Explorer.

The HTML Output Method

As with XML, you can get added control over your HTML output by designating `method="html"` with the `output` element, as in the following:

```
<xsl:output method="html" encoding="utf-8"/>
```

The `output` element, of course, lets you explicitly declare to the XSLT processor that you are shooting for HTML output. Having the `encoding` attribute at your disposal is nice, too, because you can call the character encoding shots. If you are using MSXSL, for example, you get UTF-16 output by default, which isn't very pretty in a command prompt window; `output` allows you to change that.

Indenting HTML

The default for the `indent` attribute is `yes`, rather than `no`, as with the `xml` output method. This means that the XSLT processor may add whitespace to the resulting output, as long as it won't affect how the browser (user agent) renders the document. It also means that it will take effect without using `indent` in `output`. Saxon adds a little more whitespace to its output than MSXSL, XT, and TestXSLT do.

Adding an HTML Document Type Declaration

The most recent version update to HTML is version 4.01, available since December 1999 at www.w3.org/tr/html401/. You can add legal document type declarations to your HTML 4.01 result tree with the `doctype-public` and `doctype-system` attributes in `output`. You can do this by adding an `output` element to your stylesheet with these attributes:

```
<xsl:output doctype-public="-//W3C//DTD HTML 4.01//EN"
doctype-system="http://www.w3.org/tr/html401/strict.dtd"/>
```

This will generate the following declaration in the result:

```
<!DOCTYPE HTML PUBLIC "-//W3C//DTD HTML 4.01//EN"
"http://www.w3.org/tr/html401/strict.dtd">
```

This document type declaration is for a strict interpretation of the HTML 4.01 recommendation. The strict DTD excludes elements and attributes that the W3C expects to deprecate or phase out entirely, such as the `font` element. The function and purpose of the `font` element has been outmoded by the `style` attribute and CSS font properties and, in the case of XHTML or XML, XSLFO font properties.

You can also identify the transitional identifiers for HTML 4.01. The transitional or loose DTD includes elements and attributes that are marked for phase out, such as `font`. The following instance of `output` will form a document type declaration for the transitional DTD in the result:

```
<xsl:output
doctype-public="-//W3C//DTD HTML 4.01 Transitional//EN" doctype-
    system="http://www.w3.org/TR/html401/loose.dtd"/>
```

Finally, if you want to use HTML frames in the output, you can include a declaration for the frameset DTD as well:

```
<xsl:output doctype-public="-//W3C//DTD HTML 4.01 Frameset//EN"
doctype-system="http://www.w3.org/TR/html401/frameset.dtd"/>
```

The frameset DTD is identical to the transitional DTD except that in the content model of the `html` element, the `frameset` element is used in place of the `body` element.

NOTE It is possible to output other public and system identifiers in the result tree, but they will not be compliant with the HTML 4.01 recommendation.

The Remaining Stipulations of HTML Output

There are a few other stipulations made by the XSLT recommendation on HTML output. Most of these stipulations deal with what an XSLT processor is required to produce, rather than what you put in an output element. For example, an XSLT processor should recognize the names of HTML elements no matter what case a stylesheet uses—BODY, Body, or body will all do. In addition, the version attribute of output has a default value of 4.0. You can change this value in your stylesheet to something like 3.2, but the value is not output to the result tree; it is likely that your XSLT processor does not support restricting its output to HTML version 3.2. This has interesting implications for future versions of XSLT and HTML.

NOTE If you are interested in the additional persnickety details of the quirks of the HTML output method, such as the effect of the null namespace, character escaping in the script and style elements, and the minimization of Boolean attributes, you can read about all these and more in Section 16.2 in the XSLT recommendation.

The order-html.xsl stylesheet adds a few instances of output:

```
<xsl:stylesheet version="1.0"
xmlns:xsl="http://www.w3.org/1999/XSL/Transform">
<xsl:output method="html" encoding="utf-8"/>
<xsl:output doctype-public="-//W3C//DTD HTML 4.01//EN"/>
<xsl:output doctype-system="http://www.w3.org/tr/html401/strict.dtd"/>

<xsl:template match="Order">
<html>
<head>
<title>Order from: <xsl:apply-templates select="@partner"/></title>
<style>
h1 {font-family:Verdana,Arial,Helvetica,sans-serif;font-size:18pt;text-
    align:center}
p {font-family:Verdana,Arial,Helvetica,sans-serif;font-size:12pt}
b {font-size:14pt;font-weight:bold}
</style>
</head>
<body>

<h1>Order from: <xsl:apply-templates select="@partner"/></h1>
```

```
<p><b>Date: </b><xsl:apply-templates select="Date"/></p>
<p><b>Item: </b><xsl:apply-templates select="Item"/></p>
<p><b>Quantity: </b><xsl:apply-templates select="Quantity"/></p>
<p><b>Comment: </b><xsl:apply-templates select="Comments"/></p>
<p><b>Ship By: </b><xsl:apply-templates select="ShippingMethod"/></p>
</body>
</html>

</xsl:template>
</xsl:stylesheet>
```

This stylesheet produces the following result:

```
<!DOCTYPE html PUBLIC "-//W3C//DTD HTML 4.01//EN"
"http://www.w3.org/tr/html401/strict.dtd">
<html>
<head>
<META http-equiv="Content-Type" content="text/html; charset=utf-8">
<title>Order from: 06-853-2535</title>
<style>
h1 {font-family:Verdana,Arial,Helvetica,sans-serif;font-size:18pt;text-
    align:center}
p {font-family:Verdana,Arial,Helvetica,sans-serif;font-size:12pt}
b {font-size:14pt;font-weight:bold}
</style>
</head>
<body>
<h1>Order from: 06-853-2535</h1>
<p><b>Date: </b>2001-06-01</p>
<p><b>Item: </b>0471416207</p>
<p><b>Quantity: </b>40</p>
<p><b>Comment: </b>First order this month.</p>
<p><b>Ship By: </b>USPS</p>
</body>
</html>
```

Creating an HTML Table

With a little CSS thrown in, the fields derived by transforming order.xml look ragged. You can straighten things up by creating an HTML table in the result. The stylesheet order-html-table.xsl does just that:

```
<xsl:stylesheet version="1.0"
xmlns:xsl="http://www.w3.org/1999/XSL/Transform">
<xsl:output method="html" encoding="utf-8"/>
<xsl:output doctype-public="-//W3C//DTD HTML 4.01//EN"/>
<xsl:output doctype-system="http://www.w3.org/tr/html401/strict.dtd"/>
```

```
<xsl:template match="Order">
<html>
<head>
<title>Order from: <xsl:apply-templates select="@partner"/></title>
<style>
h1 {font-family:Verdana,Arial,Helvetica,sans-serif;font-size:18pt;text-
    align:center}
p,table {font-family:Verdana,Arial,Helvetica,sans-serif;font-size:12pt}
.b {font-size:14pt;font-weight:bold}
</style>
</head>
<body>

<h1>Order from: <xsl:apply-templates select="@partner"/></h1>

<table>
<tr><td class="b" width="150">Date:</td><td><xsl:apply-templates
    select="Date"/></td></tr>
<tr><td class="b">Item:</td><td><xsl:apply-templates
    select="Item"/></td></tr>
<tr><td class="b">Quantity:</td><td><xsl:apply-templates
    select="Quantity"/></td></tr>
<tr><td class="b">Comment:</td><td><xsl:apply-templates
    select="Comments"/></td></tr>
<tr><td class="b">Ship By:</td><td><xsl:apply-templates
    select="ShippingMethod"/></td></tr>
</table>

</body>
</html>

</xsl:template>
</xsl:stylesheet>
```

Along with the HTML table tags, such as table, tr, and td, this stylesheet also adds some style. The p style rule adds the table tag (after a comma) so that it has the same rules as p. The b rule was changed into a class (now preceded by a period) so that any HTML element the attribute/value pair class="b" will take on the .b class style rules. The effect of this is shown in Figure 3.3.

Processing a Regular Structure with for-each

The table makes things look better. Sometimes you'll have a collection of data that appears in a regular structure or pattern. Processing data like this

Figure 3.3 HTML table in Navigator with CSS.

with the XSLT instruction element `for-each` is ideal. For example, take the document `country-codes.xml`. This file contains ISO 3166 two-letter country codes or abbreviations in a regular pattern. A portion of the document `country-codes.xml` is shown here. There are 243 countries in the document; the example shows only 20—the first 10 and the last 10 in the list:

```
<?xml version="1.0" encoding="utf-8" ?>

<country-codes>
 <code>
  <abbr>AD</abbr>
  <country>Andorra</country>
 </code>
 <code>
  <abbr>AE</abbr>
  <country>United Arab Emirates</country>
 </code>
 <code>
  <abbr>AF</abbr>
  <country>Afghanistan</country>
 </code>
 <code>
  <abbr>AG</abbr>
  <country>Antigua and Barbuda</country>
 </code>
```

```
<code>
 <abbr>AI</abbr>
 <country>Anguilla</country>
</code>
 ...
<code>
 <abbr>YU</abbr>
 <country>Yugoslavia</country>
</code>
<code>
 <abbr>ZA</abbr>
 <country>South Africa</country>
</code>
<code>
 <abbr>ZM</abbr>
 <country>Zambia</country>
</code>
<code>
 <abbr>ZR</abbr>
 <country>Zaire</country>
</code>
<code>
 <abbr>ZW</abbr>
 <country>Zimbabwe</country>
</code>
</country-codes>
```

This is an example of a regular structure in an XML document. The `for-each` element can process each instance of an element in a regular structure. A stylesheet that does this (`html-table-for-each.xsl`) follows:

```
<xsl:stylesheet version="1.0"
xmlns:xsl="http://www.w3.org/1999/XSL/Transform">
<xsl:output method="html" encoding="utf-8"/>

<xsl:template match="/">
<html>
<head>
<title>Two-Letter Country Codes</title>
<style>
h1 {font-family:Verdana,Arial,Helvetica,sans-serif;font-size:18pt;text-
    align:center}
p,table {font-family:Verdana,Arial,Helvetica,sans-serif;font-size:12pt}
.b {font-size:14pt;font-weight:bold}
</style>
</head>
<body>

<h1>Two-Letter Country Codes (ISO 3166)</h1>
```

```
<table>
<tr><td class="b" align="center" width="75">Code</td><td class="b">
    Country</td></tr>
<xsl:for-each select="country-codes/code">
<tr>
 <td align="center">
  <xsl:apply-templates select="abbr"/>
 </td>
 <xsl:for-each select="current()">
 <td>
  <xsl:apply-templates select="country"/>
 </td>
 </xsl:for-each>
</tr>
</xsl:for-each>
</table>

</body>
</html>

</xsl:template>
</xsl:stylesheet>
```

You see two instances of the `for-each` instruction in this stylesheet. These instructions contain templates. A template doesn't have to be defined by a `template` element alone. Other elements can contain templates, such as `for-each`, `copy`, and `if`. Generally speaking, a template is a collection of instruction elements, literal result elements, literal text, and so forth, that, taken together, form a result tree that will pass for an HTML document, an XML document, or, at the very least, a text document.

The `template` element matches the root node (`/`) in the XML document being transformed. The root node is the document node, that is, it contains all other nodes in the document. If you compare an XML document to a tree, the root node is like the unseen root structure of the tree, the root element (an element node) is like the trunk of the trees, and all other nodes, such as other element nodes, text nodes, attribute nodes, and so forth, are branches that grow out of the trunk. It's an imperfect analogy, but it will do for the moment. (You will learn more about the traditional tree data model in Chapter 12, "XSL Technology Review.")

The template in the `template` element instantiates literal result elements, such has `html`, `head`, and so forth, that are output to the result tree. After adding CSS styles and an `h1` heading and beginning an HTML table, the template encounters the first `for-each`.

This `for-each` selects what appears to be a single element node with its required `select` attribute. The element it seems to select is a `code` element, as long as it is a child of the `country-codes` element. That's what `country-codes/code` means. In the `country-codes.xml` document, `code` is always a child of `country-codes`, but the template needs to know the node's relationship to the root node. Otherwise, the template won't work.

I say that the element *seems* to select a `code` element because what is really happening is that the `select` attribute evaluates to a node-set. In this context, the node-set evaluates to the next instance of `code`, not just one instance. The `for-each` instruction in essence provides a list of nodes to the XSLT processor through which you want to step. And that's what you are about to do.

After this, the template instantiates a table row element (`tr`) and a centered table data (`td`) element. Next the `apply-templates` element selects the `abbr` element in the source, instantiates its content, and outputs it. This is followed by a `td` end-tag.

Then, lo and behold, another `for-each` appears with a template. This is legal syntax because a `for-each` element may contain another template. (A `template` element, though, cannot contain another `template` element because `template` is a top-level element, that is, it must be a child of either `stylesheet` or `transform`.) This instance of `for-each` selects the current node with the XSLT function `current()`, that is, the same node selected by the previous instance of `for-each`. You could also express this as a single period (`.`), so that:

```
<xsl:for-each select="current()">
```

and

```
<xsl:for-each select=".">
```

are equivalent. Another `td` element is instantiated, the content of `country` is instantiated, and then the `td` element is closed. After that, this `for-each` element is closed as well and the `tr` end-tag is output. The first `for-each` is closed at this point and the current node changes to the next node in the node-set, if any nodes remain in the list.

The first or outermost `for-each` will step through the entire list in document order, that is, the basic order of the start-tags in the document, until the node-set is exhausted. When you reach the end of the node-set, the remaining literal result elements in the stylesheet are instantiated and pushed out to the result tree.

NOTE   I realize that all this business about nodes and what is or isn't selected or matched or whatever can be a little overwhelming at first. Up to this point, I have introduced only enough information for you to get by, but I'll round out that knowledge in due time over succeeding chapters.

A portion of the result (`country-codes.html`) follows:

```
<html>
<head>
<META http-equiv="Content-Type" content="text/html; charset=utf-8">
<title>Two-Letter Country Codes</title>
<style>
h1 {font-family:Verdana,Arial,Helvetica,sans-serif;font-size:18pt;text-
    align:center}
p,table {font-family:Verdana,Arial,Helvetica,sans-serif;font-size:12pt}
.b {font-size:14pt;font-weight:bold}
</style>
</head>
<body>
<h1>Two-Letter Country Codes (ISO 3166)</h1>
<table>
<tr>
<td class="b" align="center" width="75">Code</td><td
    class="b">Country</td>
</tr>
<tr>
<td align="center">AD</td><td>Andorra</td>
</tr>
<tr>
<td align="center">AE</td><td>United Arab Emirates</td>
</tr>
<tr>
<td align="center">AF</td><td>Afghanistan</td>
</tr>
<tr>
<td align="center">AG</td><td>Antigua and Barbuda</td>
</tr>
<tr>
<td align="center">AI</td><td>Anguilla</td>
</tr>
...
<tr>
<td align="center">YU</td><td>Yugoslavia</td>
</tr>
<tr>
<td align="center">ZA</td><td>South Africa</td>
</tr>
<tr>
<td align="center">ZM</td><td>Zambia</td>
```

```
</tr>
<tr>
<td align="center">ZR</td><td>Zaire</td>
</tr>
<tr>
<td align="center">ZW</td><td>Zimbabwe</td>
</tr>
</table>
</body>
</html>
```

The two instances of for-each in combination will walk through every instance of abbr and country and produce a fairly good-looking result, a part of which is shown in Figure 3.4.

It doesn't take much to convert your HTML output to XHTML output. If your HTML complies with XHTML, your XSLT processor will consider it as if it were well-formed XML.

Turning Your HTML Output into XHTML

The W3C XHTML 1.0 recommendation appeared in early 2000 (see www .w3.org/tr/xhtml1) as a reformulation of HTML 4 as XML 1.0. What reformulation means is that W3C took its SGML DTD for HTML and converted it to an XML DTD. This allows you to continue to use the HTML elements,

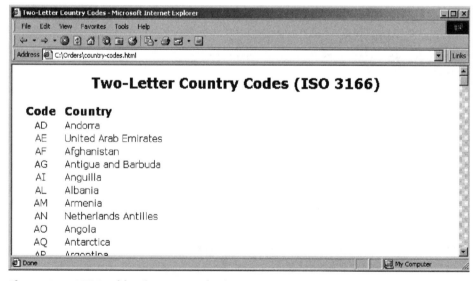

Figure 3.4   HTML table of country codes in IE.

attributes, built-in entities, and so forth within fully compliant XML documents. The next version, XHTML 1.1, will most likely become a recommendation in 2001 (see www.w3.org/tr/xhtml11/).

Several other XHTML modularization recommendations have appeared since the first. They are XHTML Basic (www.w3.org/tr/xhtml-basic/), which includes a minimal amount of modules to define an XHTML document, and Modularization of XHTML (www.w3.org/tr/xhtml-modularization/), which subsets all of XHTML into modules. The modularization effort is an attempt to break the XHTML DTD into discrete parts so that smaller platforms can handle them.

I'll cover a few basics about XHTML 1.0 and then change a previous stylesheet so that it outputs XHTML rather than HTML. There are not a tremendous number of differences between HTML and XHTML. Here are a few important ones:

- A mandatory document type declaration must appear before the `html` root element using the XHTML public identifier.

- All elements tags are must be lowercase.

- The root element `html` must include a namespace declaration for the XHTML namespace.

- Other rules of XML well-formedness apply—rules such as always pairing up tags, properly terminating empty elements, quoting attribute values, and no attribute minimization, to name a few.

I repeat here a stylesheet for HTML that you saw earlier (`order-html.xsl`) that we applied to `order.xml`. I have renamed it `order-xhtml.xsl` and have altered it so that it will output XHTML instead of HTML (note the changes in bold):

```
<xsl:stylesheet version="1.0"
xmlns:xsl="http://www.w3.org/1999/XSL/Transform"
xmlns:x="http://www.w3.org/1999/xhtml">
<xsl:output method="xml" encoding="utf-8"/>
<xsl:output indent="yes" omit-xml-declaration="yes"/>
<xsl:output doctype-public="-//W3C//DTD XHTML 1.0 Strict//EN"/>
<xsl:output doctype-system="http://www.w3.org/TR/xhtml1/DTD/
    xhtml1-strict.dtd"/>

<xsl:template match="Order">
<x:html>
<x:head>
<x:title>Order from: <xsl:apply-templates select="@partner"/></x:title>
<x:style>
```

```
h1 {font-family:Verdana,Arial,Helvetica,sans-serif;font-size:18pt;text-
    align:center}
p {font-family:Verdana,Arial,Helvetica,sans-serif;font-size:12pt}
b {font-size:14pt;font-weight:bold}
</x:style>
</x:head>
<x:body>

<x:h1>Order from: <xsl:apply-templates select="@partner"/></x:h1>
<x:p><x:b>Date: </x:b><xsl:apply-templates select="Date"/></x:p>
<x:p><x:b>Item: </x:b><xsl:apply-templates select="Item"/></x:p>
<x:p><x:b>Quantity: </x:b><xsl:apply-templates select="Quantity"/></x:p>
<x:p><x:b>Comment: </x:b><xsl:apply-templates select="Comments"/></x:p>
<x:p><x:b>Ship By: </x:b><xsl:apply-templates
        select="ShippingMethod"/></x:p>

</x:body>
</x:html>

</xsl:template>
</xsl:stylesheet>
```

Because well-formed XHTML is actually XML, I changed the output method to xml. The indent attribute has a default value of no when you use the xml output method (yes with html), so I turned indent back on. I also dropped the XML declaration in output. The document type declaration will now point to the XHTML public and system identifiers, and the namespace (http://www.w3.org/1999/xhtml) and prefix (x:) identify the proper XHTML namespace.

A version of the result tree from this stylesheet follows (order-x.html):

```
<!DOCTYPE x:html PUBLIC "-//W3C//DTD XHTML 1.0 Strict//EN"
    "http://www.w3.org/TR/xhtml1/DTD/xhtml1-strict.dtd">
<x:html xmlns:x="http://www.w3.org/1999/xhtml">
<x:head>
<x:title>Order from: 06-853-2535</x:title>
<x:style>
h1 {font-family:Verdana,Arial,Helvetica,sans-serif;font-size:18pt;text-
    align:center}
p {font-family:Verdana,Arial,Helvetica,sans-serif;font-size:12pt}
b {font-size:14pt;font-weight:bold}
</x:style>
</x:head>
<x:body>
<x:h1>Order from: 06-853-2535</x:h1>
<x:p><x:b>Date: </x:b>2001-06-01</x:p>
<x:p><x:b>Item: </x:b>0471416207</x:p>
<x:p><x:b>Quantity: </x:b>40</x:p>
```

```
<x:p><x:b>Comment: </x:b>First order this month.</x:p>
<x:p><x:b>Ship By: </x:b>USPS</x:p>
</x:body>
</x:html>
```

It doesn't look much different from the HTML output, but the output is now XHTML-conformant.

HTML Tidy

Another option you have for converting HTML to XHTML is David Raggett's HTML Tidy, available from www.w3.org/People/Raggett/tidy/. You will find documentation, downloadable executables, and source code (or links to them) at this location.

HTML Tidy not only fixes all sorts of problems with HTML, but also has an XML output option that turns an HTML document into well-formed XML. Some of the evils it corrects are missing or mismatched end-tags, badly nested tags, and adding quotation marks around attribute values.

You can run HTML Tidy on a variety of platforms (Windows, Unix, Mac, you name it) with a command-line interface. The -help (or -h) option on the command line offers the following hints:

```
tidy -help

tidy: file1 file2 ...
Utility to clean up & pretty print html files
see http://www.w3.org/People/Raggett/tidy/
options for tidy released on 30th April 2000
  -config <file>  set options from config file
  -indent or -i   indent element content
  -omit   or -o   omit optional endtags
  -wrap 72        wrap text at column 72 (default is 68)
  -upper  or -u   force tags to upper case (default is lower)
  -clean  or -c   replace font, nobr & center tags by CSS
  -raw            leave chars > 128 unchanged upon output
  -ascii          use ASCII for output, Latin-1 for input
  -latin1         use Latin-1 for both input and output
  -iso2022        use ISO2022 for both input and output
  -utf8           use UTF-8 for both input and output
  -mac            use the Apple MacRoman character set
  -numeric or -n  output numeric rather than named entities
  -modify or -m   to modify original files
  -errors or -e   only show errors
  -quiet or -q    suppress nonessential output
  -f <file>       write errors to named <file>
  -xml            use this when input is wellformed xml
  -asxml          to convert html to wellformed xml
```

```
  -slides          to burst into slides on h2 elements
  -version or -v  show version
  -help    or -h   list command line options
Input/Output default to stdin/stdout respectively
Single letter options apart from -f may be combined
as in:  tidy -f errs.txt -imu foo.html
You can also use --blah for any config file option blah
For further info on HTML see http://www.w3.org/MarkUp
```

The basic command-line syntax for converting an HTML file to XHTML is as follows:

```
tidy -asxml order.html > order-tidy.html
```

The -asxml option means *as XML*. The input file order.html is converted to XHTML and written to the file order-tidy.html.

Transforming XHTML to XML

What if you wanted to convert an XHTML document back to its original XML, bringing it around full circle? If your document is well-formed XHTML, it follows that it is likewise well-formed XML, so there is no reason why you can't transform it with XSLT. Let's look at another stylesheet that will convert order-x-prefix.html back to order.xml. The following stylesheet is called order-xhtml-back.xsl:

```
<xsl:stylesheet version="1.0"
xmlns:xsl="http://www.w3.org/1999/XSL/Transform"
xmlns:x="http://www.w3.org/1999/xhtml"
exclude-result-prefixes="x">
<xsl:output method="xml" encoding="utf-8" indent="yes"/>
<xsl:variable name="partner">
 <xsl:value-of select="substring-after(x:html/x:body/x:h1,
': ')"/>
</xsl:variable>

<xsl:template match="x:html">
<Order partner="{$partner}">
 <Date><xsl:value-of select="substring-after(x:body/x:p[1],
': ')"/></Date>
 <Item><xsl:value-of select="substring-after(x:body/x:p[2],
': ')"/></Item>
 <Quantity><xsl:value-of select="substring-
after(x:body/x:p[3],': ')"/></Quantity>
 <Comments><xsl:value-of select="substring-
after(x:body/x:p[4],': ')"/></Comments>
```

```
<ShippingMethod><xsl:value-of select="substring-
after(x:body/x:p[5],': ')"/></ShippingMethod>
</Order>

</xsl:template>
</xsl:stylesheet>
```

The stylesheet identifies the XHTML namespace (`http://www.w3
.org/1999/xhtml`) and prefix (`x:`). The prefix was my choice, and it
helps sort out where elements and so forth belong. The `exclude-
result-prefixes` attribute of `stylesheet` with a value of x means that
namespace information identified by the prefix will be excluded from the
result tree.

Throughout the stylesheet, nodes are selected with QName, such as
`x:html/x:body/x:h1`, rather than just the local part (`html/body/h1`).
A variable named `partner` is instantiated. Its value is the value of `x:h1` in
the source. An XPath function called `substring-after()` is used to
extract only a portion of what the string `h1` contains, that is, the portion of
the string following the colon and space (the DUNS number `06-853-
2535`). This value is later picked up inside `Order`'s `partner` attribute. The
braces (`{ }`) are necessary because the variable is used inside an attribute
of a literal result element.

The contents of the elements `Date`, `Item`, `Quantity`, `Comments`, and
`ShippingMethod` are all picked up by using `value-of` instead of
`apply-templates` because `value-of` returns a string value that we can
manipulate with `substring-after()`, just as we did with the `partner`
attribute. On the other hand, `apply-templates` evaluates to a node-set,
which is not what we want in this instance.

The `x:p[1]` syntax selects the first occurrence of the `x:p` element that is
a child of `x:body`. Succeeding occurrences of `x:p` are selected in the range
`[1]` through `[5]`, in document order or the order in which `x:p` element
start-tags appear in the document. The syntax inside the square brackets is
called a predicate or filter.

The result produced by this stylesheet looks like this:

```
<?xml version="1.0" encoding="utf-8"?>
<Order partner="06-853-2535">
 <Date>2001-06-01</Date>
 <Item>0471416207</Item>
 <Quantity>40</Quantity>
 <Comments>First order this month.</Comments>
 <ShippingMethod>USPS</ShippingMethod>
</Order>
```

Now the circle is complete; we are back to where we began.

Getting More Results

In the next chapter, my focus will turn back to transforming XML documents. I'll explore nodes, node-sets, and expressions in more detail, plus how to use modes and how to name and reuse a template. I will also cover how to control whitespace and how to switch namespaces. I'll show the difference between the copy and copy-of element instructions. In addition, I'll go over how to use literal result element stylesheets and embedded stylesheets.

Getting More Results

This chapter expands on earlier examples, explaining nodes, XPath location paths, patterns, expressions, and calling named templates. It covers the use of `copy` and `copy-of`, including the identity transform. It shows you how to use template modes and handle whitespace. It also teaches you how to create literal result element stylesheets and embedded stylesheets.

What's a Node, Anyway?

What is a node? The word *node* has lots of meanings in the English language. It descends to us from the Latin *nodus* or knot, such as a knot in a rope. It is also a common term in computer science, used in defining points in tree and graph data models. In XML, it applies to the basic parts of a document. XSLT relies on the XPath recommendation (www.w3.org/tr/xpath) for defining what a node is and ways to address nodes as patterns or to use them in expressions.

XPath describes seven different node types that model XML documents, each node modeling a part. These nodes are as follows:

- Root node
- Element nodes

- Text nodes
- Attribute nodes
- Namespace nodes
- Processing instruction nodes
- Comment nodes

Taken together, the nodes form a tree structure. Figure 4.1 illustrates the tree structure of the nodes that exist in `order.xml`. (This expands on the simpler concepts expressed in Figure 1.1.)

It is possible to add nodes to `order.xml`, but this is what we have so far. The root node is the root of the tree, a conceptual node that is at the root, so to speak, of the content of the entire document, including the root element `Order`. There is only one root node in any XML document. `Order`, of course, is the root or document element and is an element node.

As with the root node, there is only one root element, too. It also has an attribute node associated with it called `partner`, plus text nodes that contain only whitespace. I sometimes call them whitespace nodes. I know that these whitespace nodes are hard to see. The spaces that indent the child elements are each text nodes containing whitespace only.

The child elements that follow—`Date`, `Item`, `Quantity`, `Comments`, and `ShippingMethod`—turn out to be siblings of one another and are also element nodes. Each has a child text node that holds the content of the element. For example, the text node child of the element node `Date` holds the text content `2001-06-01`.

The sibling element nodes are indented with a single space, and each space is a text node. For the purpose of processing, whitespace text nodes that are contiguous are handled as single nodes. The whole bunch of them (all the nodes, including the root node) could be lumped together in what is known as a *node-set*.

Node-Sets

A node-set is an unordered collection of nodes. A node-set can hold all the nodes in a single tree such as a single XML document, or it can hold all the nodes from several trees or documents (sometimes referred to as a *grove* or *grove of trees*). A node-set might contain all the children of a given node in a tree, or it might include a subset of them or all the attribute nodes from a tree. It might even be empty. It is an amorphous thing that you have been using in the previous chapters perhaps without really knowing it. Basically, a node-set can hold any nodes that exist within a given context.

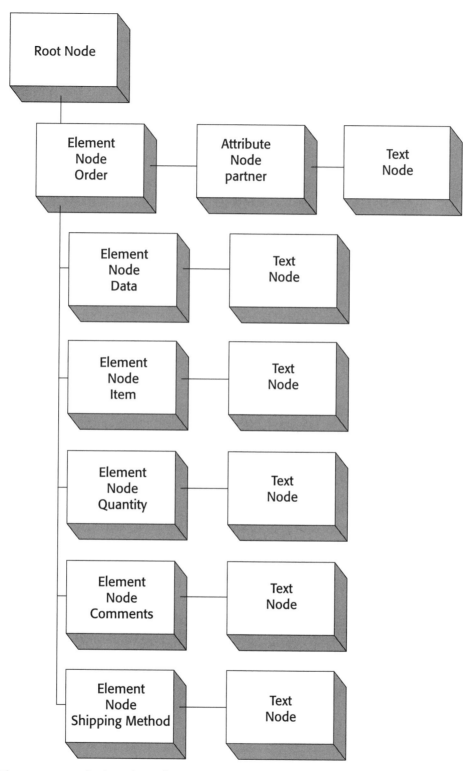

Figure 4.1 Nodes in order.xml.

The Current or Context Node

Any time you address or select a node in a tree, it becomes the context or current node. For example, given the following very boring template:

```
<xsl:template match="/">
 <xsl:apply-templates>
</xsl:template>
```

the root node (/) becomes the context node. This means that the root, and all of its children, is the context. Likewise, after this only slightly more interesting template is executed:

```
<xsl:template match="Order">
 <xsl:apply-templates select="Date">
</xsl:template>
```

the Date element, which is a child of the root element Order, becomes the context node. Generally, the XSLT recommendation uses the term *current node*, and the XPath recommendation uses *context node*. They are essentially the same thing.

Location Paths

You are no doubt aware of file paths in either the Windows or the Unix environments. Take, for example, this Unix example:

```
/Orders/06-853-2535/2001-06-01-order.xml
```

The file 2001-06-01-order.xml is in the path /Orders/06-853-2535 where / represents the root directory of the system, followed by the subdirectory Orders, followed by the subdirectory 06-853-2535. A similar directory on a Windows file system would look like the following:

```
c:\Orders\06-853-2535\2001-06-01-Order.xml
```

XSLT uses something similar in concept called the *location path*. A location path is used to address nodes or node-sets. So far, you have seen the very simplest of location paths using an abbreviated syntax. The values of both the match and select attributes in the following fragment are location paths:

```
<xsl:template match="Order">
 <ISO8601-Date>
  <xsl:apply-templates select="Date"/>
 </ISO8601-Date>
</xsl:template>
```

The location path Order, which is the value of match, addresses the Order node (the root element) in order.xml. When this location path matches Order, it selects a node-set, that is, Order, and its child nodes Date, Item, Quantity, Comments, and ShippingMethod, plus white-space-only text nodes. This then becomes the current node-set or node list.

Then the location path Date, which is the value of select, addresses the element node Date, which is in the current node-set. This selects Date, making it the context or current node. The template instantiates the literal result element ISO-8601-Date and inserts the text content of Date in the ISO-8601-Date instance in the output:

```
<ISO-8601-Date>2001-06-01</ISO-8601-Date>
```

A location path can be used in a pattern or an expression. The match attribute always contains a pattern, and the select attribute always contains an expression, a superset of the pattern. What's the difference between the two?

Patterns

A pattern is a special kind of location path, a subset of an expression. Its main job is to match a node, but with some limitations. It is limited to child or attribute nodes, in other words, child (child::) or attribute (attribute::) axes. Beside child:: and attribute::, other axes, such as the descendant-or-self:: axis, are forbidden, but patterns may use the // and / operators.

> **NOTE** The syntax for child:: and attribute:: is called an unabbreviated syntax. It is a formal, more verbose way to address nodes. You'll be introduced to this syntax later in this chapter, but more thoroughly in Chapter 9, "More XSLT."

Except in a predicate or filter ([ ]), which can contain an expression, a match attribute may contain only patterns and not expressions. Beside template, match exists in two other elements in XSLT, number and key. Table 4.1 catalogs what a pattern can match, evaluating location paths from right to left.

> **NOTE** For more information on patterns, see Section 5.2 of the XSLT recommendation.

Table 4.1 Patterns

PATTERN	DESCRIPTION
/	The root node.
*	Any element (wildcard).
element	Any given element that has the name element. An element can have a qualified name (QName) or a non-colonized name (NCName). A QName is a name qualified by a namespace URI by means of a prefix associated with a namespace (prefix:element). An NCName does not have a namespace prefix (element).
@*	Any attribute (wildcard).
@attribute	Any given attribute with the name attribute.
attribute::	Unabbreviated location path or axis that matches attribute nodes.
element/element	A given element that is a child of a given element.
element|element	A given element or another given element. The vertical line (|) is the union operator.
element//element	A given element that has another given element as an ancestor or descendant.
element[ ]	A given element that matches a predicate or filter. A predicate contains an expression. When evaluated, the node in a predicate becomes the current or context node.
child::	Unabbreviated location path (axis) that matches child nodes.
*[ ]	Any element (wildcard) that matches a predicate. A predicate contains an expression.
node()	A node test for any node that is not the root node or an attribute node (wildcard).
text()	A node test for a text node.
processing-instruction()	A node test for a processing instruction node.
comment()	A node test for a comment node.
id()	An XPath function that selects an element with a given ID attribute. The type of such an attribute must be of type ID, set in a DTD.
key()	An XLST function that selects a pattern specified with a key.

Expressions

The value of the `select` attribute in `apply-templates` may contain an expression, which includes patterns. In addition to `apply-templates`, the `select` attribute also appears in the `copy-of`, `for-each`, `param`, `sort`, `value-of`, `variable`, `with-param`. (Expressions may also occur in other attributes, such as in the `number's value` attribute.) A `match` attribute, on the other hand, cannot contain expressions except those held in a predicate. Expressions may contain whatever patterns may contain because patterns are subsets of expressions. Table 4.2 lists the additional functionality of an expression.

Table 4.2 Expressions

EXPRESSION	DESCRIPTION
`99.99`	A number.
`"literal"`	A literal, quoted string.
`.`	A current node.
`..`	A parent node.
`+`	An addition operator.
`-`, `-99`	A subtraction operator, or when combined with a number, a negative unary operator.
`*`	A multiplication operator (not the same as a wildcard).
`div`	A division operator.
`mod`	A modulus (remainder) operator.
`or`	An OR Boolean logic operator.
`and`	An AND Boolean logic operator.
`=`	An equality comparison operator.
`!=`	An inequality comparison operator.
`&lt;`	Less-than comparison operator, represented as an entity reference because of the XML rule against < in an attribute value.
`>`	Greater-than comparison operator.
`&lt;=`	Less-than or equal-to comparison operator, represented as an entity reference because of the XML rule against < in an attribute value.
`>=`	Greater-than or equal-to comparison operator.
`$variable`	A reference to a named `variable`.
`function()`	A call to a function named `function()`.

The following templates show how to address nodes in a variety of ways using the match attribute with a pattern and the select attribute with an expression or pattern. Most of the examples are given with abbreviated syntax (such as @partner), though you will see a few with unabbreviated syntax (such as attribute::partner). You will learn more about axes and unabbreviated syntax in Chapter 9.

Remember that a pattern is a subset of an expression, so in that sense, a select attribute can contain a pattern as well as an expression. On the other hand, match attributes are limited to patterns, though a predicate, when used in a pattern, may contain an expression. It sounds a bit confusing, but in practical application, it will make sense. I'd encourage you to edit the stylesheet test.xsl, trying each of these templates as you go along and experimenting with your own. These examples will make a lot more sense if you actually use them.

Here is the first template applied to country-codes.xml:

```
<xsl:template match="country-codes">
 <xsl:apply-templates select="code/abbr"/>
</xsl:template>
```

The values in match and select are location paths. They each represent a kind of node test known as a name test. The first name test is the root element country-codes found in country-codes.xml. It is a non-colonized name or NCName. An NCName does not have a namespace prefix. This NCName is the name of an element node.

The second name test, found in select, is a location path with two steps. Location paths are evaluated from right to left, so I'll start with the rightmost step, abbr, which is an NCName for an element. Next is the / operator that indicates that the first step, the name test for the abbr element, is a child of another element. The second step, the leftmost step, is a name test for the element code. This location path addresses an instance of abbr that is a direct child of code within the context of the node-set for the root element country-codes. The template outputs a stream of two-letter country codes.

The next template addresses code elements, which are children or descendants of the root element country-codes, again in country-codes.xml. It selects each occurrence of country and outputs each of them to the result tree:

```
<xsl:template match="country-codes//code">
 <xsl:apply-templates select="country"/>
</xsl:template>
```

Next, this template returns a node-set composed of all nodes in the `country-codes` root element. Then it selects the `country` element that is a child of the 32nd instance of `code`, as determined by the predicate `code[32]`, and sends the content `Bouvet Island` to the result tree:

```
<xsl:template match="country-codes">
 <xsl:apply-templates select="code[32]/country"/>
</xsl:template>
```

The following template, when applied to `order.xml`, selects an element that has an attribute with a given value:

```
<xsl:template match="Order">
 <xsl:apply-templates select="Item[@type='ISBN']"/>
</xsl:template>
```

The template matches the `Order` element, which returns a node-set containing `Order` and its children. Then `apply-templates` selects the `Item` element node in that node-set that has an attribute named `type` whose value is `ISBN` (the search or selection is case sensitive). It returns the text node child of the selected element node.

The next template applies a `text()` node test:

```
<xsl:template match="Order">
 <xsl:apply-templates select="*[text()='40']"/>
</xsl:template>
```

After finding the pattern `Order` in `order.xml`, the template hunts down any element that has a child text node with the content `40` and then returns the content to the result tree.

By the way, the `text()` syntax sort of looks like a function call, but it isn't. It is simply a node test. The same is true of `node()`, `comment()`, and `processing-instruction()`.

This template, after matching the pattern `Order`, selects the context node (`Order`) and its descendants (`//`) and outputs the attributes named with the `attribute::` axis.

```
<xsl:template match="Order">
 Partner attribute: <xsl:apply-templates select="//attribute::partner"/>
 Type attribute: <xsl:apply-templates select="//attribute::type"/>
 Class attribute: <xsl:apply-templates select="//attribute::class"/>
</xsl:template>
```

This following template matches `Order`, then, using an expression, adds the number 3 to the value of `Quantity`, outputting a string value of 43 to the result tree:

```
<xsl:template match="Order">
 <Quantity><xsl:value-of select="Quantity + 3"/></Quantity>
</xsl:template>
```

The expression in the value of `select` would not be legal as a value of `match`. The element `value-of` is used here rather than `apply-templates` because `value-of` outputs the string value of the content of the selected node (actually the string value of the first node in a node-set), rather than evaluating to a value of type node-set. This makes it possible to add a number to it because the presence of operators and operands in the expression trigger an implicit number conversion. You cannot add a value to a node-set like this without converting it to a number, whether implicitly or explicitly.

Here is another template that includes an arithmetic expression:

```
<xsl:template match="Order">
 <Quantity><xsl:value-of select="Quantity * 2"/></Quantity>
</xsl:template>
```

Again, the expression in the value of `select` would not be allowed in a `match` attribute. You have seen the use of an asterisk (*) earlier as a wildcard. In this template it is used as a multiplication operator. Any compliant XSLT processor will know that it is an operator rather than a wildcard because the preceding token is not @ :: ([, or an operator (such as +). For details on such lexical rules, see Section 3.7 of the XSLT recommendation. This expression, if applied to `order.xml`, will produce the value `80`.

This next template outputs any processing instructions that are children of the root:

```
<xsl:template match="/">
 <xsl:copy-of select="processing-instruction()"/>
</xsl:template>
```

The `copy-of` element is used in this instance in order to copy the entire PI, including `<?`, `?>`, and target name (such as `xml-stylesheet`). A `value-of` would return only the text content of the first PI as a string, and `apply-templates` evaluates to a node-set, which apparently returns nothing to the result tree. You can apply this to `order-comment.xml` to see what happens.

To pick a PI by target name, you can include an argument that specifies the target name of the PI you want to grab, as shown here:

```
<xsl:template match="/">
 <xsl:copy-of select="processing-instruction('xml-stylesheet')"/>
</xsl:template>
```

This template copies any instance of a PI that has the target name xml-stylesheet in the root of the document to which it is applied. Single quotes (') are used in the argument rather than double quotes (") to avoid irritating the XSLT processor (and breaking the stylesheet). If you want, you can try double quotes in the argument and watch what happens.

Here is a new version of order.xml with comments added. It's called order-comment.xml:

```
<?xml version="1.0" encoding="utf-8" ?>
<?xml-stylesheet href="test.xsl" type="text/xsl"?>

<Order partner="06-853-2535">
 <!-- Date (ISO 8601) the order was placed -->
 <Date>2001-06-01</Date>
 <!-- Item ordered, including type of item -->
 <Item type="ISBN">0471416207</Item>
 <!-- Number of items being ordered -->
 <Quantity>103</Quantity>
 <!-- Any comments passed on those placing the order -->
 <Comments>Send coupons, too!</Comments>
 <!-- The method by which the order is to be shipped -->
 <ShippingMethod class="4th">UPS</ShippingMethod>
</Order>
```

When applied to order-comment.xml, this template returns full comments (including < ! - - and - - >) to the result tree, all that it can find in the node-set:

```
<xsl:template match="Order">
 <xsl:copy-of select="comment()"/>
</xsl:template>
```

All comment nodes are returned to the result tree.

NOTE These patterns and expressions are only a sampling of what is possible. You will see increasingly more sophisticated location paths as you continue to progress through the book.

In the template examples, you got an introduction to copy-of. I'll expand on that introduction in the next section.

Copying Nodes

XSLT has two instruction elements whose primary purpose is to copy nodes into a result tree. Their names are copy and copy-of. These elements don't copy just the content of the node (the child text node, for example), but rather they copy markup and all, with some variations.

To illustrate the difference between these two elements, I'll apply templates for each of these to order.xml and then show you the output. To keep it fresh, here is order.xml again:

```
<?xml version="1.0" encoding="utf-8" ?>

<Order partner="06-853-2535">
 <Date>2001-06-01</Date>
 <Item type="ISBN">0471416207</Item>
 <Quantity>40</Quantity>
 <Comments>First order this month.</Comments>
 <ShippingMethod class="4th">USPS</ShippingMethod>
</Order>
```

The copy Instruction Element

Here is a stylesheet (copy-order.xsl) that uses the copy element to transform the Order element in order.xml:

```
<xsl:stylesheet version="1.0"
xmlns:xsl="http://www.w3.org/1999/XSL/Transform">
<xsl:output method="xml" encoding="utf-8" />

<xsl:template match="Order">
 <xsl:copy/>
</xsl:template>

</xsl:stylesheet>
```

The copy element does not have a select attribute, so it just copies the pattern in the match attribute of template. The result looks like this:

```
<?xml version="1.0" encoding="utf-8"?>
<Order/>
```

It isn't very interesting output, but there is a difference between copy and, say, apply-templates. In previous templates, you have been grabbing the content of child nodes, such as a text node child of an element node; copy, in this example, picks up the Order element node itself, but leaves the content children behind.

Order in order.xml has child nodes, including text nodes containing only whitespace, and element nodes (some with attribute nodes), but copy does not pick them up automatically—it just copies the current node (Order). An element node may contain attribute nodes, but these attributes are not children of the associated element node. An element node, though, is the parent of any of its attribute nodes. (See Section 5.3 of the XPath recommendation.)

If the current node has a namespace associated with it, it will copy the namespace node automatically, but not its attributes or other child nodes. The `order-ns.xml` document is the same document as `order.xml` except it has a prefixed namespace associated with the elements:

```
<?xml version="1.0" encoding="utf-8" ?>

<order:Order xmlns:order="http://www.testb2b.org/order" partner="06-853-
    2535">
 <order:Date>2001-06-01</order:Date>
 <order:Item type="ISBN">0471416207</order:Item>
 <order:Quantity>40</order:Quantity>
 <order:Comments>First order this month.</order:Comments>
 <order:ShippingMethod class="4th">USPS</order:ShippingMethod>
</order:Order>
```

The stylesheet `copy-order-ns.xsl` has a few differences from its predecessor `copy-order.xsl`:

```
<xsl:stylesheet version="1.0"
xmlns:xsl="http://www.w3.org/1999/XSL/Transform"
xmlns:order="http://www.testb2b.org/Order">
<xsl:output method="xml" encoding="utf-8" />

<xsl:template match="order:Order">
 <xsl:copy/>
</xsl:template>

</xsl:stylesheet>
```

The result is as follows:

```
<?xml version="1.0" encoding="utf-8"?>
<order:Order xmlns:order="http://www.testb2b.org/order"/>
```

The difference is that `copy` automatically picked up the namespace node for `order:Order`, but that's it. You are left to pick up the pieces or to turn to another instruction element to get the job done, such as `copy-of`, which you'll learn more about in a minute.

The `copy` element has one optional attribute, `use-attribute-sets`, which allows you to add attributes to an element copied into a result tree. As explained in Chapter 2, "XML Output," you can create a named set of attributes with the top-level element `attribute-set`. This element can define one or more attributes and can even include (chain) other attributes sets with *its* use-attribute-sets attribute. The convenient thing about this is that copy allows you to attach any named attribute set to any element you copy into output.

The following template (copy-order-att.xsl) adds a new set of attributes to the Order element:

```
<xsl:stylesheet version="1.0"
xmlns:xsl="http://www.w3.org/1999/XSL/Transform">
<xsl:output method="xml" encoding="utf-8" />
<xsl:attribute-set name="new">
 <xsl:attribute name="id">id-0001</xsl:attribute>
 <xsl:attribute name="partner-name">Wy'east
Communications</xsl:attribute>
</xsl:attribute-set>

<xsl:template match="Order">
 <xsl:copy use-attribute-sets="new"/>
</xsl:template>

</xsl:stylesheet>
```

Your output will look like the following:

```
<?xml version="1.0" encoding="utf-8"?>
<Order id="id-0001" partner-name="Wy'east Communications"/>
```

It adds the new set of attributes but leaves the original partner attribute behind.

What if you want to copy more out of a source file than just one element node? The copy-of element can help you out there. It expands on the copy element to include not only the current node but also any attribute nodes that are associated with an element node.

The copy-of Element

To get things rolling, have a look at the following little stylesheet (copy-of-order.xsl) that contains a copy-of element that selects Order in order.xml:

```
<xsl:stylesheet version="1.0"
xmlns:xsl="http://www.w3.org/1999/XSL/Transform">
<xsl:output method="xml" encoding="utf-8" />

<xsl:template match="/">
 <xsl:copy-of select="Order"/>
</xsl:template>

</xsl:stylesheet>
```

When you apply this stylesheet to order.xml, you get the following result:

```
<?xml version="1.0" encoding="utf-8"?>
<Order partner="06-853-2535">
 <Date>2001-06-01</Date>
 <Item type="ISBN">0471416207</Item>
 <Quantity>40</Quantity>
 <Comments>First order this month.</Comments>
 <ShippingMethod class="4th">USPS</ShippingMethod>
</Order>
```

Does the output look familiar? It should. It is almost an exact replica of order.xml. With copy, you get the current node plus a namespace node, if present. You also get to throw a few attributes on board if you want. But copy-of is different. It copies the current node plus other nodes that might be lying around—not only namespace nodes, but attribute nodes, text nodes, and child element nodes.

The XML declaration was not copied from the source but was generated by the XSLT processor by default. If you apply this stylesheet to order-pi.xml, which is identical to order.xml except that it has an XML stylesheet PI, you'll also notice that the stylesheet PI node will be left behind. Any comment nodes are left alone as well. You have to select PI nodes individually, as demonstrated in the following stylesheet (copy-of-order-pi.xsl):

```
<xsl:stylesheet version="1.0"
xmlns:xsl="http://www.w3.org/1999/XSL/Transform">
<xsl:output method="xml" encoding="utf-8" />

<xsl:template match="/">
 <xsl:copy-of select="processing-instruction('xml-stylesheet')"/>
 <xsl:copy-of select="Order"/>
</xsl:template>

</xsl:stylesheet>
```

When applied to order-pi.xml, the first instance of copy-of (in bold) copies the stylesheet PI and places it in the output as the following shows:

```
<?xml version="1.0" encoding="utf-8"?>
<?xml-stylesheet href="order.xsl" text="text/xsl" ?>
<Order partner="06-853-2535">
 <Date>2001-06-01</Date>
 <Item type="ISBN">0471416207</Item>
 <Quantity>40</Quantity>
 <Comments>First order this month.</Comments>
```

```
<ShippingMethod class="4th">USPS</ShippingMethod>
</Order>
```

So why else is copy-of useful? Sometimes you want to grab nodes and go. For example, if you want to place a copy of order.xml into a SOAP 1.1 envelope, you can do this easily with copy-of. As you might already know, the *Simple Object Access Protocol* (SOAP) is a protocol for packaging or enveloping XML documents, and it is a useful mechanism for exchanging documents in B2B systems, for example. (You can read about SOAP, a W3C note, at www.w3.org/tr/soap.)

The following stylesheet (order-soap.xsl) shows you how to insert order.xml into a SOAP document:

```
<xsl:stylesheet version="1.0"
xmlns:xsl="http://www.w3.org/1999/XSL/Transform">
<xsl:output method="xml" encoding="utf-8" indent="yes"/>

<xsl:template match="/">
<SOAP-ENV:Envelope
xmlns:SOAP-ENV="http://schemas.xmlsoap.org/soap/envelope/">
 <SOAP-ENV:Body>
  <xsl:copy-of select="Order"/>
 </SOAP-ENV:Body>
</SOAP-ENV:Envelope>
</xsl:template>

</xsl:stylesheet>
```

The Envelope element is the root element of a SOAP document. It has two children: an optional Header element and a mandatory Body element. A Header element, not shown, may contain authentication, payment, transaction, and other related information. The Body element holds the SOAP payload, in our case, a familiar little order form. A SOAP payload could consist of a variety of other documents, such as a reply to an order, auction information, stock quotes, or whatever. The SOAP namespace is http://schemas.xmlsoap.org/soap/envelope/ and is conventionally associated with the SOAP-ENV prefix, but you can use a different prefix if you want.

The output of this stylesheet will appear as follows:

```
<?xml version="1.0" encoding="utf-8"?>
<SOAP-ENV:Envelope
xmlns:SOAP-ENV="http://schemas.xmlsoap.org/soap/envelope/">
<SOAP-ENV:Body>
<Order partner="06-853-2535">
```

```
<Date>2001-06-01</Date>
<Item type="ISBN">0471416207</Item>
<Quantity>40</Quantity>
<Comments>First order this month.</Comments>
<ShippingMethod class="4th">USPS</ShippingMethod>
</Order>
</SOAP-ENV:Body>
</SOAP-ENV:Envelope>
```

The content of the SOAP `Body` element is now the document
`order.xml`. You can apply `order-soap-ns.xsl` to `order-ns.xml` to
include the `Order` namespace and prefix in this document, which produces similar output:

```
<?xml version="1.0" encoding="utf-8"?>
<SOAP-ENV:Envelope
xmlns:SOAP-ENV="http://schemas.xmlsoap.org/soap/envelope/"
xmlns:order="http://www.testb2b.org/Order">
<SOAP-ENV:Body>
<order:Order partner="06-853-2535">
 <order:Date>2001-06-01</order:Date>
 <order:Item type="ISBN">0471416207</order:Item>
 <order:Quantity>40</order:Quantity>
 <order:Comments>First order this month.</order:Comments>
 <order:ShippingMethod class="4th">USPS</order:ShippingMethod>
</order:Order>
</SOAP-ENV:Body>
</SOAP-ENV:Envelope>
```

NOTE SOAP 1.1 is not a W3C recommendation, though it has been submitted
to that organization as a note. W3C has no editorial control over such notes
and does not endorse them but provides them as advisory documents. W3C has
recently undertaken an activity called XML Protocol or XMLP that will build on
SOAP 1.1 (see www.w3.org/2000/xp). I hope this work will eventually yield a
W3C recommendation. Other recent notes relating to SOAP deal with MIME and
attachments (www.w3.org/tr/soap-attachments) and with digital signatures
(www.w3.org/tr/soap-dsig/).

Calling Named Templates

There are some templates that you may want to reuse, sometimes within a
single stylesheet and sometimes within other stylesheets. One way to do
this is by adding a name to a template and then calling it with the `call-
template` instruction element.

In the following fragment, the template in `copy-of-order.xsl` undergoes a small change, highlighted in bold:

```
<xsl:template name="copy-of-order">
 <xsl:copy-of select="Order"/>
</xsl:template>
```

The change is that the `match` attribute was removed and the `name` attribute was added with a value of `copy-of-order`. Without a pattern supplied by a `match` attribute, this template can't do much on its own except invoke the built-in template (see *Built-in Templates* later in this chapter).

Now have a look at the stylesheet `order-soap-named.xsl`, which makes some changes from its predecessor `order-soap.xsl` (see bold):

```
<xsl:stylesheet version="1.0"
xmlns:xsl="http://www.w3.org/1999/XSL/Transform">
<xsl:output method="xml" encoding="utf-8" indent="yes" />

<xsl:template match="/">
<SOAP-ENV:Envelope xmlns:SOAP-
ENV="http://schemas.xmlsoap.org/soap/envelope/">
 <SOAP-ENV:Body>
   <xsl:call-template name="copy-of-order"/>
 </SOAP-ENV:Body>
</SOAP-ENV:Envelope>
</xsl:template>

<xsl:template name="copy-of-order">
 <xsl:copy-of select="Order"/>
</xsl:template>

</xsl:stylesheet>
```

This stylesheet produces essentially the same result as `order-soap.xsl`, except instead of the first template invoking `copy-of`, it calls another, named template that invokes `copy-of`. Incidentally, `call-template` differs from `apply-templates` in that `call-template` does not change the current node or affect the current node-set.

I am sure that with only a glance it is evident why this is a convenient feature, but I'll throw in another twist by including the named template from a separate stylesheet. This is done with the top-level `include` element.

The include Element

This is just a brief introduction to the `include` element; Chapter 8, "Multiple Documents," covers this element (among others) more thoroughly. I offer here just a taste of how you can use it. To start, I've put a named template in a file all by itself, `copy-of-order-named.xsl`. Here is the little guy:

```
<xsl:stylesheet version="1.0"
xmlns:xsl="http://www.w3.org/1999/XSL/Transform">

<xsl:template name="copy-of-order">
 <xsl:copy-of select="Order"/>
</xsl:template>

</xsl:stylesheet>
```

In the stylesheet `order-soap-include.xsl`, you'll notice the `include` element near the top:

```
<xsl:stylesheet version="1.0"
xmlns:xsl="http://www.w3.org/1999/XSL/Transform">
<xsl:output method="xml" encoding="utf-8" indent="yes" />
<xsl:include href="copy-of-order-named.xsl"/>

<xsl:template match="/">
<SOAP-ENV:Envelope
xmlns:SOAP-ENV="http://schemas.xmlsoap.org/soap/envelope/">
 <SOAP-ENV:Body>
   <xsl:call-template name="copy-of-order"/>
 </SOAP-ENV:Body>
</SOAP-ENV:Envelope>
</xsl:template>

</xsl:stylesheet>
```

The `href` attribute of `include` references the `copy-of-order-named.xsl` stylesheet, which holds the template named `copy-of-order`. This template is called with `call-template` from within `order-soap-include.xsl`. The XSLT processor is able to see the named template because of `include`. With `include`, you can reuse a named template in any stylesheet you wish. This is kind of handy for common functionality such as is found in the identity transform.

The Identity Transform

The XSLT recommendation discusses an identity transform in Section 7.5. The stylesheet `identity.xsl`, unsurprisingly, holds an identity transform in a template, shown here:

```
<xsl:stylesheet version="1.0"
xmlns:xsl="http://www.w3.org/1999/XSL/Transform">
```

```
<xsl:output encoding="utf-8"/>

<xsl:template name="identity" match="@*|node()">
 <xsl:copy>
  <xsl:apply-templates select="@*|node()"/>
 </xsl:copy>
</xsl:template>

</xsl:stylesheet>
```

The template is named `identity`, but it also bears a `match` attribute with only wildcards. There is nothing specific in this transform that applies to any particular document, so it can be applied to any XML document.

> **NOTE** This transform does not work with XT because it has not implemented the use of `node()` completely. Whether it ever will be implemented in XT is unclear.

If you include the stylesheet by means of the `include` element, you can then use the template named `identity` to copy all nodes (`node()`), including all attribute nodes (`@*`), from any document to which it is applied.

When applied directly to `order.xml`, the `identity.xsl` stylesheet produces the following result tree:

```
<?xml version="1.0" encoding="utf-8"?>


<Order partner="06-853-2535">
 <Date>2001-06-01</Date>
 <Item type="ISBN">0471416207</Item>
 <Quantity>40</Quantity>
 <Comments>First order this month.</Comments>
 <ShippingMethod class="4th">USPS</ShippingMethod>
</Order>
```

If you apply the same stylesheet to `order-ns.xml`, you will get this result:

```
<?xml version="1.0" encoding="utf-8"?>


<order:Order xmlns:order="http://www.testb2b.org/order" partner="06-853-
2535">
 <order:Date>2001-06-01</order:Date>
 <order:Item type="ISBN">0471416207</order:Item>
 <order:Quantity>40</order:Quantity>
 <order:Comments>First order this month.</order:Comments>
```

```
<order:ShippingMethod class="4th">USPS</order:ShippingMethod>
</order:Order>
```

Built-in Templates

By default, an XSLT processor also includes built-in template rules. These rules are applied to a document if the other rules fail to match a pattern. In some instances, it is sort of a failsafe mechanism that ensures you'll get something to output, even if erroneous template rules flop.

The `apply-templates` instruction may not only resolve to a node-set but it may also search for another template in the stylesheet that processes the node in `select`. If such a template is not present and the selected node or node-set is not present in the XML document that is processed, nothing happens. Without the `select` attribute, though, the built-in template rules will kick in, that is, `apply-templates` applies the built-in template rules.

Essentially, the built-in template rules will select all elements or the root node, all text or attribute nodes, and all modes. (For more information on modes, see the *Modes* section a little later in this chapter.) The built-in rules also address processing instruction, comment, and namespace nodes, but they produce nothing.

If you apply a stylesheet without any matching template rules, you will kick in the built-in rules. For example, if you apply the following mindless stylesheet to `order.xml`:

```
<xsl:stylesheet version="1.0"
xmlns:xsl="http://www.w3.org/1999/XSL/Transform">

<xsl:template match="/">
 <xsl:apply-templates/>
</xsl:template>

</xsl:stylesheet>
```

it will apply the built-in rules and give you back the following:

```
<?xml version="1.0" encoding="utf-8"?>
 2001-06-01
 0471416207
 40
 First order this month.
 USPS
```

You get the XML declaration by default because you don't have an `output` element forbidding it with the `omit-xml-declaration="yes"` attribute/value pair. The content of all the elements—the text node children of elements—are output as well. It's hard to see, but whitespace text nodes are also retrieved, such as the whitespace before each of the child elements of Order and the line feeds and carriage returns after the elements.

The stylesheet built-in.xsl expresses the built-in template rules with equivalent templates, as shown here:

```
<xsl:stylesheet version="1.0"
xmlns:xsl="http://www.w3.org/1999/XSL/Transform">

<xsl:template match="*|/">
 <xsl:apply-templates/>
</xsl:template>

<xsl:template match="*|/" mode="m">
 <xsl:apply-templates mode="m"/>
</xsl:template>

<xsl:template match="text()|@*">
 <xsl:value-of select="."/>
</xsl:template>

<xsl:template match="processing-instruction()|comment()"/>

</xsl:stylesheet>
```

This stylesheet is completely unnecessary, as its template rules are already built in to any XSLT 1.0 compliant processor. I provide it merely to show you what is happening behind the scenes in XSLT.

> **NOTE** TestXSLT complains about the redundancy of the * | / pattern, but the other processors do not. See Section 5.8 in the XSLT recommendation for more information on built-in template rules.

Modes

Sometimes you'd like to process a node in an XML document more than once, each time producing a different result. The way to do this is with modes. The template and apply-templates elements each have an optional mode attribute. These attributes are what make modes work. Let's look at an example.

Imagine that you have received an order in the form of an order.xml document, and you want to send a receipt back to the sender—a common B2B system scenario. One option is to transform the received document to produce a receipt and then to send that document back, whether by HTTP, SMTP, or FTP. The example that follows does just this.

In the following stylesheet (modes.xsl), you will find a template that matches a node in order.xml twice, each time using another template with a different mode. It also uses a global parameter named newid that allows you to pass in a value to the stylesheet at runtime.

```
<xsl:stylesheet version="1.0"
xmlns:xsl="http://www.w3.org/1999/XSL/Transform">
<xsl:output method="xml" encoding="utf-8" indent="yes"/>
<xsl:param name="newid" select="1000"/>

<xsl:template match="Order">
 <OrderReceipt>
   <xsl:apply-templates select="Date" mode="date"/>
   <xsl:apply-templates select="Date" mode="rcptID"/>
 </OrderReceipt>
</xsl:template>

<xsl:template match="Date" mode="date">
 <OrderDate>
  <xsl:value-of select="current()"/>
 </OrderDate>
</xsl:template>

<xsl:template match="Date" mode="rcptID">
 <OrderReceiptID>MSG-ID-<xsl:value-of select="current()"/>-<xsl:value-of
     select="$newid"/>
 </OrderReceiptID>
</xsl:template>

</xsl:stylesheet>
```

Assuming that the document is applied to order.xml, the following is an example of the result:

```
<?xml version="1.0" encoding="utf-8"?>
<OrderReceipt>
 <OrderDate>2001-06-01</OrderDate>
 <OrderReceiptID>MSG-ID-2001-06-01-1000</OrderReceiptID>
</OrderReceipt>
```

How did it happen? First I'll cover modes, then I'll touch on how this stylesheet uses a parameter. This stylesheet uses modes because it wants to process the same element node (Date) twice in a single template, each time in a different way.

In the first template, which matches Order in order.xml, you see two instances of apply-templates, each selecting the Date child of Order, but each in a different mode. The date mode attribute in the first instance tells the XSLT processor to look for a template that has the same value in its mode attribute. The second instance tells the processor to look for the rcptID mode.

The template with the mode value of date uses the XSLT function current() to select the string value of Date. Actually, it returns the current node, which is converted to a string with value-of. You could also just use a single period (.) in place of current() as you have already seen before.

The template with the mode value of rcptID processes the Date node a bit differently. It is forming an identification number. To do so, it uses a literal result element to create a prefix (MSG-ID), grabs the string value of Date (2001-06-01), just as in the previous template, and then finally tacks on a value stored in the parameter $newid, resulting in MSG-ID-2001-06-01-1000.

The param Element

When the global parameter newid is defined, it is given a value of 1000 by using the select attribute, which is in essence a default. I say *global* because the parameter is defined at the top level of the stylesheet, making it available throughout the stylesheet. You can also define parameters within templates and make them effectively local. You will learn more about how to do this in Chapter 7, "Variables and Parameters."

You can easily change the value of the newid parameter at runtime by passing the new value in on the command line. All four of the command-line processors used to test examples in this book, namely XT, Saxon, MSXSL, and TestXSLT, have an option for doing this. XT, Saxon, and MSXSL each use the param=value syntax as the last value on a command line, whereas TestXSLT uses a -param switch.

Let's process the example with XT and change the parameter value while we are at it. If you use the command line:

```
xt order.xml modes.xsl newid=987654321
```

you will get this following result:

```
<?xml version="1.0" encoding="utf-8"?>
<OrderReceipt>
<OrderDate>2001-06-01</OrderDate>
<OrderReceiptID>MSG-ID-2001-06-01-987654321</OrderReceiptID>
</OrderReceipt>
```

MSXSL and Saxon have identical syntax except for the processor name. TestXSLT's command-line syntax is different and would look like the following:

```
testxslt -in order.xml -xsl modes.xsl -param newid 987654321
```

This is what you will get back:

```
========= Parsing modes.xsl ==========
Parse of modes.xsl took 0 milliseconds
========= Parsing order.xml ==========
Parse of order.xml took 0 milliseconds
=============================
Transforming...
<?xml version="1.0" encoding="utf-8"?>
<OrderReceipt>
<OrderDate>2001-06-01</OrderDate>
<OrderReceiptID>MSG-ID-2001-06-01-987654321</OrderReceiptID>
</OrderReceipt>

transform took 10 milliseconds

Total time took 10 milliseconds
```

Again, you'll learn more about parameters and variables in Chapter 7. Now let's move on to handling whitespace in your result tree.

Controlling Whitespace

Whitespace is important in presentation, but it's not so important in stored data, especially if next to no one sees it. Whitespace in XML consists of spaces, tabs, carriage returns, and linefeeds.

In regard to what whitespace adds visually, I am sure you will agree that your ability to quickly comprehend the following:

```
<?xml version="1.0" encoding="utf-8"?><Order partner="06-853-
2535"><Date>2001-06-01</Date><Item
type="ISBN">0471416207</Item><Quantity>40</Quantity><Comments>First
order this month.</Comments><ShippingMethod
class="4th">USPS</ShippingMethod></Order>
```

is much improved by the introduction of whitespace:

```
<?xml version="1.0" encoding="utf-8"?>

<Order partner="06-853-2535">
 <Date>2001-06-01</Date>
 <Item type="ISBN">0471416207</Item>
 <Quantity>40</Quantity>
 <Comments>First order this month.</Comments>
 <ShippingMethod class="4th">USPS</ShippingMethod>
</Order>
```

Let's review the ways you have already used whitespace previously in this book and cover some new ways you can control whitespace. Whitespace handling varies from XSLT processor to XSLT processor, so you should test the methods presented in this section until you get what you are after.

The output Element's indent Attribute

One way to improve presentation is to use a yes value in the indent attribute of output when transforming XML (indent="yes" is the default for HTML output). This means that an XSLT processor may add whitespace to a result tree, in addition to the whitespace already present in the literal text items in the stylesheet, to make the output look nice. You saw the effect of this earlier in Chapter 2.

Adding Linefeed and Carriage Return Characters Directly

You can insert whitespace in a stylesheet in a number of ways and with a variety of results. You can use the text element, for example, to insert carriage returns or linefeeds directly. For example, the following snippets will output a linefeed by using character references:

```
<xsl:text>&#xa;</xsl:text>
```

```
<xsl:text>&#10;</xsl:text>
```

The first character reference is a hexadecimal reference (xa), and the second is a decimal reference (10), but they both will expand to the linefeed character in output.

The 128-character US-ASCII character set has the same characters as the first 128 characters mapped in the ISO-8859-1, Unicode, or ISO/IEC 10646 Universal Character Set (UCS) standards. So the 10th character in each set, the linefeed character, maps to 10 in decimal or A in hexadecimal (hexadecimal numbers, which use the letters A through F, are case insensitive).

In the lower range of characters, that is, 0–127 (0–7F), the US-ASCII, ISO-8859-1, Unicode, and UCS character sets each have 33 control characters: 0–31 (0–1F) and 127 (7F). Only the horizontal tab (9 or 9), linefeed (10 or A), and carriage return (13 or D) are legal in XML documents. Beyond the traditional US-ASCII character range, control characters in the range 128–159 (80–9F) are also illegal.

The following snippets, using hexadecimal first then decimal, introduce carriage returns into the output:

```
<xsl:text>&#xd;</xsl:text>

<xsl:text>&#13;</xsl:text>
```

Another way to introduce a carriage return/linefeed (CR/LF) sequence into an XML file is with the following:

```
<xsl:text>
</xsl:text>
```

End-of-Line Normalization

The interpretation of these whitespace characters varies between XLST processors and on different platforms. Because different platforms handle ends of lines differently, under XML 1.0, end-of-line handling must be normalized (see www.w3.org/tr/rec-xml.html#sec-line-ends). Windows uses a carriage return/linefeed sequence for a newline. Unix uses a single linefeed, and Macintosh uses a single carriage return. In brief, the way XML processors normalize line ends is by converting carriage return/linefeed sequences (Windows newline) and carriage returns not followed by a linefeed (Mac newline) to a single linefeed character (like the Unix newline) in XML documents.

The xml:space Attribute

The XML 1.0 recommendation specifies the xml:space attribute (see www.w3.org/tr/rec-xml.html#sec-white-space). This attribute may be included in an element start-tag to signal to a processing application how you want whitespace handled.

The xml:space attribute has two possible values, either default or preserve. A value of default lets the application know that it can use its default for whitespace handling, whatever that may be. The preserve value indicates that you want whitespace preserved as it appears in the source document.

In XSLT, you can place instances of xml:space in literal result elements or define them with the attribute element. You might also pass an instance from a source to a result.

To see the difference that xml:space will make by adding it to a literal result element, let's start out with the following stylesheet:

```
<xsl:stylesheet version="1.0"
xmlns:xsl="http://www.w3.org/1999/XSL/Transform">
<xsl:output method="xml" encoding="utf-8" />
```

```
<xsl:template match="Order">
<newOrder>
 <newDate><xsl:value-of select="Date"/></newDate>
</newOrder>
</xsl:template>

</xsl:stylesheet>
```

As it stands, if this stylesheet were applied to order.xml, most processors would give you a result that looks like this:

```
<?xml version="1.0" encoding="utf-8"?>
<newOrder><newDate>2001-06-01</newDate></newOrder>
```

But if you add xml:space with a value of preserve to newOrder, as shown in whitespace.xsl:

```
<xsl:stylesheet version="1.0"
xmlns:xsl="http://www.w3.org/1999/XSL/Transform">
<xsl:output method="xml" encoding="utf-8" />

<xsl:template match="Order">
<newOrder xml:space="preserve">
 <newDate><xsl:value-of select="Date"/></newDate>
</newOrder>
</xsl:template>

</xsl:stylesheet>
```

your output will appear as follows with whitespace intact:

```
<?xml version="1.0" encoding="utf-8"?>
<newOrder xml:space="preserve">
 <newDate>2001-06-01</newDate>
</newOrder>
```

Sometimes you don't want to keep or add whitespace—you want to get rid of it. You can do this with the top-level element strip-space.

The strip-space and preserve-space Elements

The strip-space element strips whitespace-only text nodes out of elements. To help you understand where such text nodes lurk, I'll apply a basic, garden-variety stylesheet to order.xml. This stylesheet:

```
<xsl:stylesheet version="1.0"
xmlns:xsl="http://www.w3.org/1999/XSL/Transform">
```

```
<xsl:output method="xml" encoding="utf-8"/>

<xsl:template match="/">
 <xsl:copy-of select="Order"/>
</xsl:template>

</xsl:stylesheet>
```

yields these results:

```
<?xml version="1.0" encoding="utf-8"?>
<Order partner="06-853-2535">
 <Date>2001-06-01</Date>
 <Item type="ISBN">0471416207</Item>
 <Quantity>40</Quantity>
 <Comments>First order this month.</Comments>
 <ShippingMethod class="4th">USPS</ShippingMethod>
</Order>
```

There are whitespace-only text nodes loitering after each these elements, such as a newline character after a tag and the space before a tag. Now if you add an instance of strip-space at the top level of this stylesheet, you can easily strip those text nodes away. I'll show you how.

Here is the stylesheet strip-space.xsl:

```
<xsl:stylesheet version="1.0"
xmlns:xsl="http://www.w3.org/1999/XSL/Transform">
<xsl:output method="xml" encoding="utf-8"/>
<xsl:strip-space elements="Order"/>

<xsl:template match="/">
 <xsl:copy-of select="Order"/>
</xsl:template>

</xsl:stylesheet>
```

and here is the result of applying it to order.xml:

```
<?xml version="1.0" encoding="utf-8"?><Order partner="06-853-
2535"><Date>2001-06-01</Date><Item
type="ISBN">0471416207</Item><Quantity>40</Quantity><Comments>First
order this month.</Comments><ShippingMethod
class="4th">USPS</ShippingMethod></Order>
```

Those text nodes just disappeared. The strip-space element has only one required attribute; it's called elements. The value of elements is a list of one or more elements from which you want to strip whitespace-only text nodes. If the list has more than one element, the list is delimited by (of all things) whitespace. Only text nodes that contain whitespace only are stripped. Text nodes with at least one non-whitespace character remain in the result.

To illustrate this a little better, I am going to apply the following to `order.xml`:

```
<xsl:stylesheet version="1.0"
xmlns:xsl="http://www.w3.org/1999/XSL/Transform">
<xsl:output method="xml" encoding="utf-8" omit-xml-declaration="yes"/>

<xsl:template match="Order/*">
 Position: <xsl:value-of select="position()"/> Node: <xsl:copy-of
select="."/>
</xsl:template>

</xsl:stylesheet>
```

This stylesheet matches all elements that are children of `Order` (`Order/*`). The `position()` function in `select` returns each element's position, in document order, as output. *Document order* means the order in which the start-tag for each element appears in the document.

The `copy-of` element selects the current node with the single period (`.`), but you could also use `current()` just as well. It outputs each element node selected in turn. The output, when this stylesheet is applied to `order.xml`, is:

```
Position: 2 Node: <Date>2001-06-01</Date>

Position: 4 Node: <Item type="ISBN">0471416207</Item>

Position: 6 Node: <Quantity>40</Quantity>

Position: 8 Node: <Comments>First order this month.</Comments>

Position: 10 Node: <ShippingMethod class="4th">USPS</ShippingMethod>
```

Why did this yield only even numbers for the positions of the elements? You might expect that it would give you numbers 1 through 5 for the five element children of `Order`, but the output recognizes the whitespace text nodes, and that's why you only get even numbers. Figure 4.2 labels the positions of the text and element child nodes of `order.xml` so that you can see what's really going on.

The gray numbers label contiguous text nodes that contain only whitespace. These contiguous text nodes consist of the newlines and spaces, joined together and counted as one (1, 3, 5, 7, and 9). The element nodes, together with their text node children, are in positions 2, 4, 5, 6, 8, and 10.

You can strip away these text nodes from the result by applying `count-nodes.xsl`, which follows:

```
        <?xml version="1.0" encoding="utf-8" ?>

        <Order partner="06-853-2535">
                        2
1       <Date>2001-06-01</Date>
                        4
3       <Item type="ISBN">0-471-41620-7</Item>
                        6
5       <Quantity>40</Quantity>
                        8
7       <Comments>First order this month.<?Comments>
                        10
9       <ShippingMethod class-"4th">USPS</ShippingMethod>

        </order>
```

Figure 4.2   Node positions.

```
<xsl:stylesheet version="1.0"
xmlns:xsl="http://www.w3.org/1999/XSL/Transform">
<xsl:output method="xml" encoding="utf-8" omit-xml-declaration="yes"/>
<xsl:strip-space elements="Order"/>

<xsl:template match="Order/*">
 Position: <xsl:value-of select="position()"/> Node: <xsl:copy-of
select="."/>
</xsl:template>

</xsl:stylesheet>
```

With the text nodes removed, the result tree will return the position of each element node without being thrown off by invisible text nodes:

```
Position: 1 Node: <Date>2001-06-01</Date>
Position: 2 Node: <Item type="ISBN">0471416207</Item>
Position: 3 Node: <Quantity>40</Quantity>
Position: 4 Node: <Comments>First order this month.</Comments>
Position: 5 Node: <ShippingMethod class="4th">USPS</ShippingMethod>
```

The `strip-space` element has a companion element, `preserve-space`. This element has the whitespace delimited attribute value for elements, containing the names of elements where you want to preserve text nodes. Here is a fragment showing an instance of `preserve-space`:

```
<xsl:preserve-space elements="Order"/>
```

A Literal Result Element Stylesheet

Without much fuss, you can create a stylesheet that almost looks like a regular XML or HTML document. This is possible because XSLT supports a stylesheet whose root element is a literal result element rather than a `stylesheet` or `transform` element. With a few little modifications, you can get it to work.

Following is an example (`order-ns-literal-ss.xml`), created from `order-ns.xml`, of an XML document that is a literal result element stylesheet:

```
<?xml version="1.0" encoding="utf-8" ?>

<order:Order partner="06-853-2535"
 xmlns:order="http://www.testb2b.org/Order"
 xml:space="preserve" xsl:version="1.0"
 xmlns:xsl="http://www.w3.org/1999/XSL/Transform">
 <order:Date><xsl:value-of
select="order:Order/order:Date"/></order:Date>
 <xsl:variable name="type"
select="order:Order/order:Item/@type"/><order:Item
type="{$type}"><xsl:value-of
select="order:Order/order:Item"/></order:Item>
  <order:Quantity><xsl:value-of
select="order:Order/order:Quantity"/></order:Quantity>
  <order:Comments><xsl:value-of
select="order:Order/order:Comments"/></order:Comments>
  <xsl:variable name="class"
select="order:Order/order:ShippingMethod/@class"/><order:ShippingMethod
class="{$class}"><xsl:value-of
select="order:Order/order:ShippingMethod"/></order:ShippingMethod>
</order:Order>
```

When applied to `order-ns.xml`, the result will be:

```
<?xml version="1.0" encoding="utf-8"?>

<order:Order partner="06-853-2535" xml:space="preserve"
xmlns:order="http://www.testb2b.org/order">
  <order:Date>2001-06-01</order:Date>
  <order:Item type="ISBN">0471416207</order:Item>
  <order:Quantity>40</order:Quantity>
  <order:Comments>First order this month.</order:Comments>
  <order:ShippingMethod class="4th">USPS</order:ShippingMethod>
</order:Order>
```

To get an XSLT processor to recognize XSLT elements, you add the XSLT namespace declaration and version number to the root element, in this case, `order:Order`. The XSLT namespace declaration and version number disappear in the output. The XML stylesheet PI is also not reproduced (you'd need `copy-of` to do that).

You don't have to include the `xml:space` attribute, but I threw it in to preserve line breaks in the output. Normally, I use `indent="yes"` in the XSLT `output` element to help the result look better, but that's not an option here because you cannot use top-level elements in literal result element stylesheets. In fact, because you don't use `template` elements or the `stylesheet` or `transform` element, you'll find other limitations to what you can include in these simple stylesheets.

What else is happening here? An XSLT processor interprets the XML or HTML document as a single template rule in and of itself, with the root node (/) as its pattern. You can't include top-level elements, such as `output`, inside a template, so you have to leave them behind. So why would anyone want to use a literal result element stylesheet?

One reason why is that they are simple. For example, let's say you manage a series of documents that all look alike except for element or attribute content. You could convert a copy of this document into a literal result element stylesheet to create a paradigm document. This makes it pretty easy to figure out what goes where in the result tree.

You may have noticed that some of the attributes are replaced with variables, but the attribute `partner` in the root element is not. The reason? First of all, you have to use variables to extract attribute values for literal result elements because you cannot use `apply-template` or `value-of` elements in a literal result element attribute value. Because an XSLT `variable` element can be used at the top level and within templates, you can use `variable` as a child of the document element (`order:Order`), which an XSLT processor interprets as the beginning of the template. Because you can't define a variable before the document or root element, the processor won't see a later definition so it will chew you out.

Variable definitions for `type` and `class` both work later on because they are children of `order:Order` and they are defined before they are used, so everything works out fine. But you can't get a variable to work for the root element because you can't define it before it's needed.

You will notice the use of braces (`{  }`) in the literal result element attribute values—as in `{$type}` and `{$class}`. These are called *attribute value templates* (see Section 7.6.2 of the XSLT recommendation). Attribute value templates can contain expressions, not just variable references. You will learn more about variables and parameters in Chapter 7.

You can turn an HTML document into a literal result element stylesheet, too. You can apply the following HTML literal result element stylesheet (`order-ns-literal-ss.html`) to `order-ns.xml`:

```
<html xmlns:xsl="http://www.w3.org/1999/XSL/Transform" xsl:version="1.0"
xmlns:order="http://www.testb2b.org/order">
<head>
<title>Order from: <xsl:value-of select="order:Order/@partner"/></title>
</head>
<body>
<h1>Order from: <xsl:value-of select="order:Order/@partner"/></h1>
<p><b>Date: </b><xsl:value-of select="order:Order/order:Date"/></p>
<p><b>Item: </b><xsl:value-of select="order:Order/order:Item"/><b> Type:
    </b><xsl:value-of select="order:Order/order:Item/@type"/></p>
<p><b>Quantity: </b><xsl:value-of
select="order:Order/order:Quantity"/></p>
<p><b>Comment: </b><xsl:value-of
select="order:Order/order:Comments"/></p>
<p><b>Ship By: </b><xsl:value-of
select="order:Order/order:ShippingMethod"/><b> Class: </b><xsl:value-of
    select="order:Order/order:ShippingMethod/@class"/></p>
</body>
</html>
```

The HTML result tree will look like this:

```
<html xmlns:order="http://www.testb2b.org/order">
<head>
<META http-equiv="Content-Type" content="text/html; charset=UTF-8">
<title>Order from: 06-853-2535</title>
</head>
<body>
<h1>Order from: 06-853-2535</h1>
<p>
<b>Date: </b>2001-06-01</p>
<p>
<b>Item: </b>0471416207<b> Type: </b>ISBN</p>
<p>
<b>Quantity: </b>40</p>
<p>
<b>Comment: </b>First order this month.</p>
<p>
<b>Ship By: </b>USPS<b> Class: </b>4th</p>
</body>
</html>
```

An Embedded Stylesheet

It is also possible to embed an XSLT stylesheet right in an XML document. Under some circumstances you may want to let an XML document carry its own stylesheet in its back pocket. With a couple of easy steps, you can make it happen.

First of all, the XML stylesheet PI identifies a stylesheet with the href pseudo-attribute. Normally, the stylesheet PI would appear something like this:

```
<?xml-stylesheet href="order.xsl" type="text/xsl" ?>
```

In order to use an embedded stylesheet, you have to use a fragment identifier that is preceded by a #:

```
<?xml-stylesheet href="#embed" type="text/xsl" ?>
```

An XSLT processor such as Saxon will recognize the fragment identifier and try to match it with a value of an id attribute with a type of ID, as defined in a DTD. The following example (order-embed.xml) uses an internal subset DTD to declare that the attribute id associated with the stylesheet element is of type ID. The stylesheet is placed in the document before the root element end-tag:

```
<?xml version="1.0" encoding="utf-8" ?>
<?xml-stylesheet href="#embed" type="text/xsl" ?>
<!DOCTYPE order:Order SYSTEM "order-ns.dtd" [
 <!ATTLIST xsl:stylesheet id ID #IMPLIED>
]>

<order:Order xmlns:order="http://www.testb2b.org/order"
 partner="06-853-2535">
 <order:Date>2001-06-01</order:Date>
 <order:Item type="ISBN">0471416207</order:Item>
 <order:Quantity>40</order:Quantity>
 <order:Comments>First order this month.</order:Comments>
 <order:ShippingMethod class="4th">USPS</order:ShippingMethod>
  <xsl:stylesheet id="embed" version="1.0"
     xmlns:xsl="http://www.w3.org/1999/XSL/Transform">
  <xsl:output method="text" indent="yes"/>
   <xsl:template match="order:Order" xml:space="preserve">
    <xsl:text>Order #</xsl:text><xsl:apply-templates
      select="order:Date"/><xsl:text>-0001
    </xsl:text>
    <xsl:text>Date: </xsl:text><xsl:apply-templates
select="order:Date"/>
    <xsl:text>Partner: </xsl:text><xsl:apply-templates
      select="@partner"/>
    <xsl:text>Item: </xsl:text><xsl:apply-templates
      select="order:Item"/>
    <xsl:text>Type: </xsl:text><xsl:apply-templates
      select="order:Item/@type"/>
    <xsl:text>Quantity: </xsl:text><xsl:apply-templates
      select="order:Quantity"/>
    <xsl:text>Comments: </xsl:text><xsl:apply-templates
```

```
        select="order:Comments"/>
      <xsl:text>Shipper: </xsl:text><xsl:apply-templates
        select="order:ShippingMethod"/>
      <xsl:text>Class: </xsl:text><xsl:apply-templates
        select="order:ShippingMethod/@class"/>
    </xsl:template>
  </xsl:stylesheet>
</order:Order>
```

To get this to work with Saxon, use:

```
saxon -a order-embed.xml
```

The `-a` option instructs the XSLT processor to use the XML stylesheet PI in `order-embed.xml`. The output produced by the embedded stylesheet follows:

```
Order #2001-06-01-0001

Date: 2001-06-01
Partner: 06-853-2535
Item: 0471416207
Type: ISBN
Quantity: 40
Comments: First order this month.
Shipper: USPS
Class: 4th
```

The stylesheet creates a plain text document that extracts the content of all the elements and attributes. It also adds an identification number to the top of the document by adding a value to the date.

Sorting Things Out

Hey, by now you're probably getting pretty good at this. Let's press on then. In the next chapter we'll move on to creating lists—sorting and numbering them—as well as formatting numbers.

Sorting and Numbering Lists

According to set theory, sets are inherently unordered. A node-list—a set of nodes in XSLT—is likewise inherently unordered. Chaos can be fun (especially for a one-year-old), but most of us need order to make some sense out of the world. With XSLT, you can at least make sense out of part of your world, that is, by creating a new, ordered list from an unordered node-set or from elements in document order. This chapter will tell you how. One way to do this is the sort instruction element.

Sorting by Text

The sort element instructs the XSLT processor to sort nodes based on a given criteria. That criteria is known as a sort key. By default—that is, with no attributes—the sort element sorts in ascending order on the current node. In English, ascending order means from A to Z. It also sorts on text datatypes by default, rather than on numbers. It is also possible to sort the same node-list with more that one instance of sort.

Let's dig up something to sort. The catalog.xml document will do us fine. Here it is:

```xml
<?xml version="1.0" encoding="utf-8"?>

<Catalog>
 <Item id="AHA-133040">
  <Name>Pen Calligraphy Manual</Name>
  <Description>This basic calligraphy manual includes
   alphabets, projects and more. For beginners of all
   ages.</Description>
  <Price currency="USD">19.95</Price>
 </Item>
 <Item id="SPD-3066">
  <Name>Elementary Alphabet Book</Name>
  <Description>Twenty-four page book, authored by Ross F.
   George, features basic alphabets, drafting alphabets and
   manuscript. By Speedball.</Description>
  <Price currency="USD">3.95</Price>
 </Item>
 <Item id="SPD-3067">
  <Name>Speedball Textbook</Name>
  <Description>This bestseller among lettering books is a
   practical 96-page manual on all lettering and poster forms.
   An excellent instruction and reference book offering a wide
   variety of letter styles. Edited by Ross F. George. 23rd
   edition.</Description>
  <Price currency="USD">8.95</Price>
 </Item>
 <Item id="SPD-3092">
  <Name>Abe Lincoln Italic Workbook</Name>
  <Description>This workbook by Speedball is perfect for
   classroom use and lesson planning. Easy-to-follow
   instructions, prepared in simple form.</Description>
  <Price currency="USD">14.50</Price>
 </Item>
 <Item id="TAP-081182">
  <Name>McDonald Calligraphy Book</Name>
  <Description>Presents 26 alphabets and variations from the
   basic Roman capital through Uncial, Gothic, Batarde and
   Italic hands with explanations of their appropriate
   applications. By Parkwest Publishing.</Description>
  <Price currency="USD">5.99</Price>
 </Item>
</Catalog>
```

This document is an XML version of just a small part of a real online catalog from C^{2}F, Inc. (www.c2f.com), an arts and crafts supply wholesaler.
The name of the items, contained in the Name element, are not in alphabetical order. To alphabetize at least the names, let's apply the stylesheet
sort.xsl to catalog.xml. This stylesheet uses sort in about as fundamental a way as you can. Here is the stylesheet:

```
<xsl:stylesheet version="1.0"
xmlns:xsl="http://www.w3.org/1999/XSL/Transform">
<xsl:output method="text" encoding="utf-8" omit-xml-declaration="yes"/>

<xsl:template match="Catalog">
 <xsl:apply-templates select="Item/Name">
  <xsl:sort/>
 </xsl:apply-templates>
</xsl:template>

</xsl:stylesheet>
```

The result of applying this stylesheet to `catalog.xml` is as follows:

Abe Lincoln Italic Workbook Elementary Alphabet Book**McDonald Calligraphy Book**Pen Calligraphy Manual**Speedball Textbook**

It's not very pretty as is, but you can see that the stylesheet put the names in alphabetical order. I've set off the names in alternating bold so that you can distinguish them better. The template matches the `Catalog` element (the document element), then the location path in the `select` attribute of `apply-templates` finds `Name`, a child element of `Item`, which is a child of `Catalog`.

Up until now, this book has used `apply-templates` only as an empty element, that is, an element without content. You can see here that `apply-templates` can have `sort` in its content. (It can also have `with-param` as content, but I won't discuss this until Chapter 7, "Variables and Parameters.")

The `sort` element selects the current node by default, as if it had a `select` element with a value of `.` or `current()`. It also sorts on text by default rather than numbers, as if the attribute/value pair `data-type="text"` were present.

sort's lang Attribute

In addition, `sort` can have a `lang` attribute with values that indicate the language in use, so it can know how to sort on text. For example, the Greek and Cyrillic languages, which, of course, use different alphabets than English, are going to have different sort orders than English. The value for `lang` might be `en` for English, `de` for German (Deutsch), `fr` for French, and so forth. If the `lang` attribute is not present, the XSLT processor can query the environment of the system it is running on to try to determine the language. At this time, unfortunately, there is little apparent support by XSLT processors for languages other than English.

Let's see if we can get better results with `sort-names.xsl`:

```
<xsl:stylesheet version="1.0"
xmlns:xsl="http://www.w3.org/1999/XSL/Transform">
<xsl:output method="text" encoding="utf-8" omit-xml-declaration="yes"/>

<xsl:template match="/">
 <xsl:apply-templates select="Catalog/Item">
  <xsl:sort/>
 </xsl:apply-templates>
</xsl:template>

<xsl:template match="Item">
Name: <xsl:apply-templates select="Name"/>
</xsl:template>

</xsl:stylesheet>
```

This stylesheet adds another template that helps process the nodes that are identified. The XSLT processing model allows nodes to be processed recursively, and that's what is happening in this example. The first template, similar to the template that's in `sort.xsl`, matches the root node, selects the `Item` children of `Catalog` (the only child of root), and then sorts the `Item` children. The other template processes the sorted children of `Item`, selecting the `Name` children of each `Item` and prepending the literal text `Name:` to each instance of `Name`. This is what the result tree looks like, nicely sorted in alphabetical order:

```
Name: Abe Lincoln Italic Workbook
Name: Elementary Alphabet Book
Name: McDonald Calligraphy Book
Name: Pen Calligraphy Manual
Name: Speedball Textbook
```

Sorting Text by Descending Order: The order Attribute

With just a flip of a switch, so to speak, you can change the order in which the `Name` elements are sorted. By default, the `sort` element sorts by ascending order, that is, from A to Z in English. This is as if the attribute/value pair `order="ascending"` were present in the `sort` tag. An XSLT processor assumes that it's there if it's not.

You can also sort in descending order—from Z to A in English. If you want to sort this way, you add the `order` attribute to the `sort` tag explicitly with a value of `descending`. The stylesheet `sort-names-`

descending.xsl is only slightly different from sort-names.xsl in that it adds the order attribute. Here is a fragment showing the small difference between the two:

```
<xsl:sort order="descending"/>
```

The presence of order with a value of descending has this effect when applied to catalog.xml:

```
Name: Speedball Textbook
Name: Pen Calligraphy Manual
Name: McDonald Calligraphy Book
Name: Elementary Alphabet Book
Name: Abe Lincoln Italic Workbook
```

The result shows that the alphabetical order has reversed such that the letter *A* is now last instead of first.

Sorting Text by Case: The case-order Attribute

Another sort attribute, case-order, determines whether text in uppercase is sorted before lowercase—or if the opposite is true. To demonstrate this, I'll add three duplicate items, all with lowercase names, to the catalog file. The new file is called catalog-lc.xml. Here is a fragment of catalog-lc.xml showing these changes:

```
<Item id="SPD-3092">
  <Name>abe lincoln italic workbook</Name>
  <Description>This workbook by Speedball is perfect for classroom use
and lesson planning. Easy-to-follow instructions, prepared in simple
form.</Description>
  <Price currency="USD">14.50</Price>
 </Item>
 <Item id="SPD-3066">
  <Name>elementary alphabet book</Name>
  <Description>Twenty-four page book, authored by Ross F. George,
features basic alphabets, drafting alphabets and manuscript. By
Speedball.</Description>
  <Price currency="USD">3.95</Price>
 </Item>
 <Item id="AHA-133040">
  <Name>pen calligraphy manual</Name>
  <Description>This basic calligraphy manual includes alphabets,
projects and more. For beginners of all ages.</Description>
  <Price currency="USD">19.95</Price>
 </Item>
```

You can see in bold the three duplicate instances of the `Item` element, each with a `Name` child whose content is all lowercase. Now I will add a small change to the `sort-names.xsl` stylesheet and call the new version `sort-names-lc.xsl`. Here is the tiny change:

```
<xsl:sort case-order="lower-first"/>
```

When you apply `sort-names-lc.xsl` to `catalog-lc.xml`, you will get the following result:

```
Name: abe lincoln italic workbook
Name: Abe Lincoln Italic Workbook
Name: elementary alphabet book
Name: Elementary Alphabet Book
Name: McDonald Calligraphy Book
Name: pen calligraphy manual
Name: Pen Calligraphy Manual
Name: Speedball Textbook
```

See the effect? Bold sets off the instances of lowercase names that appear *before* their uppercase counterparts that sport at least some uppercase characters. You can flip this around by writing a stylesheet with an `upper-first` value for the `case-order` attribute in the `sort` element. Such is the case with the stylesheet `sort-names-uc.xsl`, which, when applied to `catalog-lc.xml`, gives you the following result:

```
Name: Abe Lincoln Italic Workbook
Name: abe lincoln italic workbook
Name: Elementary Alphabet Book
Name: elementary alphabet book
Name: McDonald Calligraphy Book
Name: Pen Calligraphy Manual
Name: pen calligraphy manual
Name: Speedball Textbook
```

In this result, the same lines are highlighted in bold as in the previous result, but this time they appear *after* the lines containing uppercase. The order of case—that is, what comes first, either uppercase or lowercase—varies from language to language, so the XSLT recommendation allows case order to be language dependent.

NOTE XT, Saxon, and MSXSL sort reliably by case order, but, at the time of this writing, TestXSLT (Xalan C++) has not yet implemented `sort`'s `case-order` attribute.

Sorting by Numbers: The data-type Attribute

By default, the sort element sorts on text data, as if the attribute/value pair data-type="text" were present in the sort start-tag. You can also sort by numbers with data-type="number" present, with an ascending count from 1 to x (by default or by using order="ascending" explicitly) or a descending count from x to 1 (by using order="descending").

Where is a number in catalog.xml that we could sort by? The content of the Price elements will work. Here is a new stylesheet that will sort from the lowest price to the highest (sort-numbers.xsl):

```
<xsl:stylesheet version="1.0"
xmlns:xsl="http://www.w3.org/1999/XSL/Transform">
<xsl:output method="text" encoding="utf-8" omit-xml-declaration="yes"/>

<xsl:template match="/">
 <xsl:apply-templates select="Catalog//Price">
  <xsl:sort data-type="number"/>
 </xsl:apply-templates>
</xsl:template>

<xsl:template match="Price">
Price: <xsl:value-of select="."/>
</xsl:template>

</xsl:stylesheet>
```

When applied to catalog.xml, this stylesheet yields the following result:

```
Price: 3.95
Price: 5.99
Price: 8.95
Price: 14.50
Price: 19.95
```

As you can see, the items in catalog.xml are sorted based on the number content of Price, in ascending order by default. The location path Catalog//Price finds any Price elements that are descendents of Catalog. If the data-type attribute were set to text, the sort instruction would give you a different result (try it and see).

You can change to descending order by adding the order attribute with a value of descending. With the following change to a single line:

```
<xsl:sort data-type="number" order="descending"/>
```

the stylesheet `sort-numbers-descending.xsl` gives you this output:

```
Price: 19.95
Price: 14.50
Price: 8.95
Price: 5.99
Price: 3.95
```

The prices are now sorted from the highest to the lowest price.

Sorting Twice

You can use `sort` multiple times within a template or within several templates. In addition, the `sort` element can be a child of either `apply-templates` or `for-each`. The `sort-twice.xsl` stylesheet sorts `catalog-price-expanded.xml` on two sort keys: (1) the alphabetic order of `Name` elements and (2) the alphabetic order of `Currency` elements. Here is an instance of `Item` within `catalog-price-expanded.xml`:

```
<Item id="SPD-3067">
 <Name>Speedball Textbook</Name>
 <Description>This bestseller among lettering books is a practical 96-
page manual on all lettering and poster forms. An excellent instruction
and reference book offering a wide variety of letter styles. Edited by
Ross F. George. 23rd edition.</Description>
 <Price><Currency>USD</Currency><Amount>8.95</Amount></Price>
 <Price><Currency>GBP</Currency><Amount>6.22</Amount></Price>
 <Price><Currency>CAN</Currency><Amount>14.00</Amount></Price>
 <Price><Currency>EUR</Currency><Amount>9.90</Amount></Price>
</Item>
```

This version of the C^{2}F catalog has four different prices, each in a different currency, and uses elements rather than attributes to hold the currency abbreviation. Here is the `sort-twice.xsl` stylesheet:

```
<xsl:stylesheet version="1.0"
xmlns:xsl="http://www.w3.org/1999/XSL/Transform">
<xsl:output method="text" encoding="utf-8" omit-xml-declaration="yes"/>

<xsl:template match="/">
 <xsl:apply-templates select="Catalog"/>
</xsl:template>

<xsl:template match="Catalog">
 <xsl:apply-templates select="Item">
  <xsl:sort select="Name"/>
 </xsl:apply-templates>
```

```
</xsl:template>

<xsl:template match="Item">
 <xsl:for-each select="Price">
  <xsl:sort select="Currency"/>
  <xsl:value-of select="preceding-sibling::Name"/>:
<xsl:value-of select="Currency"/>-<xsl:value-of
select="Amount"/><xsl:text>&#xa;</xsl:text>
 </xsl:for-each>
</xsl:template>

</xsl:stylesheet>
```

The first template matches the root node and selects `Catalog`. The next template matches `Catalog`, selects `Item` children, and sorts on `Name` children of `Item`. The final template matches `Item` elements. Then for each `Price` element, it instantiates a template that sorts on `Currency` and outputs the string value of each `Name`, the content of `Currency`, the content of `Amount`, and a linefeed. The result follows:

```
Abe Lincoln Italic Workbook: CAN-22.68
Abe Lincoln Italic Workbook: EUR-16.05
Abe Lincoln Italic Workbook: GBP-10.08
Abe Lincoln Italic Workbook: USD-14.50
Elementary Alphabet Book: CAN-6.18
Elementary Alphabet Book: EUR-4.37
Elementary Alphabet Book: GBP-2.75
Elementary Alphabet Book: USD-3.95
McDonald Calligraphy Book: CAN-9.37
McDonald Calligraphy Book: EUR-6.63
McDonald Calligraphy Book: GBP-4.16
McDonald Calligraphy Book: USD-5.99
Pen Calligraphy Manual: CAN-31.20
Pen Calligraphy Manual: EUR-22.08
Pen Calligraphy Manual: GBP-13.87
Pen Calligraphy Manual: USD-19.95
Speedball Textbook: CAN-14.00
Speedball Textbook: EUR-9.90
Speedball Textbook: GBP-6.22
Speedball Textbook: USD-8.95
```

With two instances of `sort`, the output is in alphabetical order based on the content of each `Name` element, and the currency names are in alphabetical order based on the content of each `Currency` element as well. You certainly could tweak this stylesheet and make it prettier, but as is, it serves to show you some added possibilities with multiple sorts.

Now that you understand the basics of sorting, I'll show how to generate numbers.

Generating Numbers

The `number` instruction element allows you to insert numbers into a result tree. You can format these numbers in several ways and at multiple levels as well. The `number` element has nine attributes, but none of them is required. You'll learn about each of these attributes in this section.

As usual, let's get started with a simple example that builds on the `sort-names.xsl` stylesheet. It's called `number-names.xsl`:

```
<xsl:stylesheet version="1.0"
xmlns:xsl="http://www.w3.org/1999/XSL/Transform">
<xsl:output method="text" encoding="utf-8" omit-xml-declaration="yes"/>

<xsl:template match="/">
 <xsl:apply-templates select="Catalog/Item">
  <xsl:sort/>
 </xsl:apply-templates>
</xsl:template>

<xsl:template match="Item">
Name: <xsl:number value="position()"/> <xsl:apply-templates
select="Name"/>
</xsl:template>

</xsl:stylesheet>
```

The only difference between `sort-names.xsl` and `number-names.xsl` is the addition of an instance of the `number` element along with an attribute/value pair (`value="position()"`), highlighted in bold. The `value` attribute must contain an expression; in our example, the expression is the XPath function `position()` that returns the position of the current node in the current node list. The current node list was selected when `apply-templates` was called. You could use any legal expression as a value for this attribute, such as `value="position() + 1000"` or `value="position() != 1"`.

Apply this stylesheet to `catalog.xml` and you add sequential numbering to the list in the output (note bold):

```
Name: 1Abe Lincoln Italic Workbook
Name: 2Elementary Alphabet Book
Name: 3McDonald Calligraphy Book
Name: 4Pen Calligraphy Manual
Name: 5Speedball Textbook
```

It's clear that you can number a list from this output, but I admit it isn't very attractive yet. The expression in `value` is evaluated and the value for `position()`, based on the previous sort, is returned. This value or object is converted into a number, just as if it were processed by calling the XPath function `number()` (see Section 4.4 of the XPath recommendation). This number is rounded to an integer (almost always a positive integer) and then converted to a string.

To improve the output's good looks, I'll add the `format` attribute to number and see what happens. Here is the changed line:

```
<xsl:number value="position()" format="&#xa; 0. "/>
<xsl:apply-templates select="Name"/>
```

The change is in the stylesheet `number-names-format.xsl`. If you apply it to `catalog.xml`, the output will be as follows:

```
1. Abe Lincoln Italic Workbook
2. Elementary Alphabet Book
3. McDonald Calligraphy Book
4. Pen Calligraphy Manual
5. Speedball Textbook
```

For starters, notice that I removed the literal text `Name:`. The `format` attribute contains a linefeed character reference (`&#xa;`), which adds a linefeed at the beginning of a line in the result tree and is yet another way to add whitespace to output. (This is not mandatory by any means—don't get the idea that you are forced to use it—but it is a convenient way to improve the appearance of your output with whitespace.)

The attribute also adds a space before the resulting number, with a period (.) and space after it. The zero digit (0) indicates that the number will be an integer. It does not set the start of the numbering sequence at zero (0), only that the number will be of a certain type. The numbering sequence comes from the `value` attribute, at least in this instance of `number`.

You can also format a list to generate a sequence based on letters or roman numerals. Both these forms can be either uppercase or lowercase. For example, if you change the `format` attribute value to a lowercase *a* (`format="&#xa; a. "`) in `number-names-format.xsl`, the output will look like this:

```
a. Abe Lincoln Italic Workbook
b. Elementary Alphabet Book
c. McDonald Calligraphy Book
d. Pen Calligraphy Manual
e. Speedball Textbook
```

Try the following values in `number-names-format.xsl` and test to see what the results look like:

- `format="&#xa; A. "` (uppercase letters)
- `format="&#xa; I "` (uppercase Roman numerals)
- `format="&#xa; i. "` (lowercase Roman numerals)
- `format="&#xa; 000. "` (numeral prefix)
- `format="&#xa; 1-"` (integer/hyphen prefix)

There is no reason why you can't experiment with other formats besides these. Pull the linefeed out (`&#a;`) and watch what happens, or try other character references. Results will vary depending on what XSLT processor you use.

Here is an additional example you can run with this command line:

```
saxon currency.xml number-currency.xsl
```

The result of this transform will be as follows:

```
 1 Afghanistan
 2 Albania
 3 Algeria
 4 American Samoa
 5 Andorra
 6 Angola
 7 Anguilla
 8 Antarctica
 9 Antigua and Barbuda
10 Argentina
11 Armenia
12 Aruba
13 Australia
14 Austria
15 Azerbaijan
```

The document `currency.xml` contains information about the currencies that are used in different countries. The `number-currency.xsl` stylesheet has a default, global parameter that helps pull out all the names of countries that begin with the letter *A* in document order and number those country names upon output. You can change the letter by changing the parameter value on the command line, like this:

```
saxon currency.xml number-currency.xsl letter=D
```

This command changes the `letter` parameter from *A* (default) to *D*. You must use uppercase letters. With `letter=D`, the output will be:

```
 1 Denmark
 2 Djibouti
```

```
3 Dominica
4 Dominican Republic
```

This is just a little introduction to sorting based on parameters. I will explore parameters more thoroughly in Chapter 7.

Numbering Levels

Perhaps you will want to organize your output with different levels of numbering, such as in the sections and subsections of a specification document, namely 1.1, 1.2, 1.3 or 1.1.1, 1.1.2, 1.1.3, and so forth. You can do this manually or let the processor do the counting for you by using the `level` attribute.

I'll start by showing you how to format number levels by hand in `number-names-level-manual.xsl`. It's pretty easy to do. I have highlighted in bold the critical lines in the stylesheet:

```
<xsl:stylesheet version="1.0"
xmlns:xsl="http://www.w3.org/1999/XSL/Transform">
<xsl:output method="text" encoding="utf-8" omit-xml-declaration="yes"/>

<xsl:template match="/">
 <xsl:apply-templates select="Catalog/Item">
  <xsl:sort/>
 </xsl:apply-templates>
</xsl:template>

<xsl:template match="Catalog/Item">
 <xsl:number value="1" format="&#xa; 1."/>
 <xsl:number value="position()" format="0 "/>
 <xsl:apply-templates select="Name"/>
</xsl:template>

</xsl:stylesheet>
```

Apply this to `catalog.xml` and you get the following:

```
1.1 Abe Lincoln Italic Workbook
1.2 Elementary Alphabet Book
1.3 McDonald Calligraphy Book
1.4 Pen Calligraphy Manual
1.5 Speedball Textbook
```

The first instance of `number` sets the value for the first number to 1 with the `value` attribute. The `format` attribute inserts a linefeed and sets up the numbering format: An integer (namely the digit 1) preceded by a space and followed by a period. The second instance of `number` uses the incremental position number (value="position()") formatted as an integer followed by a space. Combined, these manually formatted numbers yield multileveled numbers 1.1 through 1.5.

By using additional instances of number, you could develop increasingly deeper numbering levels. The following fragment adds a couple of number elements to the previous stylesheet:

```
<xsl:template match="Catalog/Item">
 <xsl:number value="1" format="&#xa; 1."/>
 <xsl:number value="2" format="0."/>
 <xsl:number value="3" format="0."/>
 <xsl:number value="position()" format="0 "/>
 <xsl:apply-templates select="Name"/>
</xsl:template>
```

and generates output like this when applied to catalog.xml:

```
1.2.3.1 Abe Lincoln Italic Workbook
1.2.3.2 Elementary Alphabet Book
1.2.3.3 McDonald Calligraphy Book
1.2.3.4 Pen Calligraphy Manual
1.2.3.5 Speedball Textbook
```

You can experiment by adding or changing instances of number to your heart's content; however, by adding the level attribute to number, you can put the XSLT processor to work for you.

number's level Attribute

By default, the level attribute of number is set to single, as if level="single" were present in the number element, which also acts as if the count attribute were present with a value equal to, in essence, the current node. In plain terms, this means that the processor counts all ancestor nodes in the tree that match the current node, plus itself, matching the ancestor-or-self axis (you will learn more about this and other axes in Chapter 9, "More XSLT").

If level has a value of multiple, on the other hand, the processor counts all ancestors that match count. This has the effect of having multiple running numbers for a given node. To help you understand this a little better, let's jump into an example so you can see what it does.

The document catalog-price.xml adds more instances of the Price element so that the price of the item is represented in four different currencies: US dollars (USD), British or UK pounds sterling (GBP), Canadian dollars (CAD), and the Euro (EUR) of the European Monetary Union.

A snippet from `catalog-price.xml` shows the additional `Price` elements:

```
<Price currency="USD">19.95</Price>
<Price currency="GBP">13.87</Price>
<Price currency="CAN">31.20</Price>
<Price currency="EUR">22.08</Price>
```

The following stylesheet, `number-price-level-multiple.xml`, pulls the values of each `Price` and gives each one a multilevel number.

```
<xsl:stylesheet version="1.0"
xmlns:xsl="http://www.w3.org/1999/XSL/Transform">
<xsl:output method="text" encoding="utf-8" omit-xml-declaration="yes"/>

<xsl:template match="/">
 <xsl:apply-templates select="Catalog//Price"/>
</xsl:template>

<xsl:template match="Price">
 <xsl:number level="multiple" count="Item|Price" format="&#xa;1.1 "/>
<xsl:apply-templates/> (<xsl:value-of select="./@currency"/>)<xsl:if
test="./@currency='EUR'">
---------------</xsl:if>
</xsl:template>

</xsl:stylesheet>
```

The stylesheet creates the following result:

```
1.1 19.95 (USD)
1.2 13.87 (GBP)
1.3 31.20 (CAN)
1.4 22.08 (EUR)
---------------
2.1 3.95 (USD)
2.2 2.75 (GBP)
2.3 6.18 (CAN)
2.4 4.37 (EUR)
---------------
3.1 8.95 (USD)
3.2 6.22 (GBP)
3.3 14.00 (CAN)
3.4 9.90 (EUR)
---------------
4.1 14.50 (USD)
4.2 10.08 (GBP)
4.3 22.68 (CAN)
4.4 16.05 (EUR)
---------------
```

```
5.1 5.99 (USD)
5.2 4.16 (GBP)
5.3 9.37 (CAN)
5.4 6.63 (EUR)
----------------
```

The second template in the stylesheet recursively matches `Price` elements. The `number` instruction element includes the `level` attribute with a value of `multiple`. This means that the XSLT processor creates a node-list from *all* the ancestors of the current node in document order and then selects those nodes that match the pattern in count (that is, `Item` or `Price`).

The processor then figures out a count for these nodes by adding the number of preceding siblings plus 1. The format token `1.1` tells the processor that you want to output these numbers as a multilevel section number, so for each `Item` (1 through 5) you get 1 through 4 instances of `Price`. The templates are applied so that the content of each instance of `Price` is output, followed by the content of `currency` attribute, surrounded by parentheses. With an `if` element, the processor tests to find out if the instance of the `currency` attribute contains the text EUR; if it does, it separates the list with a group of hyphens (you'll learn more about `if` in the next chapter). It then moves on to process the next `Item` in the list and its `Price` elements, until the list of nodes is exhausted.

It's sometimes hard, I know, to follow all these fancy-pants descriptions of what the processor is doing, and perhaps it is not that important to you. What you really want is results, and, in my opinion, the quickest way to get results is to imitate examples. In this vein, I'll give you yet another example where you will see the `Label` element appear at different depths in the tree representing the catalog. The example will then map and output a multilevel number for each instance of `Label`.

The new version of the catalog file is `catalog-label.xml`. Following is the first instance of `Item` (and its children) with the `Label` elements highlighted in bold. One of the main differences is that `Name`, `Description`, and `Price` are no longer siblings, but each is a child of the element that precedes it: `Price` is a child of `Description`, `Description` is a child of `Name`, and `Name` is a child of `Item`. `Label` appears as a child of any and all of these.

Here is a fragment of `catalog-label.xml`, the first instance of `Item`:

```
<Item id="AHA-133040"><Label>Item</Label>
  <Name>Pen Calligraphy Manual<Label>Name</Label>
   <Description>This basic calligraphy manual includes alphabets,
projects and more. For beginners of all ages.<Label>Description</Label>
    <Price currency="USD">19.95<Label>Price</Label></Price>
```

```
      <Price currency="GBP">13.87<Label>Price</Label></Price>
      <Price currency="CAN">31.20<Label>Price</Label></Price>
      <Price currency="EUR">22.08<Label>Price</Label></Price>
    </Description>
  </Name>
</Item>
```

Now here is the fairly simple stylesheet that I will apply to catalog-label.xml. It's called number-label-level-multiple.xsl:

```
<xsl:stylesheet version="1.0"
xmlns:xsl="http://www.w3.org/1999/XSL/Transform">
<xsl:output method="text" encoding="utf-8" omit-xml-declaration="yes"/>

<xsl:template match="/">
 <xsl:apply-templates select="Catalog//Label"/>
</xsl:template>

<xsl:template match="Label">
<xsl:number level="multiple" count="Item|Name|Description|Price"
format="&#xa;1.1 "/>
<xsl:apply-templates/>
</xsl:template>


</xsl:stylesheet>
```

The first template matches the root node and then selects all the Label elements that have Catalog as an ancestor, creating a node-list. The next template recursively processes the Label elements in this node-list, ascribing a multilevel number to each instance of Label, based on the count of elements in the count attribute. The format attribute sets the format of the multilevel number. Following is the result of applying this stylesheet to catalog-label.xml:

```
1 Item
1.1 Name
1.1.1 Description
1.1.1.1 Price
1.1.1.2 Price
1.1.1.3 Price
1.1.1.4 Price
2 Item
2.1 Name
2.1.1 Description
2.1.1.1 Price
2.1.1.2 Price
2.1.1.3 Price
2.1.1.4 Price
3 Item
```

```
3.1 Name
3.1.1 Description
3.1.1.1 Price
3.1.1.2 Price
3.1.1.3 Price
3.1.1.4 Price
4 Item
4.1 Name
4.1.1 Description
4.1.1.1 Price
4.1.1.2 Price
4.1.1.3 Price
4.1.1.4 Price
5 Item
5.1 Name
5.1.1 Description
5.1.1.1 Price
5.1.1.2 Price
5.1.1.3 Price
5.1.1.4 Price
```

The XSLT processor successfully numbered the `Label` elements at their proper depth, even when multiple instances of a parent element showed up. You have now seen several ways to number multilevel items, both manually and automatically; now I'll show you one other value for `level`: any.

The any Level

I'll show you the effect of a small change to an earlier stylesheet (`number-price-level-multitple.xsl`) from `multiple` to `any`. The new stylesheet is `number-price-level-any.xsl`, and the change is highlighted in bold:

```
<xsl:stylesheet version="1.0"
xmlns:xsl="http://www.w3.org/1999/XSL/Transform">
<xsl:output method="text" encoding="utf-8" omit-xml-declaration="yes"/>

<xsl:template match="/">
 <xsl:apply-templates select="Catalog//Price"/>
</xsl:template>

<xsl:template match="Price">
 <xsl:number level="any" format="&#xa;1.1 "/>
<xsl:apply-templates/> (<xsl:value-of select="./@currency"/>)<xsl:if
test="./@currency='EUR'">
----------------</xsl:if>
</xsl:template>

</xsl:stylesheet>
```

All I did was change the value of level from multiple to any and then deleted the count attribute. Now I will apply the stylesheet to catalog-price.xml and show you the result:

```
1  19.95  (USD)
2  13.87  (GBP)
3  31.20  (CAN)
4  22.08  (EUR)
---------------
5  3.95  (USD)
6  2.75  (GBP)
7  6.18  (CAN)
8  4.37  (EUR)
---------------
9  8.95  (USD)
10  6.22  (GBP)
11  14.00  (CAN)
12  9.90  (EUR)
---------------
13  14.50  (USD)
14  10.08  (GBP)
15  22.68  (CAN)
16  16.05  (EUR)
---------------
17  5.99  (USD)
18  4.16  (GBP)
19  9.37  (CAN)
20  6.63  (EUR)
---------------
```

With a few changes to number, the XSLT processor numbered all the Price elements sequentially, rather than counting them in multiple levels. Perhaps a good way to explain the any value of level is to compare or contrast the values single and multiple with any.

What's the Difference between single, multiple, and any?

The level single is the default, that is, if number has no level attribute, the XSLT processor must assume a level of single. When instantiated with single, this level stipulates that the processor find the first node that matches the ancestor-or-self axis. This axis includes the context node in its search of all ancestor nodes, including the root node. What the processor will look for in its search is a node that matches the value of count; however, if count is not present, it matches on the current node. Once it finds the match, it will count up all the matching nodes it finds in the preceding sibling axis plus 1.

The preceding-sibling axis looks for matches that are siblings, that is, having the same parent, as the current node or the node in count. All this counting produces a list with only one item: A count of 1 plus all the preceding siblings that match either the value of count or the current node (the current node by default if no count attribute is present). In other words, the processor counts up the desired nodes and eventually presents a string representation of a number, that is, the number of nodes in question. (The preceding-sibling axis does not count attribute or namespace nodes.)

If the from attribute is present, it throws a little curve at the processor. It tells the processor where to start counting from, rather than counting all nodes.

That spells out single. How then does multiple work? The multiple method constructs not a list of length 1 (one item) but rather a list of all the nodes that are ancestors of the current node, in document order (document order, you'll remember, is the actual order of element start-tags in the document). After creating this list, the processor then selects from that list all the nodes that match the nodes represented in count. The from attribute applies to multiple just as it does to single.

The next step in the process maps the number of preceding siblings (siblings have the same parent) plus 1 for each node that matches count. This produces a count for each node in count, so a multiple count is possible. You have to use count with level="multiple" because counting only those preceding siblings that match the current node—the default behavior—will count only one node and so cannot yield multiple numbers.

Now let's look at the any value for level. Like single, any also constructs a list of length 1. This list of one will contain the number of nodes that match count and that match the result of the union of the preceding-sibling axis and the ancestor-or-self axis—in other words, the current node and all nodes before the current node, on any level of the document, in document order (attribute and namespace nodes are not counted). The from attribute applies as well.

Looking back at the previous example that implemented any, you can now see why it numbered all the Price elements contiguously, rather than restarting the numbering with each instance of Item. With any, you count all nodes, including and preceding the current node, rather than numbering the nodes separately, in effect, as with multiple.

I'll now demonstrate how to use the from attribute when numbering with the any level. The following stylesheet, number-price-level-any-from.xsl, adds a from attribute to the stylesheet used in the previous example:

```
<xsl:stylesheet version="1.0"
xmlns:xsl="http://www.w3.org/1999/XSL/Transform">
<xsl:output method="text" encoding="utf-8" omit-xml-declaration="yes"/>

<xsl:template match="/">
 <xsl:apply-templates select="Catalog//Price"/>
</xsl:template>

<xsl:template match="Price">
 <xsl:number level="any" from="Item" format="&#xa;1.1 "/>
<xsl:apply-templates/> (<xsl:value-of select="./@currency"/>)<xsl:if
test="./@currency='EUR'">
----------------</xsl:if>
</xsl:template>

</xsl:stylesheet>
```

This stylesheet will produce the count of `Price` (the current node) from within each `Item` element, giving you a result tree as follows:

```
1 19.95 (USD)
2 13.87 (GBP)
3 31.20 (CAN)
4 22.08 (EUR)
---------------
1 3.95 (USD)
2 2.75 (GBP)
3 6.18 (CAN)
4 4.37 (EUR)
---------------
1 8.95 (USD)
2 6.22 (GBP)
3 14.00 (CAN)
4 9.90 (EUR)
---------------
1 14.50 (USD)
2 10.08 (GBP)
3 22.68 (CAN)
4 16.05 (EUR)
---------------
1 5.99 (USD)
2 4.16 (GBP)
3 9.37 (CAN)
4 6.63 (EUR)
---------------
```

Even though the `format` attribute still accommodates multilevel numbers (1.1), it formats the numbers as if they are on a single level. The instances of `Price` are counted within `Item` (four per `Item`) because of the presence of `from` with a value of `Item`.

NOTE From a processing standpoint, it is a fair assumption that `single` takes fewer CPU cycles to do its counting, with `multiple` in second place, and then `any` in last place. Therefore, if performance is important in your application of XSLT, you may want to use `number` sparingly, consuming as few cycles as possible with single, and making other adjustments to avoid more complex numbering. Nevertheless, if the appearance of the output, rather than performance, is more important to you, then use whatever numbering scheme makes the most sense.

Before moving on, I should mention the other attributes of `number`. The `lang` attribute allows you to specify the language for the numbering. If no `lang` attribute is specified, the XSLT processor should be able to determine the language from the system where it is running. The English language uses Arabic numerals; however, some languages use their alphabet for numbering. You can specify this with the `letter-value` attribute, using either the value `traditional` or `alphabetic`. The default value is implementation specific, that is, it depends on the language and the XSLT processor.

The following fragment shows you how to use these attributes:

```
<xsl:number value="1" lang="heb" letter-value="traditional"
    format="&#x5d0;"/>
```

By default, this instance of `number` assumes `level="single"` and that `count` is the current node. The value `heb` of `lang` is the ISO 639-2:1998 Alpha-3 code for the Hebrew language. The `letter-value` attribute specifies `traditional`, which is actually alphabetic! Can you see why this value is implementation-specific? It can get a bit circular. The format token in the `format` attribute is a character reference for the Unicode value of aleph (א), the first character in the Hebrew alphabet, and the first number in the traditional Hebrew sequence.

Commonly, natural numbers are grouped with three places, separated with a comma (,) such as at the thousands place, as in 1,234. (Three is the default.) This may be changed with the `grouping-size` attribute. Likewise, you can change the grouping separator (by default a comma) with the `grouping-separator` attribute. For example, say you wanted to change the grouping size to four digits, with a period as the grouping separator. You could specify the number with the following:

```
<xsl:number grouping-separator="." grouping-size="4"/>
```

Again, `level` and `count` are defaulted. With these attributes in place, you could expect output like:

```
4.0000
4.0001
4.0002
4.0003
```

and so on. Now let's move on to formatting numbers a little differently.

Formatting Numbers

The XSLT function `format-number()` formats a number based on a pattern and according to a decimal format set by default or by the `decimal-format` top-level element. (You'll remember that a top-level element must be a child of the `stylesheet` or `transform` element.) This function/element combination produces numbers that are modeled after the Java version 1.1 DecimalFormat class. (You can read more about the Decimal-Format class at http://java.sun.com/products/jdk/1.1/docs/api/java .text.DecimalFormat.html.)

> **NOTE** As of this writing, TestXSLT (Xalan C++) does not fully support `format-number()`; however, XT, Saxon, and MSXSL all do.

Let's format the number 1,000,000,000,000 (that's a trillion in the American numbering system, a billion in the British). Here is a fragment that uses `format-number()` to format this large number:

```
<xsl:value-of select="format-number(1000000000000,'#')"/>
```

XSLT and XPath functions are called in expressions, such as a value of a `select` attribute. The `format-number()` function has three possible arguments; the first two shown in the example are required.

The first argument is the number you want to format; in this example, the number is `1000000000000`. The second is a format pattern string whereby you specify the format of the outputted number. The example specifies a single #, which merely specifies a digit placeholder. The third argument (missing in the fragment) is optional and is the name of a `decimal-format` instance, which you will see in a few paragraphs.

This particular instance would produce the following output:

```
1000000000000
```

Without any commas separating groups of three zeros, this is sort of hard to read. I'll change `format-number()` slightly to make an improvement:

```
<xsl:value-of select="format-number(1000000000000,',###')"/>
```

After adding a comma and placeholders for three digits, this format pattern string will produce this output:

```
1,000,000,000,000
```

Now that's looking a little better. If you wanted to express the number as dollars, you could change the format pattern to this:

```
<xsl:value-of select="format-number(1000000000000,'$,###.00')"/>
```

which would yield the following result:

```
$1,000,000,000,000.00
```

I added a dollar sign ($) to the beginning of the format pattern string plus a decimal point and two zeros (.00) at the end, which gave us a monetary output. A zero (0) replaces digits that are absent in the number, and # just holds a place for digits that already exist in the number being formatted.

Are you ready to dive into a more complex example? I have no doubt that you are ready. Here is a stylesheet, format-number-price.xsl, that formats the value of a Price element in one of four different currencies. It transforms the entire content of catalog-price.xml but with each Price represented with its proper currency symbol. Here is the stylesheet:

```
<xsl:stylesheet version="1.0"
xmlns:xsl="http://www.w3.org/1999/XSL/Transform">
<xsl:output method="xml" encoding="utf-8" indent="yes"/>

<xsl:template match="/">
<xsl:processing-instruction name="xml-
stylesheet">href="catalog.css" type="text/css"</xsl:processing-
instruction>
 <Catalog>
  <Item>
   <xsl:apply-templates select="Catalog"/>
  </Item>
 </Catalog>
</xsl:template>

<xsl:template match="Item">
 <xsl:variable name="price-1" select="Price[1]"/>
 <xsl:variable name="price-2" select="Price[2]"/>
 <xsl:variable name="price-3" select="Price[3]"/>
 <xsl:variable name="price-4" select="Price[4]"/>
   <xsl:copy-of select="Name"/>
```

```
   <xsl:copy-of select="Description"/>
   <Price>
   <xsl:value-of select="format-number(number($price-
1),'$#####.00')"/> (<xsl:value-of select="Price[1]/@currency"/>)</Price>
   <Price>
   <xsl:value-of select="format-number(number($price-
2),'&#xa3;#####.00')"/> (<xsl:value-of
select="Price[2]/@currency"/>)</Price>
   <Price>
   <xsl:value-of select="format-number(number($price-3),'$#####.00')"/>
(<xsl:value-of select="Price[3]/@currency"/>)</Price>
   <Price>
   <xsl:value-of select="format-number(number($price-
4),'&#x20ac;#####.00')"/> (<xsl:value-of
select="Price[4]/@currency"/>)</Price>
   </xsl:template>

</xsl:stylesheet>
```

Here's what's going on in this stylesheet. The `output` element turns on indent (`indent="yes"`) so that the result will be a bit more attractive and readable. The first template matches the document root (/) and then instantiates an XML stylesheet PI for a CSS stylesheet (you'll see what that does a little later). It also selects the `Catalog` element, that is, all child nodes of `Catalog`, and instantiates several literal result elements (`Catalog` and `Item`).

The second template matches `Item` elements returned in the node-set of the first template. It then instantiates four variables, one for each of the `Price` elements in an `Item` element. The predicate, that is, the `[1]` part of `Price[1]`, in the `select` attribute of the first variable instructs the processor to select the first instance of `Price` that is a child of `Item`. The predicate in the second variable selects the second occurrence of `Price`, and so forth. Each variable holds the string value that is in the content of the `Price` element it selects. (You will learn more about variables in Chapter 7.)

The instances of `copy-of` copies the `Name` and `Description` content, tags and all, to the result tree. Then comes the heavy lifting.

After instantiating a literal result element for `Price`, an instance of `value-of` returns the string value of the result of calling `format-number()`. Because each variable contains a string value, it must be converted to number so that `format-number()` can accept the value as its first argument. This is done with the `number()` function, an XPath function that converts an object into a number (as in `number($price-1)`). This number is then formatted according to the format pattern string in the second argument, each with a different currency symbol ($ for dollar,

£ for pound sterling [£], and € for the Euro [€]). The currency abbreviation is thrown into the value of Price for convenience in identifying the currency.

Here is a chunk of the output:

```
<Price>$5.99 (USD)</Price>
<Price>T£4.16 (GBP)</Price>
<Price>$9.37 (CAN)</Price>
<Price>[é¼46.63 (EUR)</Price>
```

Oops. If you transform this from a Windows command prompt, wow—it's ugly. What happened? When the output is displayed in an MS-DOS window, it reads the characters as individual bytes and outputs them as such. The Unicode characters are represented in several bytes by UTF-8, not just single bytes, as are the 128 characters in US-ASCII. The MS-DOS code page doesn't handle the multibyte characters properly and spits out two or three characters instead.

All is not lost. If you redirect the output to a file and then view the file with an up-to-date browser, it should interpret the characters correctly. For example, if you create an output file with XT as follows:

```
xt catalog-price.xml format-number-price.xsl new-price.xml
```

you can then view the file with a browser such as Internet Explorer (IE) 5.5. That's where the stylesheet PI for a CSS stylesheet comes in handy. Figure 5.1 shows a browser window displaying new-price.xml formatted for display with the help of catalog.css. The currency symbols are displayed correctly.

A Few Notes on CSS

The CSS stylesheet that modifies the presentation of this XML document follows:

```
/* catalog.css */

Name {
  display:block;
  margin-top:4mm;
  font-size:14pt;
  font-family:Tahoma,Verdana,Arial,Helvetica,san-serif;
  font-weight:bold
}

Description {
  display:block;
```

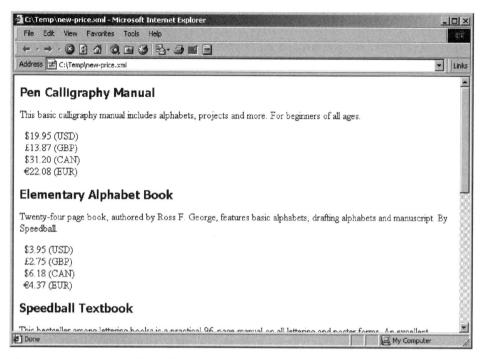

Figure 5.1   Internet Explorer displaying new-price.xml with catalog.css.

```
margin-top:4mm;
margin-bottom:4mm
}

Price {
display:block;
margin-left:2mm
}
```

With a C-style comment at the top showing the filename (/* cata-
log.css */), this CSS stylesheet defines presentation rules for the content
of catalog.xml or documents with similar elements. Any Name element
is displayed in block format, as bold, in 14 points, and with a sans-serif font
with fonts in a prioritized order of preference, based on availability. It also
has a small margin at the top (4 millimeters). Description and Price
elements are also displayed as blocks and with some margins. By the way,
a block format is formatted like a separate paragraph (as with the p element
in XHTML), as opposed to an inline format (display:inline), which
formats text on a line, such as a bold format (as with the b element
in XHTML).

The decimal-format Element

Without a third argument, the format-number() function displays numbers according to the default decimal format settings. The default values of the decimal-format element are shown in the following snippet:

```
<xsl:decimal-format
decimal-separator="."
grouping-separator=","
infinity="Infinity"
minus-sign="-"
NaN="NaN"
percent="%"
per-mille="‰"
zero-digit="0"
digit="#"
pattern-separator=";"/>
```

This is illustrative but is quite unnecessary because all the defaults are set by, well, default. It is important to know that these defaults don't automatically set up your number formats. What they do is help the XSLT processor to interpret the format pattern string in the second argument of format-number(). For example, if a format pattern string is ',###.00' and you are depending on the default decimal format, your XSLT processor will know that the period or full stop (.) is the decimal separator, that the comma (,) is the grouping separator, and that the pound sign (#) represents a digit. If you change these defaults (I'll show you an example a little later), the processor will interpret format patterns according to the new settings.

Each of the attributes of decimal-format is explained further in Table 5.1. All of these attributes represent the special characters and pattern parts that are in the Java version 1.1 DecimalFormat; however, the currency sign feature in DecimalFormat is not supported in XSLT. One thing that this feature does, for example, is replace a currency sign (¤) in a format pattern with an appropriate currency symbol (such as $) in the formatted number.

The name Attribute in decimal-format

Missing from the previous fragment instance of the defaults for decimal-format is the name attribute, which names a decimal format so that you can reference it in the third argument of format-number(). The following fragment defines three decimal formats, each changing the values of some of the attributes. The name of each format is a two-letter country code for a different nation: Germany is de, France is fr, and Russia is ru.

Table 5.1 Decimal-Format Attributes

ATTRIBUTE	DESCRIPTION
name	The name of the decimal format, referenced by the third argument of `format-number()`.
decimal-separator	The decimal point, as in $64.00 (default is `.`).
grouping-separator	The character that separates groups of digits (default is `,`).
infinity	A string representing infinity (default is `Infinity`).
minus-sign	A character representing the minus sign or negative unary operator (default is `-`).
NaN	A string representing *Not a Number* (default is `NaN`).
percent	The percent sign (default is `%`); also, multiply by 100.
per-mille	The per thousand sign (default is `‰`); also, multiply by 1000.
zero-digit	The digit representing zero (default is `0`). A zero in a format pattern string will replace an absent digit in a number with a 0. For example, `'##.00'` will format `10` as `10.00`.
digit	A character representing any digit in a format pattern string (default is `#`). This character is a digit placeholder, representing the placement of a corresponding digit in a number. For example, `'#,###'` will format `1000` as `1,000`.
pattern-separator	A character that separates positive patterns from negative subpatterns in a format pattern string (default is `;`). For example, `'##.00;(-##.00)'` will represent `10` as `10.00` and `-10` as `(-10.00)`.

```
<xsl:decimal-format name="de" decimal-separator="," grouping-
    separator="."/>
<xsl:decimal-format name="fr" decimal-separator="," grouping-separator="
    "/>
<xsl:decimal-format name="ru" decimal-separator=" " grouping-
    separator="."/>
```

The following instances of `value-of` return the string value of three formatted numbers, each with different format pattern strings reflecting a different country's decimal and grouping separators:

```
German: <xsl:value-of select="format-number(1000000,'.###,00', 'de')"/>
French: <xsl:value-of select="format-number(1000000,' ###,00', 'fr')"/>
Russian: <xsl:value-of select="format-number(1000000,'.### 00', 'ru')"/>
```

These would give you the following output, correct in turn for each country's numeration conventions:

```
German: 1.000.000,00
French: 1 000 000,00
Russian: 1.000.000 00
```

On to Conditional Processing

In this chapter we discussed how to sort lists with `sort`, how to number lists with `number`, how to format numbers with the `format` attribute of `number`, the `format-number()` function, and the `decimal-format` element. In the next chapter, we will go over ways to process stylesheet input conditionally with several mechanisms that are familiar from traditional programming.

Conditional Processing

There are two instruction elements in XSLT that allow you to instantiate a template based on certain tests. These elements are if and choose. In this chapter, I will explain how to use these elements and compare them to similar conditional statements in modern programming languages. I will also expand on what you have already learned about expressions. And even though you have already seen it a few times, I'll discuss the for-each instruction element as well.

If you are a C++ or Java programmer, conditional statements are not foreign to you; however, if you are not a programmer, don't sweat it. I'll do my best to make sense out of conditional statements for you.

The if Element

Let's start out with the XLST if element. Before I discuss the if element, though, I want to show you a few examples of if statements. Here is a simple if statement in Java:

```
if (currency == 'EUR' )
     usd = 1.0000 * 0.9032;
```

If you are an experienced programmer, you already know what is going on here in this little morsel. If you don't understand it, read on and I'll try to clear things up.

An `if` statement contains a Boolean expression. George Boole, the nineteenth-century British mathematician, is credited with creating a system of logical comparisons, as with the Boolean operators such as AND, OR, and NOT. Such logic is very important in computer science. In a Boolean expression, if a test is true (or returns true), the statement following it is executed; if it is false (returns false), it is skipped. It's fairly straightforward to get a machine to imitate this kind of logic.

Before the actual `if` statement, assume that the program has laid some groundwork by assigning values to variables, such as assigning a string value to `currency`. The Java statement tests whether `currency` and `'EUR'` have the same value with an equality comparison operator (`==`). A single equal sign (`=`) has the effect of assigning a value to a variable rather than comparing values.

That's what's going on in the line immediately following the `if`: The result of multiplying two real numbers (`1.0000` and `0.9032`) is assigned to the variable `usd`. In other words, if the currency is Euros, assign a value to `usd` that may be used to calculate U.S. dollars based on the value of Euros.

You could also trigger a series of actions by adding braces (`{ }`) to the Java statement, like so:

```
if (currency == 'EUR' ) {
    usd = 1.0000 * 0.9032;
    new_price = price * usd;
    System.out.println("The price in USD is " + new_price);
}
```

A series of statements is known as a block or a block of statements. If the expression in the `if` statement evaluates to true, then all the statements in the block are executed. With a few lines of code, a new price is calculated in U.S. dollars based on Euros, and a bit of text to that effect is printed on standard output, which is usually the screen.

The `if` element in XSLT is similar. You saw an example of `if` in the last chapter. Do you remember it? It first appeared in the stylesheet `number-price-level-multiple.xsl`. Here is a little piece of that stylesheet:

```
<xsl:if test="./@currency='EUR'">
----------------</xsl:if>
```

This template is saying that if the current node (a `Price` element represented by a `.`) has a `currency` attribute whose content is the string `'EUR'`

(Euros), the processor will output a handful of hyphens to the result tree to split up the result visually.

The test Attribute

The `if` element's `test` attribute is required. It states a Boolean expression and, if the expression is true, instantiates any template that the `if` element might contain. If it returns false, it does nothing, and the XSLT processor just happily moves on.

Following is a simple stylesheet (`if.xsl`) whose one and only template contains an `if` instruction. It tests to see if `order.xml` has a `Date` element whose content is the text `2001-06-01`.

```
<xsl:stylesheet version="1.0"
xmlns:xsl="http://www.w3.org/1999/XSL/Transform">
<xsl:output method="text" encoding="utf-8" omit-xml-declaration="yes"/>

<xsl:template match="Order">
 <xsl:if test="Date[. = '2001-06-01']">
  <xsl:text>Order Date: June 1, 2001</xsl:text>
 </xsl:if>
</xsl:template>

</xsl:stylesheet>
```

The template matches `Order` and so can process any of the child nodes of `Order`, one of which is `Date`. The `if` element is within a `template` element; this is a must. In this example, the `test` attribute uses a predicate to check whether the `Date` element has as its content a string matching `'2001-06-01'`, which it does. Because this is true, the rule in `if` is instantiated, or, in this case, the `text` element outputs text to the result tree, as shown:

```
Order Date: June 1, 2001
```

Following are a series of stylesheet relics that show a variety of if-then tests. The following test checks to see if the content of `Date` in `order.xml` does *not* match the given date:

```
<xsl:if test="Date[not(. = '2001-06-01')]">
 <xsl:message>Wrong order!</xsl:message>
</xsl:if>
```

The `not()` function is a Boolean function from XPath (see Section 4.3 of the XPath recommendation). The logic of `not()` is a flip-flop, if you will— it evaluates as true if its argument is false and returns false if its argument is true. The content of message is output by the XSLT processor, not in the result tree, but as an error notification to standard output. (You will learn more about the message element in Chapter 9, "More XSLT.")

This next test checks if the content of the Quantity element in order.xml is less than 50. If so, a Discount element is output to the result tree with a bit of bad news:

```
<xsl:if test="Quantity[. &lt; 50]">
 <Discount>None.</Discount>
</xsl:if>
```

XPath expressions—including predicates—must use the entity reference < when the logic calls for a less-than symbol (<). In XML, the symbol < is not allowed in an attribute value, and attribute values are where expressions are expressed in XSLT. When an XSLT processor parses an expression, it can figure out what to do with < or <= given the context. Furthermore, the content of Quantity is treated as if it were a number rather than just a string value representing a number, so that the logical, less-than comparison can be made with good effect. (See Section 3.4 of the XPath recommendation.)

This next if element tests to see if the Order element in order.xml evaluates to true on two conditions, compared with the Boolean operator and (also in Section 3.4 of the XPath recommendation). The conditions that must pass muster are these: (1) the Order element must have a partner attribute with a value '06-853-2535' and (2) a Date child of Order must have the string '2001-06-01' as content (or a text node child).

```
<xsl:template match="Order">
<xsl:if test="@partner='06-853-2535' and Date[.='2001-06-01']">
 <xsl:copy-of select="self::Order"/>
</xsl:if>
</xsl:template>
```

If the test evaluates to true, the Order element and its children—including any attributes accompanying its element children—are copied to the result tree with copy-of. The self:: axis used with Order, as in self::Order, is the same as using either . or current().

Next we have a similar test that uses the or XPath Boolean operator:

```
<xsl:template match="Order">
<xsl:if test="@partner='06-853-2535' or Date[.='2001-06-01']">
 <xsl:copy-of select="self::Order"/>
</xsl:if>
</xsl:template>
```

This test verifies whether the first condition or the second condition is true. If either of the conditions is true, the Boolean expression returns true, so you are aiming to get one true condition and at best two true conditions.

Now it's time to fry bigger fish.

Searching country-codes.xml

The document archive for this book contains a file based on the ISO standard for representing countries with two-letter abbreviations (ISO 3166-1:1997). The document is called `country-codes.xml`. (This document certainly isn't an authoritative version of the standard; it is merely an approximation of ISO 3166 written in XML.) This file has about 1000 lines in it, and it isn't very convenient to scroll through to find a country code for a country or the name of a country that goes with a code.

One way you could approach this document is with the stylesheet `country-codes-if.xsl`. When processing the document with the stylesheet, you submit a parameter with either a country name or a country code. If you provide a country name, you get a country code as a result (provided that the country name is correct and it is in the document). If you submit a valid country code, you will get a country name in return. You have seen it before, but here is a glimpse of what the document `country-codes.xml` looks like (I won't reproduce the whole file here for want of space):

```
<?xml version="1.0" encoding="utf-8"?>

<country-codes>
 <code>
  <abbr>AD</abbr>
  <country>Andorra</country>
 </code>
 <code>
  <abbr>AE</abbr>
  <country>United Arab Emirates</country>
 </code>
 <code>
  <abbr>AF</abbr>
  <country>Afghanistan</country>
 </code>
 <code>
  <abbr>AG</abbr>
  <country>Antigua and Barbuda</country>
 </code>
 <code>
```

```
 <abbr>AI</abbr>
 <country>Anguilla</country>
</code>
<code>
 <abbr>AL</abbr>
 <country>Albania</country>
</code>
<code>
 <abbr>AM</abbr>
 <country>Armenia</country>
</code>
...
```

Each instance of code contains a single instance of abbr (the two-letter country code) and a single instance of country (the country name). Now have a look at the stylesheet country-codes-if.xsl:

```
<xsl:stylesheet version="1.0"
xmlns:xsl="http://www.w3.org/1999/XSL/Transform">
<xsl:output method="text" encoding="utf-8"/>
<xsl:param name="country"/>
<xsl:param name="code"/>

<xsl:template match="/">
 <xsl:apply-templates select="country-codes"/>
</xsl:template>

<xsl:template match="country-codes">
 <xsl:apply-templates select="code"/>
</xsl:template>

<xsl:template match="code">
  <xsl:if test="country[. = $country]">
   The country code for <xsl:value-of select="country"/> is <xsl:value-
     of select="abbr"/>.
  </xsl:if>
  <xsl:if test="abbr[. = $code]">
   The country for the code <xsl:value-of select="abbr"/> is <xsl:value-
     of select="country"/>.
  </xsl:if>
</xsl:template>

</xsl:stylesheet>
```

The output method for this stylesheet is text. At the top level, the stylesheet defines two global parameters, country and code. These parameters will come in handy later.

In the third template are two instances of the if element. The first if tests if the value of the parameter $country is the same as the content of any country element in the node-set. (The node-set at this point contains all code elements and their abbr and country element children.) If it finds matching content, the template will output a line containing the string value of a matching country name (country) and its accompanying country code (abbr). In the second instance of if, it checks to see if the value of the parameter $code is the same as the content of an instance of abbr. If so, the template outputs a line giving the matching abbr and its accompanying country.

For example, if you issue a command with a country parameter, such as:

```
msxsl country-codes.xml country-codes-if.xsl country=Lesotho
```

it will produce the following output:

```
The country code for Lesotho is LS.
```

Likewise, you could enter the following for a code parameter (uppercase is a must):

```
saxon country-codes.xml country-codes-if.xsl code=LS
```

and get this result:

```
The country for the code LS is Lesotho.
```

If the name of a country has more than one word, you have to enclose the name in single or double quotes, like this example:

```
xt country-codes.xml country-codes-if.xsl country="United States"
```

and it will generate this result:

```
The country code for United States is US.
```

TestXSLT requires a bit more typing. An example follows:

```
testxslt -in country-codes.xml -xsl country-codes-if.xsl -param country
    'Germany'
```

A parameter value Germany, surrounded by single quotes, and the parameter name country do not need an equal sign as in other implementations. You'll see output like this (unless you shut off all the processor reports with the –q command-line option):

```
========= Parsing country-codes-if.xsl ==========
Parse of country-codes-if.xsl took 10 milliseconds
========= Parsing country-codes.xml ==========
```

```
Parse of country-codes.xml took 20 milliseconds
==============================
Transforming...

    The country code for Germany is DE.

transform took 30 milliseconds

Total time took 80 milliseconds
```

> **NOTE** The required use of single quotes with a parameter value in TestXSLT is inconsistent. I suspect there is a bug in the version I used (1.1.0). I suggest trying a similar example with and without single quotes. I have gotten it to work both ways.

Perhaps you will want to test more than one condition at a time, with multiple expressions, making your template a little more efficient. For this you can use the choose element.

The choose Element

An if instruction can test at most one expression. Granted, that expression may test more than one condition, but you are limited to instantiating the content of only one template. So what if you have more than one situation that you want to test? This is where the choose instruction element can come into play.

The Java if-else Statement

Near the beginning of the chapter, you saw a very elementary if-then statement in Java. One thing I did not mention there is that you can test multiple conditions by adding an else keyword. Here is the Java:

```
if (currency == 'EUR' ) {
    usd = 1.0000 * 0.9032;
    new_price = price * usd;
    System.out.println("The price in USD is " + new_price);
}
else {
    System.out.println("Currency not in Euros.");
}
```

The else statement provides an escape hatch, so to speak. In other words, if the condition in the if statement immediately preceding else is not true, the statement in else is executed. You can also write this in a way that tests more than one condition, as shown next:

```
if (currency == 'EUR' ) {
    usd = 1.0000 * 0.9032;
    new_price = price * usd;
    System.out.println("The price in USD is " + new_price);
}
else if (currency == 'GBP' ) {
    usd = 1.0000 * 1.4425;
    new_price = price * usd;
    System.out.println("The price in USD is " + new_price);
}
else {
    System.out.println("Currency not in Euros or pounds.");
}
```

A Java interpreter will look at each `if` or `else if` statement. When it finds one whose expression is true, it drops out of the if-else statement and continues processing on the next line, after the statement. If none of the if-else statements is true, the interpreter will execute the statements in the `else` block and then move on.

To illustrate how this kind of processing is done similarly in XSLT, here is a stylesheet called `country-codes-choose.xsl`, which is based on the previous example. It works just like `country-codes-if.xsl` but has a tidier syntax. Changes are shown in bold:

```
<xsl:stylesheet version="1.0"
xmlns:xsl="http://www.w3.org/1999/XSL/Transform">
<xsl:output method="text" encoding="utf-8"/>
<xsl:param name="country"/>
<xsl:param name="code"/>

<xsl:template match="/">
 <xsl:apply-templates select="country-codes"/>
</xsl:template>

<xsl:template match="country-codes">
 <xsl:apply-templates select="code"/>
</xsl:template>

<xsl:template match="code">
 <xsl:choose>
  <xsl:when test="country[. = $country]">
   The country code for <xsl:value-of select="country"/> is
<xsl:value-of select="abbr"/>.
  </xsl:when>
  <xsl:when test="abbr[. = $code]">
   The country for the code <xsl:value-of select="abbr"/> is <xsl:value-
      of select="country"/>.
  </xsl:when>
 </xsl:choose>
```

```
</xsl:template>

</xsl:stylesheet>
```

Instead of two `if` elements, one right after the other, this stylesheet uses the `choose` instruction element. A `choose` element must contain at least one `when` element, but it could contain just about as many as you want. Although `choose` can offer a number of alternative choices (expressions) through any number of `when` elements, it can instantiate the content of only one `when` element. These `when` elements are similar to the initial `if` and following `else if` statements in Java.

Test out the results. If you enter this command line:

```
saxon country-codes.xml country-codes-choose.xsl country="Sri Lanka"
```

you will get output looking like:

```
The country code for Sri Lanka is LK.
```

The otherwise Element

The `choose` element can also contain a single instance of the `otherwise` element. This `otherwise` element works like the final `else` statement in Java by instantiating its template content if none of the expressions in the preceding `when` elements is true. (If none of the `when` elements evaluates to true and there is no `otherwise` element, a `choose` element will have no effect on the result tree.) Likewise, the `otherwise` element must come last in `choose`. An instance of `choose` is shown in the following piece based on the previous stylesheet:

```
<xsl:template match="code">
 <xsl:choose>
  <xsl:when test="country[. = $country]">
   The country code for <xsl:value-of select="country"/> is
<xsl:value-of select="abbr"/>.
  </xsl:when>
  <xsl:when test="abbr[. = $code]">
   The country for the code <xsl:value-of select="abbr"/> is <xsl:value-
     of select="country"/>.
  </xsl:when>
  <xsl:otherwise>
    Sorry. No matching country name or country code.
  </xsl:otherwise>
 </xsl:choose>
</xsl:template>
```

If you add an `otherwise` element to the previous stylesheet, you will discover some interesting things about the way XSLT processors work. The expected behavior is that the template will examine a code element, including its children. This template matches a node-set containing all 243 code elements in country-codes.xml, so you will see results like this:

```
Sorry. No matching country name or country code.

Sorry. No matching country name or country code.

Sorry. No matching country name or country code.

Sorry. No matching country name or country code.

Sorry. No matching country name or country code.

Sorry. No matching country name or country code.

Sorry. No matching country name or country code.

...
```

You would see this line of text repeated over and over because the template is mulling over every instance of code in the node-set. For each choose that does not return true on an expression in a when element, the content of otherwise is output, that is, 242 times if just one code element contains a hit! The following stylesheet limits the scope within the context of code elements. It's called country-codes-choose-otherwise.xsl:

```
<xsl:stylesheet version="1.0"
xmlns:xsl="http://www.w3.org/1999/XSL/Transform">
<xsl:output method="text" encoding="utf-8"/>
<xsl:param name="country"/>
<xsl:param name="code"/>
<xsl:param name="letter"/>

<xsl:template match="/">
 <xsl:apply-templates select="country-codes"/>
</xsl:template>

<xsl:template match="country-codes">
 <xsl:apply-templates select="code[starts-with(country,$letter) or
    starts-with(abbr,$letter)]"/>
</xsl:template>

<xsl:template match="code">
 <xsl:choose>
  <xsl:when test="country[. = $country]">
    The country code for <xsl:value-of select="country"/> is
<xsl:value-of select="abbr"/>.
  </xsl:when>
  <xsl:when test="abbr[. = $code]">
```

```
    The country for the code <xsl:value-of select="abbr"/> is <xsl:value-
       of select="country"/>.
  </xsl:when>
  <xsl:otherwise>
   Sorry. No matching country name or country code. (<xsl:value-of
      select="country"/>, <xsl:value-of
 select="abbr"/>)
  </xsl:otherwise>
 </xsl:choose>
</xsl:template>

</xsl:stylesheet>
```

This stylesheet adds a parameter called letter. This parameter is put into service in the second template, which calls the XPath function starts-with() in a predicate, as in code[starts-with(country,$letter)] or code[starts-with(abbr,$letter)]. What this does is select those code elements whose country or abbr child elements start with a letter given in the parameter $letter, thereby limiting the scope of the node-set. Let's say you provide the letter *F* and then search the node-set for France. This is how you could do it:

```
saxon country-codes.xml country-codes-choose-otherwise.xsl letter=F
       country=France
```

As you can see, you enter two parameters at the command line, letter and country (uppercase and lowercase characters matter). Here then is what you would get back:

```
Sorry. No matching country name or country code. (Finland, FI)

Sorry. No matching country name or country code. (Fiji, FJ)

Sorry. No matching country name or country code. (Falkland Islands
      (Malvinas), FK)

Sorry. No matching country name or country code. (Micronesia, FM)

Sorry. No matching country name or country code. (Faroe Islands, FO)

The country code for France is FR.

Sorry. No matching country name or country code. (France, Metropolitan,
      FX)

Sorry. No matching country name or country code. (French Guiana, GF)

Sorry. No matching country name or country code. (French Polynesia, PF)
```

```
Sorry. No matching country name or country code. (French Southern
    Territories, TF)
```

I added a pair of `value-of` elements to the content of `otherwise` so that you could see what was getting skipped. You'll see that one country (Micronesia) was included in the node-set because its country code (`abbr`) starts with *F* (FM).

Conditional Processing with for-each

You have already seen the `for-each` element in action in previous examples (such as `html-table-for-each.xsl` in Chapter 3, "HTML and XHTML Output"). The `for-each` element does things a little differently than `apply-templates`, and I'd like to draw some of those distinctions more clearly here.

Both `for-each` and `apply-templates` are instruction elements, so they must not be children of `stylesheet` (or `transform`). They must be part of a template, which usually means they are children of the `template` element, but not always. They could also be children of other template elements, such as `if` or `when`.

Both `for-each` and `apply-templates` evaluate to a node-set, based on the value of a `select` attribute (an expression); however, `for-each` requires the `select` attribute, but `apply-templates` does not. Without a `select` attribute, `apply-templates` will just process all the children of the current node, such as those in the `match` attribute of `template`; with `select`, it processes the node-set to which the expression evaluates.

The XSLT processor then must hunt around to see if there are any templates in the stylesheet whose `match` attribute is the same as the expression in `select`. What appears to be one template "dropping down" its node-set to another is really an instance of `apply-templates` finding an applicable template elsewhere in the stylesheet. All nodes are processed in document order unless there is a `sort` element child; if so, it processes the nodes in the sorted order. I know it is all a bit mind-boggling, but after a while it will start to make sense.

The `for-each` element, on the other hand, is a little simpler in its processing approach. It must evaluate to a node-set with the expression in its `select` attribute, so it doesn't bother with the children of the current node, as does `apply-templates` without `select`, only those nodes that present themselves in the node-set. In addition, `for-each` concerns itself only with the node-set at hand and doesn't have to cast about for applicable templates. It just processes each node in the node-set, in document order or, if the node-set is sorted with a `sort` element, in the sorted order.

Some think that a `for-each` element iterates like a loop through the node-set and then breaks out given a certain condition. It sort of acts like that, but that's not really what's happening. I think it's fair to use the term *iteration* in relation to `for-each`, but it can be deceiving.

Comparing the Java For Loop

To understand the difference between `for-each` and a traditional for loop, let's examine the following Java for loop:

```
int i = 0;
int j = 0;

for (int counter = 0; counter < 244; counter++) {
  System.out.println(country[i] + " " + abbr[j]);
  i++;
  j++;
}
```

The integer variables `i` and `j` are set to `0`. These will be used to increment through a couple of arrays. The `counter` variable in the for loop is also initialized to `0`.

Then the loop tests to see if `counter` is less than 244. If this is true, `counter` increments by 1 (`counter = 0 + 1`) and then executes the statements in the loop. The first statement prints a country name from position 0 of an array named `country[]` and also a country code (two-letter abbreviation) from position 0 of an array named `abbr[]`. Both of these arrays have 243 members (0 through 242). After printing these out, the `i` and `j` variables are incremented by one (`i = 0 + 1` and `j = 0 + 1`), and the loop starts all over again. The loop continues to iterate until the value of `counter` exceeds 243. At that point, the arrays `country[]` and `abbr[]` should be exhausted and all 243 country names and codes should have been printed out.

With `for-each`, there is no incrementing or looping going on at all. It is just applying templates repeatedly to nodes in a list until each node in the list has been processed. In that sense, it is analogous to a for loop, but that's where the similarity ends. In addition, you can't get an XSLT processor to break out of a loop when it finds a certain condition because there really is no loop to break out of. You can get it to process fewer nodes in the list, but you can't really do a break.

I think the `for-each` element better resembles the Unix C shell command `foreach`. The `foreach` command basically executes commands on a list until the list is exhausted. Following is an example:

```
% foreach i (*.xml)
?   cat $i >> all.xml
? end
```

The first line of this example declares the variable i and, by using a wild-card (*.xml), creates a list to do its work on, namely, a list of all the XML files in the current directory. The Unix command cat concatenates or appends all these XML files (represented by the variable reference $i) into one file called all.xml. After it does this to every file in the list, the com-mand ends.

This, to my way of thinking, is a better allegory for the for-each ele-ment than a for loop. Nevertheless, it is possible to mimic the behavior of a for loop further, not by breaking out of a loop when a certain condition is met, but by processing fewer of the nodes in the current node-set condi-tionally. I offer an example to illustrate.

The stylesheet is country-codes-for-each.xsl. A for-each ele-ment processes all the nodes in the current node list, unless a parameter is passed in to the stylesheet. In such a case, only the nodes qualified by the parameter are processed; otherwise, all nodes are processed:

```
<xsl:stylesheet version="1.0"
xmlns:xsl="http://www.w3.org/1999/XSL/Transform">
<xsl:output method="text" encoding="utf-8"/>
<xsl:param name="letter"/>

<xsl:template match="/">
 <xsl:apply-templates select="country-codes"/>
</xsl:template>

<xsl:template match="country-codes">
 <xsl:apply-templates select="code"/>
</xsl:template>

<xsl:template match="code">
 <xsl:if test="country[starts-with(.,$letter)]">
  <xsl:for-each select="."><xsl:value-of select="country"/> [<xsl:value-
    of select="abbr"/>]
 </xsl:for-each>
 </xsl:if>
</xsl:template>

</xsl:stylesheet>
```

If the test returns false, that is, if $letter is empty, then for-each processes all the nodes in the set, but if the test returns true, it processes only those nodes that match the test, namely, those country names that start with the letter provided on the command line.

The test in if will evaluate as false with this command (no parameter):

```
msxsl country-codes.xml country-codes-for-each.xsl
```

Here are just 20 lines of the overwhelming result:

```
Andorra [AD]
United Arab Emirates [AE]
Afghanistan [AF]
Antigua and Barbuda [AG]
Anguilla [AI]
Albania [AL]
Armenia [AM]
Netherlands Antilles [AN]
Angola [AO]
Antarctica [AQ]
Argentina [AR]
American Samoa [AS]
Austria [AT]
Australia [AU]
Aruba [AW]
Azerbaijan [AZ]
Bosnia and Herzegovina [BA]
Barbados [BB]
Bangladesh [BD]
Belgium [BE]
...
```

The test will evaluate as true if you submit a parameter value on the command line, such as the following:

```
msxsl country-codes.xml country-codes-for-each.xsl letter=Z
```

which will produce this as a result:

```
Zambia [ZM]
Zaire [ZR]
Zimbabwe [ZW]
```

Variables and Parameters

Numerous examples in this book have already been introduced of how to use variables and parameters. The next chapter will cover them in more detail.

Variables and Parameters

You have already seen variables and parameters in action in a number of examples in this book. This chapter is dedicated to settling the details of how to use them. If you are a programmer, the concept of declaring variables is not new to you, but you may find the way XSLT uses them a bit strange.

To get started, I'll talk about how to assign variables in Java and then compare that process to the way you set values for variables or parameters in XSLT.

Declaring Variables in Java

What's a software program without a variable? One of the reasons why variables are used in programming is that they allow data to be dynamic, so you can manage data or perform arithmetic on variables rather than just numbers, for example. The following bit of Java code declares a few variables and assigns values to them:

```
int counter = 1;
double gbp = 1.4425;
double usd = 1.0000;
String currency = "GBP";
```

The variable named `counter` has a type of `int`. A variable of this type in Java must be a signed, 32-bit integer. This one is assigned a value of 1. The two variables `gbp` and `usd` are assigned 64-bit, floating-point values. The last variable, `currency`, is assigned a string of characters.

In Java, you can do all sorts of operations on these variables. In the case where the types are numbers, you can add, subtract, multiply, and divide the variables:

```
new = usd * gbp;
```

In the case of strings, you can concatenate them or reproduce them at various places:

```
System.out.println(currency + ": pounds sterling (UK).");
```

Variables represent a convenience without which computing itself would prove difficult if not dreadfully verbose. Because of their convenience, I'm glad that XSLT includes variables and parameters. But to use them properly—and to avoid some pitfalls—you need to get better acquainted with them. Let's get on with it.

What's the Difference?

XSLT offers two similar elements, `variable` and `param`, both of which have comparable syntax. Both have a mandatory `name` attribute and an optional `select` attribute. You have already seen them defined, so none of this will be a surprise, I hope. One thing I think we should get out of the way early is the difference between the two.

You can bind a value to a name in XSLT with either the `variable` or `param` element. You have seen declarations like this before in this book:

```
<xsl:variable name="partner"/>
```

```
<xsl:param name="letter"/>
```

By defining them in this way, you have bound each to an empty string, which has the same effect as:

```
<xsl:variable name="partner" select="''"/>
```

```
<xsl:param name="letter" select="''"/>
```

Not very interesting, really. What do you do with an empty string? Actually, an empty string is not of much value in a `variable`, but the value bound by `param` is considered only a default or initial value because you can later pass a new value to a parameter either from outside of the stylesheet, such as from the command line, or from another template using the `with-param` element (see the section titled *The with-param Element* near the end of this chapter).

With parameters, you are in good shape even with an empty-string declaration: You just have to pass a value in later, as you have already seen in earlier chapters. As for the value of `variable`, as a general rule, once it is set, it is set, and you can't change it dynamically. Nevertheless, there are special conditions under which you can change the value of variables in templates.

A value bound by `variable`, though, cannot be changed as a parameter value can be changed. Under certain conditions, though, you can change the value of a local variable in a template. If you remember the `format-number-price.xsl` stylesheet in Chapter 5, "Sorting and Numbering Lists," you'll recognize this template:

```
<xsl:template match="Item">
 <xsl:variable name="price-1" select="Price[1]"/>
 <xsl:variable name="price-2" select="Price[2]"/>
 <xsl:variable name="price-3" select="Price[3]"/>
 <xsl:variable name="price-4" select="Price[4]"/>
  <xsl:copy-of select="Name"/>
  <xsl:copy-of select="Description"/>
  <Price>
   <xsl:value-of select="format-number(number($price-1),'$#####.00')"/>
(<xsl:value-of select="Price[1]/@currency"/>)</Price>
  <Price>
   <xsl:value-of select="format-number(number($price-
2),'&#xa3;#####.00')"/> (<xsl:value-of select=
"Price[2]/@currency"/>)</Price>
  <Price>
   <xsl:value-of select="format-number(number($price-3),'$#####.00')"/>
(<xsl:value-of select="Price[3]/@currency"/>)</Price>
  <Price>
   <xsl:value-of select="format-number(number($price-
4),'&#x20ac;#####.00')"/> (<xsl:value-of
select="Price[4]/@currency"/>)</Price>
</xsl:template>
```

For each instance of `Item` and its `Price` child elements, the value bound to the variables `price-1`, `price-2`, `price-3`, and `price-4` changes each time the template is instantiated. In this sense, you can change the values of variables.

Global and Local Variables

The concept of local and global variables is another familiar notion to programmers. XSLT can't be accurately described as a general-purpose programming language, but it does some of the things such programming languages do, such as scoped variables.

Depending on where you define them, `variable` and `param` bindings are visible to and usable within an entire stylesheet or just part of it. If they are defined at the top level, that is, as children of `stylesheet` (or `transform`), variables or parameters are visible (in scope, really) for the entire stylesheet and can be used anywhere. If they are defined within a template, though, they are usable only within that template. The following stylesheet, `order-param-var.xsl`, defines both:

```
<xsl:stylesheet version="1.0"
xmlns:xsl="http://www.w3.org/1999/XSL/Transform">
<xsl:output method="xml" encoding="utf-8" indent="yes"/>
<xsl:variable name="jan" select="31"/>
<xsl:variable name="feb" select="28"/>
<xsl:variable name="febl" select="29"/>
<xsl:variable name="mar" select="31"/>
<xsl:variable name="apr" select="30"/>
<xsl:variable name="may" select="31"/>
<xsl:variable name="jun" select="30"/>
<xsl:variable name="jul" select="31"/>
<xsl:variable name="aug" select="31"/>
<xsl:variable name="sep" select="30"/>
<xsl:variable name="oct" select="31"/>
<xsl:variable name="nov" select="30"/>
<xsl:variable name="dec" select="31"/>
<xsl:variable name="elapsed" select="1 + $may + $apr + $mar + $feb +
    $jan"/>
<xsl:variable name="remaining" select="29 + $jul + $aug + $sep + $oct +
    $nov + $dec"/>
<xsl:param name="monthCount" select="0"/>
<xsl:param name="dayOrderCount" select="0"/>

<xsl:template match="/">
 <xsl:apply-templates select="Order"/>
</xsl:template>

<xsl:template match="Order">
<xsl:variable name="monthID" select="$monthCount * 100000"/>
<xsl:variable name="newID" select="$dayOrderCount + $monthID"/>
<xsl:variable name="orderID">ORD-ID-<xsl:value-of select="Date"/>-
    <xsl:value-of select="$newID"/></xsl:variable>
<xsl:choose>
```

```
<xsl:when test="not($dayOrderCount = 0 or $monthCount = 0)">
<Order orderID="{$orderID}">
 <SalesYear>
  <Days elapsed="{$elapsed}" remaining="{$remaining}" total="{$elapsed +
    $remaining}"/>
  <DayOrderCount><xsl:value-of select="$dayOrderCount"/></DayOrderCount>
 </SalesYear>
 <xsl:copy-of select="Date"/>
 <xsl:copy-of select="Item"/>
 <Partner>
  <DUNS><xsl:value-of select="@partner"/></DUNS>
  <Location>
   <Address>
    <Company>Wy'east Communications</Company>
    <Mailing>P.O. Box 537</Mailing>
    <City>West Linn</City>
    <State>Oregon</State>
    <ZIPCode>97068-0537</ZIPCode>
    <Country>United States<Code>US</Code></Country>
   </Address>
  </Location>
 </Partner>
 <xsl:copy-of select="Quantity"/>
 <xsl:copy-of select="Comments"/>
 <xsl:copy-of select="ShippingMethod"/>
</Order>
</xsl:when>
<xsl:otherwise>
<xsl:text>
Document not processed.
Must use dayOrderCount and monthCount parameters.
</xsl:text>
</xsl:otherwise>
</xsl:choose>
</xsl:template>

</xsl:stylesheet>
```

When applied to `order.xml` without giving a `dayOrderCount` and `monthCount` parameter on the command line, as follows:

```
saxon order.xml order-param-var.xsl
```

the stylesheet (and processor) gives you back this error message:

```
Document not processed.
Must use dayOrderCount and monthCount parameters.
```

If you add the required parameters on the command line, to pass them in to the stylesheet at runtime, in this way:

```
saxon order.xml order-param-var.xsl dayOrderCount=1 monthCount=6 >
    order-new.xml
```

you will get a file that looks like the following:

```
<?xml version="1.0" encoding="utf-8"?>
<Order orderID="ORD-ID-2001-06-01-600001">
    <SalesYear>
        <Days elapsed="152" remaining="213" total="365"/>
        <DayOrderCount>1</DayOrderCount>
    </SalesYear>
    <Date>2001-06-01</Date>
    <Item type="ISBN">0471416207</Item>
    <Partner>
        <DUNS>06-853-2535</DUNS>
        <Location>
            <Address>
                <Company>Wy'east Communications</Company>
                <Mailing>P.O. Box 537</Mailing>
                <City>West Linn</City>
                <State>Oregon</State>
                <ZIPCode>97068-0537</ZIPCode>
                <Country>United States<Code>US</Code>
                </Country>
            </Address>
        </Location>
    </Partner>
    <Quantity>40</Quantity>
    <Comments>None.</Comments>
    <ShippingMethod class="4th">USPS</ShippingMethod>
</Order>
```

With this result tree, it appears that order.xml is growing up a bit. Before I get into that, I want to talk about the difference between global and local variables.

At the beginning of the stylesheet, you see that a number of variables are instantiated, 12 with names such as jan, feb, mar, and so forth. There is also one called elapsed and another called remaining. These variables, based on the number of days in calendar months, are used to calculate the day in the sales year that orders occur. (In place of feb, use febl in the elapsed declaration if the year is a leap year.) Each of the 12 month variables binds a number to an abbreviated name of a month by using the select attribute, which contains an expression.

The elapsed variable does a little math to count the number of days elapsed in the sales year (a non-leap year), including the current day (day of the order). The remaining variable counts the days remaining for the rest of the sales year, not counting the day of the order. A numeric operator, such as +, converts the operands (such as 1 and $jan) to numbers, as if the number() function were called.

There are also two parameter declarations on the top level, one named dayOrderCount and another named monthCount. If these parameters are not defined or are defined with a value of 0, then the stylesheet will produce some error text. If values are bound and passed in at runtime, the stylesheet produces a result tree, an enhanced version of order.xml called order-new.xml.

All of these variables and the single parameter are declared on the top level, as children of stylesheet. These are then global variables. Their names and the values bound to their names are visible or in scope throughout the entire stylesheet. They are available on the top level and within any templates in the stylesheet as well. For example, the elapsed and the remaining variables both derive their values from other variables on the top level:

```
<xsl:variable name="elapsed" select="1 + $may + $apr + $mar + $feb +
    $jan"/>
<xsl:variable name="remaining" select="29 + $jul + $aug + $sep + $oct +
    $nov + $dec"/>
```

Accordingly, the monthID variable, defined later in a template, gets its value by multiplying the value of the top-level parameter monthCount by 100000:

```
<xsl:variable name="monthID" select="$monthCount * 100000"/>
```

Yet, if you attempted to reference a variable or parameter declared in a template at the top level, it would generate an error. Likewise, if you attempted to reference a variable or parameter from within a deeper template (such as one defined in another template within the template element), this too will generate an error. Variables and parameters declared in templates are available or visible only within the templates where they are declared and to templates underneath or deeper than the originating template. Think of them as having a cascading effect: They can spill down from the top level to a template, to a template within that template, and so on, but they cannot spill upward!

NOTE Another important characteristic to mention is that, when defined in templates, a variable can be declared anywhere within the template but that a parameter must be declared at the beginning of a template.

Enhancing order.xml

The second template matches the pattern Order, which means that it will produce a node-set consisting of the element Order and its children. Before processing any of the nodes in this list, a when element checks to see if dayOrderCount and monthCount got passed into the stylesheet with this test:

```
<xsl:when test="not($dayOrderCount = 0 or $monthCount = 0)">
```

If dayOrderCount or monthCount are equal to 0, as declared at the top level, you then will see the error reported. You must pass non-zero values in to the stylesheet, as you saw earlier, to get it to work right:

```
saxon order.xml order-param-var.xsl dayOrderCount=1 monthCount=6
```

The template declares three variables: monthID, newID, and orderID. The monthID and newID variables rely on the values of parameters set at the top level. In addition, newID depends on a variable from within the template (monthID) as does orderID (newID). The newID variable adds the value of monthID, defined just before it, and orderID relies on newID, also defined immediately before it.

Order of declaration is important, too, no matter the level of definition. Though you can define them anywhere on the top level or anywhere that an instruction element can be given in a template, you cannot reference a variable unless it has already been declared, in order from top to bottom.

The order of variable declarations shown in this fragment of order-param-var.xsl is significant, in that the variables are not referenced (as in $monthID and $newID) until after they have been declared:

```
<xsl:variable name="monthID" select="$monthCount * 100000"/>
<xsl:variable name="newID" select="$dayOrderCount + $monthID"/>
<xsl:variable name="orderID">ORD-ID-<xsl:value-of select="Date"/>-
<xsl:value-of select="$newID"/></xsl:variable>
```

Together these variables help form the value of a new attribute for the Order element, orderID. There is nothing really ingenious about the mathematics here; it's just a way to come up with a unique number that can be easily calculated. It is also easy to find the factors and the sums, thus making the steps simple for assigning and retrieving a sequence of numbers, each identifying a unique order.

To determine the meaning of the last six digits of an orderID, you just take the number of the month when the order took place and multiply it by

100000 (for example, June is month 6; multiply it by 100000, and you get 600000). Then subtract this number from the last six digits and get the total number of orders for the month (for example, 600342 minus 600000 equals 342 orders for the month of June). Furthermore, if you test against the ISO 8601 date in `orderID`, you also will know how many orders took place on a given day (for example, if before incrementing to the next date, `orderID` equals `ORD-ID-2001-06-01-600001` through `ORD-ID-2001-06-01-600007`, you know that there were seven orders on the first day of June in 2001).

Attribute Value Templates

You probably noticed the braces ({ }) in the value of the `orderID` attribute. Using this syntax means that whatever is inside the braces is evaluated as an expression. Therefore, an attribute value template, such as the following:

```
<Order orderID="{$orderID}">
```

is expanded, so to speak, in the result tree as:

```
<Order orderID="ORD-ID-2001-06-01-600001">
```

When an attribute value template is evaluated, its result is converted to a string in the result tree. Not all attributes values in a stylesheet can handle this. The following attributes cannot be set with attribute value templates:

- XSLT attributes that contain patterns or expressions (such as `select` in `apply-templates`)
- XSLT attributes of any top-level XSLT elements (such as `elements` in `strip-space`)
- XSLT attributes that refer to named objects in XSLT (such as the `name` attribute of `template`)
- Namespace declarations with `xmlns`

The literal result element `Days` also uses the attribute value templates in its attributes:

```
<Days elapsed="{$elapsed}" remaining="{$remaining}" total="{$elapsed +
$remaining}"/>
```

You can read about attribute value templates in Section 7.6.2 of the XSLT recommendation.

> **NOTE** Whenever you use the numeric operator for subtraction in an
> expression, the operator must have at least one space on either side so that it
> is not interpreted as a unary operator such as for a negative number. (See the
> first note in Section 3.5 of the XPath recommendation.)

New Elements in order-new.xml

In addition to using `copy-of` to copy elements from the source tree (for
`Date`, `Item`, `Quantity`, `Comments`, and `ShippingMethod`), this new
version of an order adds a number of elements. The `SalesYear` element
and its children, `Days` and `DayOrderCount`, help keep track of sales
information over the course of the year. `DayOrderCount` is intended to
carry a running total for the day's orders.

Also on board is a new `Partner` element. It contains a DUNS element—
DUNS, again, stands for Data Universal Number System from Dun &
Bradstreet (see www.dnb.com/dunsno/dunsno.htm)—and it was extracted
from the `partner` attribute in `order.xml`. Another child, `Location`,
contains `Address` and other related elements, such as `Company`, `Mail-
ing`, `City`, and so forth, describing the physical location of the purchasing
entity.

Datatypes

One thing that I haven't discussed much in the book is that variables and
parameters can be bound to values of five different datatypes:

- Node-set
- String
- Number
- Boolean
- Result tree fragment

You are already familiar with the first four, which are common types in
XSLT. The last type, the result tree fragment, is specific to variables and
parameters. I'll review each type with examples.

Node-Set Type

A variable can have a value that is a node-set. For example, if you were to
apply the following variable declaration and template against `order.xml`:

```
<xsl:variable name="order" select="Order"/>

...

<xsl:template match="/">
 <xsl:apply-templates select="$order/Date"/>
</xsl:template>
```

you would get this output:

```
2001-06-01
```

In other words, the variable reference $order is interpreted as being a node-set Order. The Date element is a child of Order. The output generated by apply-templates yields the text node child of Date.

Remember, you can use variable references, such as $order, in an expression but not in a pattern. This means that you cannot use the reference $order in the value of a match attribute, but you can use it in the value of a select attribute (or any other attribute that can handle an expression). Also, a variable reference works only at the beginning of a location path expression, not later on—for example, select="Order/$date" will generate an error.

Here is another example that selects the Company element in order-new.xml and a template that outputs the text node child of Company:

```
<xsl:variable name="addr"
select="Order/Partner/Location/Address/Company"/>

...

<xsl:template match="/">
 <xsl:apply-templates select="$addr"/>
</xsl:template>
```

The result when applied to order-new.xml is:

```
Wy'east Communications
```

Of course, a trimmer way to handle this would be with the // operator, as in:

```
<xsl:variable name="addr" select="Order//Company"/>

...

<xsl:template match="/">
 <xsl:apply-templates select="$addr"/>
</xsl:template>
```

This says, in essence, to select the `Company` descendents of `Order`, no matter what child elements intervene.

In this final example, all `Partner` elements that are descendants of the current node (.) and its children are copied to the result tree:

```
<xsl:variable name="desc" select=".//Partner"/>


...


<xsl:template match="Order">
 <xsl:copy-of select="$desc"/>
</xsl:template>
```

When you transform `order-new.xml` with this template, the result tree will be truncated as follows:

```
<Partner>
 <DUNS>06-853-2535</DUNS>
 <Location>
  <Address>
   <Company>Wy'east Communications</Company>
   <Mailing>P.O. Box 537</Mailing>
   <City>West Linn</City>
   <State>Oregon</State>
   <ZIPCode>97068-0537</ZIPCode>
   <Country>United States<Code>US</Code>
   </Country>
  </Address>
 </Location>
</Partner>
```

The `.` location step is the same as `self::node()`, which is the current node.

String Type

Instead of using node-sets with their attendant housekeeping, you may prefer to use a string, if you are interested only in actual text. This section will show you how to define string variables.

I'll start out with a simple example using the XPath function `string()`. If a stylesheet contained the following:

```
<xsl:variable name="true" select="string(true())"/>
<xsl:variable name="false" select="string(false())"/>


...


<xsl:value-of select="$true"/> (1)<xsl:text>
</xsl:text><xsl:value-of select="$false"/> (0)
```

you would get the following:

```
true (1)
false (0)
```

Of course, you could get the same result with:

```
<xsl:value-of select="true()"/> (1)<xsl:text>
</xsl:text><xsl:value-of select="false()"/> (0)
```

but it wouldn't be nearly as much fun as jumping through the extra hoop of creating two new variables. Near the beginning of the chapter, you saw a variable defined with an empty string, like this:

```
<xsl:param name="company"/>
```

which has the same effect as this:

```
<xsl:param name="company" select="''"/>
```

This is, in effect, an initial, default setting that can be changed later from the command line or some other parameter-binding mechanism (how parameters are passed into a stylesheet is not defined by XSLT). Here is how to bind a string value to a variable:

```
<xsl:variable name="company" select="'IBM'"/>
```

You can transpose the quotations so that single quotes come first, then double quotes:

```
<xsl:variable name="company" select='"IBM"'/>
```

Another way to do this is with the `string()` function, which is somewhat more verbose:

```
<xsl:variable name="company" select="string('IBM')"/>
```

NOTE If you want use strings that contain markup and other special characters, you can use a result tree fragment (see the section titled *Result Tree Fragment Type* later in this chapter).

Number Type

You can declare a variable that has a number as a value. Let's start with a simple example using the XPath function `number()`. Given the declarations and rules from a stylesheet:

```
<xsl:variable name="treu" select="number(true())"/>
```

```
<xsl:variable name="falsch" select="number(false())"/>

...

Treu ist <xsl:value-of select="$treu"/> und falsch ist <xsl:value-of
select="$falsch"/>.
```

you get the following output in German:

```
Treu ist 1 und falsch ist 0.
```

You saw several variables with a number type in order-param-var.xsl. Here are a few:

```
<xsl:variable name="elapsed" select="1 + $may + $apr + $mar + $feb +
$jan"/>
<xsl:variable name="remaining" select="29 + $jul + $aug + $sep + $oct +
$nov + $dec"/>
```

Bound to the elapsed and remaining variables are sums from integers and other variables. The sum values are numbers. You are assured of this because the presence of numeric operators in the select attribute converts the operands to numbers, as if each operand were an argument of the number() function.

What if you wanted to add up the numeric content of a group of nodes? You can do this with the sum() function, as demonstrated next. Say that you have a document that contains a record of the number of orders for a week (counter.xml):

```
<?xml version="1.0" encoding="utf-8"?>
<Counter month="June" year="2001">
 <Count day="1">7</Count>
 <Count day="2">0</Count>
 <Count day="3">0</Count>
 <Count day="4">11</Count>
 <Count day="5">9</Count>
 <Count day="6">21</Count>
 <Count day="7">8</Count>
</Counter>
```

The root element Counter has two attributes that indicate the month and year the orders are being counted. Each Count element has a day attribute that represents the day of the month when the orders arrived, with the number in the content of the element signifying the number of orders received on that day.

In the next example we have a stylesheet to apply to counter.xml called counter. xsl:

```
<xsl:stylesheet version="1.0"
xmlns:xsl="http://www.w3.org/1999/XSL/Transform">
<xsl:output method="xml" encoding="utf-8" indent="yes"/>
<xsl:attribute-set name="counter.atts">
 <xsl:attribute name="month">June</xsl:attribute>
 <xsl:attribute name="year">2001</xsl:attribute>
</xsl:attribute-set>
<xsl:variable name="sumit" select="sum(Counter/Count)"/>

<xsl:template match="Counter">
 <xsl:copy use-attribute-sets="counter.atts">
  <xsl:copy-of select="Count"/>
  <Sum day="{count(Count)}"><xsl:value-of select="$sumit"/></Sum>
 </xsl:copy>
</xsl:template>

</xsl:stylesheet>
```

Using a combination of `copy` and `copy-of`, along with `attribute-set`, the stylesheet reproduces the existing document and adds a new element, `Sum`. When you apply this stylesheet, you will produce this output:

```
<?xml version="1.0" encoding="utf-8"?>
<Counter month="June" year="2001">
 <Count day="1">7</Count>
 <Count day="2">0</Count>
 <Count day="3">0</Count>
 <Count day="4">11</Count>
 <Count day="5">9</Count>
 <Count day="6">21</Count>
 <Count day="7">8</Count>
 <Sum day="7">56</Sum>
</Counter>
```

The variable `sumit` declaration sums the content of all the `Count` elements in `counter.xml`. It uses the variable to insert the sum in a literal result element `Sum`. It also uses the `count()` function to count up all the `Count` elements in the document and place this value in `Sum`'s `day` attribute by using an attribute value template.

Boolean Type

A variable or parameter can also be of type Boolean, which has only two possible values, true or false. Here is a pretty simple example.

You could set up a stylesheet so that you instantiate a template based on whether a parameter is passed in from outside the stylesheet, with any value. The following is an empty-string declaration for the `okay` parameter (in `boolean.xsl`):

```
<xsl:param name="okay" select="''"/>
```

The following template will not be instantiated unless `okay` is passed in with some kind of value; any value—even 0—will do. The `boolean()` function in the `test` attribute of `when` tests the parameter value `okay`. If the value of `okay` is an empty string (as defined by default), `boolean()` evaluates to `false()`, and the stylesheet makes its exit. If it does have a value, `boolean()` evaluates to `true()`, and the template is instantiated.

```
<xsl:template match="Counter">
<xsl:choose>
 <xsl:when test="boolean($okay)">
 <xsl:copy use-attribute-sets="counter.atts">
  <xsl:copy-of select="Count"/>
 </xsl:copy>
 </xsl:when>
 <xsl:otherwise>
  Error. Must use okay parameter (with any value) to apply
template.
 </xsl:otherwise>
</xsl:choose>
</xsl:template>
...
```

If there is a value passed in, such as with:

```
xt counter.xml boolean.xsl okay=0
```

the processor returns the following output:

```
<?xml version="1.0" encoding="utf-8"?>
<Counter month="June" year="2001">
    <Count day="1">7</Count>
    <Count day="2">0</Count>
    <Count day="3">0</Count>
    <Count day="4">11</Count>
    <Count day="5">9</Count>
    <Count day="6">21</Count>
    <Count day="7">8</Count>
</Counter>
```

Result Tree Fragment Type

Variables and parameters permit yet another type beyond the standard four (node-set, string, Boolean, and number). It is called the result tree fragment. A result tree fragment is a chunk of text—a string—that can contain markup and what not. From the processor's perspective, it is treated as if it were a node-set with just a root node.

You don't define a result tree fragment with the `select` attribute; rather, it is declared as content of either the `variable` or `param` element. You can perform operations on a result tree fragment as if it were a string, but you can't use the operators /, //, or [] on them as you could with a regular set of nodes. The way you get a result tree fragment into a result tree is with the `copy-of` instruction element.

NOTE In general, if you use the `select` attribute, the `variable` and `param` elements are empty elements (no content); otherwise, if you don't use `select` and the `variable` and `param` element declarations have content, that content is a result tree fragment.

Here is a result tree fragment declaration. The bold text is the actual fragment:

```
<xsl:variable name="frag">
<Count day="29">17</Count>
</xsl:variable>
```

There is no `select` attribute. You are not selecting a node and using an expression to produce a number. You are creating arbitrary text suitable for a result tree. If you applied the following stylesheet to `counter.xml` (`fragment.xsl`):

```
<xsl:stylesheet version="1.0"
xmlns:xsl="http://www.w3.org/1999/XSL/Transform">
<xsl:output method="xml" encoding="utf-8" indent="yes"/>
<xsl:attribute-set name="counter.atts">
 <xsl:attribute name="month">June</xsl:attribute>
 <xsl:attribute name="year">2001</xsl:attribute>
</xsl:attribute-set>
<xsl:variable name="frag">
<Count day="29">17</Count>
</xsl:variable>

<xsl:template match="Counter">
 <xsl:copy use-attribute-sets="counter.atts">
  <xsl:copy-of select="Count"/>
  <xsl:copy-of select="$frag"/>
 </xsl:copy>
</xsl:template>

</xsl:stylesheet>
```

you would knock out the following result tree with an added element:

```
<?xml version="1.0" encoding="utf-8"?>
<Counter month="June" year="2001">
```

```
<Count day="1">7</Count>
<Count day="2">0</Count>
<Count day="3">0</Count>
<Count day="4">11</Count>
<Count day="5">9</Count>
<Count day="6">21</Count>
<Count day="7">8</Count>
<Count day="29">17</Count>
</Counter>
```

The with-param Element

Remember how I said earlier in the chapter that variables and parameters that are declared in templates (not at the top level) are not visible or available in other templates? In some cases, there is a workaround for this, at least as far as parameters are concerned. It's called the with-param element.

Just as with variable and param, with-param has two attributes: name, which is required, and the optional select.

Of course, a parameter declared at the top level can be seen by templates throughout a stylesheet. Sometimes, though, you want to pass a parameter off to use for some other processing. Following is one example of how you do this.

The stylesheet summary.xsl uses a couple of named templates, sum-orders and count-days. When these templates are called, with-param replaces the value of sumit with its own value for sumit, one collecting the sum of orders placed (sum-orders), another counting the number of days (count-days). These values are tucked into Sum elements in the output:

```
<xsl:stylesheet version="1.0"
xmlns:xsl="http://www.w3.org/1999/XSL/Transform">
<xsl:output method="xml" encoding="utf-8" indent="yes"/>

<xsl:template match="Counter">
<Summary month="{@month}" year="{@year}">
 <xsl:call-template name="sum-orders">
  <xsl:with-param name="sumit" select="sum(Count)"/>
 </xsl:call-template>
 <xsl:call-template name="count-days">
  <xsl:with-param name="sumit" select="count(Count)"/>
 </xsl:call-template>
</Summary>
</xsl:template>

<xsl:template name="sum-orders">
```

```
<xsl:param name="sumit" select="''"/>
<Sum sum="orders"><xsl:value-of select="$sumit"/></Sum>
</xsl:template>

<xsl:template name="count-days">
<xsl:param name="sumit" select="''"/>
<Sum count="days"><xsl:value-of select="$sumit"/></Sum>
</xsl:template>

</xsl:stylesheet>
```

Here is the output the stylesheet generates when applied against counter.xml:

```
<?xml version="1.0" encoding="utf-8"?>
<Summary month="June" year="2001">
 <Sum sum="orders">56</Sum>
 <Sum count="days">7</Sum>
</Summary>
```

The param declarations in the named templates don't collide with each other because they can't see each other, so to speak. When the named templates are called, the with-param values replace those of the parameter sumit.

This example shows with-param as a child of call-template. It can also be used as a child of apply-templates. If applicable when arriving at a value, with-param uses the current node and current node list from the instance of call-template or apply-template that contains it. If a template does not have a given parameter and you try to pass one into it by using with-param, this will not generate an error, but the parameter will be ignored.

Using Multiple Documents

Beside a few introductory examples, we have been tackling our tasks with single stylesheets. It is also possible to use multiple stylesheets at once as well as multiple XML documents. The next chapter shows you how.

Multiple Documents

You are not limited to working with just one XML document or one XSLT stylesheet at a time. You can access additional XML source documents with the XSLT function document(). You can also include additional stylesheets in a stylesheet with the include element. Likewise, you can import stylesheets with the import element. Import operations are different from include operations. Stylesheets brought in with import have precedence rules applied to them, but those included with the include element are affected only by normal stylesheet rules, not import precedence rules. I'll explain this later in the chapter.

You had a brief introduction to include in Chapter 4, "Getting More Results." I'll start this chapter by talking about the document() element. Then I'll move on to including stylesheets. Following that, I'll discuss what rules go into effect when you import stylesheets, including the consequence of using the apply-imports element.

Processing Additional XML Documents

The document() function allows you to retrieve XML documents and the nodes they contain, besides the one you are processing directly. The function may be called from any attribute that can contain an expression, such as the `select` attribute of `value-of`. I'll start out by calling this function in its simplest form, that is, with a URI as a single string argument.

Here is a little XML document. It's called `2001-06-orders.xml`, and there isn't much to it. It's well formed, but what else can I say about it?

```
<?xml version="1.0" encoding="utf-8" ?>

<Orders month="June" year="2001" href="order.xml">

</Orders>
```

As it turns out, this document is really just a placeholder. The intent is that it will hold orders that occur during June 2001. How do you get those orders into this placeholder? The best way I can think of doing it in XSLT is with the `document()` function.

The following stylesheet, `get-one-order.xsl`, uses `document()` to bring a single order into the placeholder file:

```
<xsl:stylesheet version="1.0"
xmlns:xsl="http://www.w3.org/1999/XSL/Transform">
<xsl:output method="xml" encoding="utf-8" indent="yes"/>

<xsl:template match="Orders">
 <xsl:copy>
  <xsl:copy-of select="document('order.xml')"/>
 </xsl:copy>
</xsl:template>

</xsl:stylesheet>
```

The `copy` element copies the `Orders` element, but leaves its attributes behind. The `copy-of` element copies all the content of `order.xml` into the result tree (except the XML declaration), starting with the root node and on down the line. The `document()` function retrieves the local resource `order.xml`. The XSLT processor parses the retrieved resource as an XML document and builds a tree based on it. The output will appear as follows:

```
<?xml version="1.0" encoding="utf-8"?>
<Orders>
<Order partner="06-853-2535">
 <Date>2001-06-01</Date>
 <Item type="ISBN">0471404012</Item>
 <Quantity>40</Quantity>
 <Comments>None.</Comments>
 <ShippingMethod class="4th">USPS</ShippingMethod>
</Order>
</Orders>
```

Base URI

The XSLT processor knows where to find the local file `order.xml` in the current directory because an XSLT processor assigns every node its own base URI. You can't see them on the surface, but they are there. Where these base URIs come from is spelled out in Table 8.1 (compare Section 3.2 of the XSLT recommendation).

If an element node, for example, comes from an external entity, that element will have the same base URI as the external entity. An external entity is usually an external file, referenced in an XML document by means of an entity reference to this file, such as `&add-ins;`. Such an entity reference refers to an external entity that must be declared in a DTD in a way similar to this: `<!ENTITY add-ins SYSTEM "add-ins.xml">`.

Usually, a document entity is really a document file. A document or root node will have the same base URI as the document entity or file. Likewise, an element, including a root element, has the same base URI as this file. An attribute, whose parent is an element, has the same base URI as the element with which it is associated; that element, in turn, has the base URI of the document or external entity that holds it.

In general, a base URI for a node is relative to the base URI of the document from which it comes. A relative URI, such as the one suggested in `document('order.xml')`, is in the same directory as the current node under consideration. Base URIs help the processor figure out absolute URIs for objects as well.

Table 8.1   Base URIs

NODE	BASE URI
Root or document node	Has the same base URI as the document entity
Element	Has the same base URI as the document or external entity from which it came
Processing instruction	Has the same base URI as the document or external entity from which it came
Attribute	Has same the same base URI as its parent node, which is always an element
Text	Has the same base URI as its parent node
Comment	Has the same base URI as its parent node
Namespace	Has the same base URI as its parent node

You are not limited to accessing only local files: You can retrieve remote files as well, using absolute URIs. Here is a part of a stylesheet that references a remote document (`get-one-remote-order.xsl`):

```
<xsl:copy-of
select="document('http://www.testb2b.org/B2B/order.xml')"/>
```

The `document()` function can have at most two arguments, but usually you see only one. The first argument can be either a string or a node-set, but the second one, if used, is always a node-set. How these arguments are interpreted depends on how you use them.

You have seen what happens when you use only one string argument: The processor interprets this as a URI for a document you want to retrieve. Now I'll show you what happens if the argument is not a string but a node-set.

A Node-Set Argument to document()

This is the stylesheet `get-one-href-order.xsl`. It uses the `href` attribute in the `Orders` element of `2001-06-orders.xml` to retrieve desired order documents:

```
<xsl:stylesheet version="1.0"
xmlns:xsl="http://www.w3.org/1999/XSL/Transform">
<xsl:output method="xml" encoding="utf-8" indent="yes"/>

<xsl:template match="Orders">
 <xsl:copy>
  <xsl:copy-of select="document(@href)"/>
 </xsl:copy>
</xsl:template>

</xsl:stylesheet>
```

Because the template matches `Orders`, the root element of `2001-06-orders.xml`, the processor knows where to look for the attribute node identified by `@href`. When it finds it in the source document's (`2001-06-orders.xml`) root element start-tag, it interprets it as a URI and retrieves it as a resource, giving identical output as the `get-one-order.xsl` stylesheet did.

Here is yet another example that uses a list of URIs found in a set of nodes pointed to by the first argument of `document()`. The new document containing this list of URIs is `2001-06-orders-list.xml`:

```
<?xml version="1.0" encoding="utf-8" ?>
```

```
<Orders month="June" year="2001" href="order.xml">

<OrderList>
 <OrderURI href="2001-06-01-600001-order.xml"/>
 <OrderURI href="2001-06-01-600002-order.xml"/>
 <OrderURI href="2001-06-01-600003-order.xml"/>
 <OrderURI href="2001-06-01-600004-order.xml"/>
</OrderList>

</Orders>
```

If you now apply `get-list-href-order.xsl` to this XML document, you will get a result filled with the first four orders of June 2001. Here then is the stylesheet:

```
<xsl:stylesheet version="1.0"
xmlns:xsl="http://www.w3.org/1999/XSL/Transform">
<xsl:output method="xml" encoding="utf-8" indent="yes"/>

<xsl:template match="Orders">
 <xsl:copy>
  <xsl:copy-of select="document(OrderList/OrderURI/@href)"/>
 </xsl:copy>
</xsl:template>

</xsl:stylesheet>
```

The node-set or location path in the argument of the `document()` function looks for those URIs in `href` attributes associated with `OrderURI` elements, which are children of `OrderList`. These resources are retrieved and placed in the result tree. This is what the beginning of the output looks like:

```
<?xml version="1.0" encoding="utf-8"?>
<Orders>
<Order orderID="ORD-ID-2001-06-01-60001" partner="06-853-2535">
<Date>2001-06-01</Date>
<Item type="ISBN">0471416207</Item>
<Quantity>7</Quantity>
<Comments>None.</Comments>
<ShippingMethod>UPS</ShippingMethod>
</Order>
<Order orderID="ORD-ID-2001-06-01-60002" partner="06-853-2535">
<Date>2001-06-01</Date>
<Item type="ISBN">0471416207</Item>
<Quantity>244</Quantity>
<Comments>Apply special quantity discount.</Comments>
<ShippingMethod class="1st">USPS</ShippingMethod>
</Order>
...
```

Two Node-Set Arguments to document()

If you want to perform a transformation using a remote source file, you'd have to do things a bit differently. For example, let's say that you wanted to use the same source file as in the last example, that is, `2001-06-orders-list.xml`, but the file is not local: It's on a Web server at the address `http://www.testb2b.org/B2B/2001-06-orders-list.xml`. Though it is at a different location, the document is precisely the same as the example you saw earlier:

```
<?xml version="1.0" encoding="utf-8" ?>

<Orders month="June" year="2001" href="order.xml">

<OrderList>
 <OrderURI href="2001-06-01-600001-order.xml"/>
 <OrderURI href="2001-06-01-600002-order.xml"/>
 <OrderURI href="2001-06-01-600003-order.xml"/>
 <OrderURI href="2001-06-01-600004-order.xml"/>
</OrderList>

</Orders>
```

The problem is that the XSLT processor assumes that the documents referenced in the `href` attributes are in the same location as the base URI of the current node, but they are not. They, too, are on the remote host, so the stylesheet that I used earlier will be broken.

What we have to do is let the processor know where those files are. We can do so with a second argument to `document()`, as shown in `get-list-remote-href-order.xsl`:

```
<xsl:stylesheet version="1.0"
xmlns:xsl="http://www.w3.org/1999/XSL/Transform">
<xsl:output method="xml" encoding="utf-8" indent="yes"/>

<xsl:template match="Orders">
 <xsl:copy>
  <xsl:copy-of select="document(OrderList/OrderURI/@href,document(.))"/>
 </xsl:copy>
</xsl:template>

</xsl:stylesheet>
```

You can apply the stylesheet like this:

```
saxon http://www.testb2b.org/B2B/2001-06-orders-list.xml get-list-
remote-href-order.xsl
```

This second argument, that is, `document(.)`, lets the processor know that you want to look for those documents in `href` relative to the source document being processed, that is `http://www.testb2b.org/B2B/2001-06-orders-list.xml`. The four order documents are located in the same place on the Web server as this document. The argument `document(.)` points this out to the processor, and you get the output you expect.

If the second argument were `document('')` instead of `document(.)`, that would tell the processor that those order documents you are looking for are in the same place as the actual stylesheet. For more information, see the section titled *Referring to the Stylesheet with document()*, later in this chapter.

Adding a Node-Set after document()

Another way you can call `document()` is with a location path immediately following the function call. The argument to `document()` is a URI represented by a string, and following that is a location path—a node-set argument—in the document being retrieved. In other words, it is as if you are feeding the processor a location path, with the first part being a document and the second part being a continuation of the location path in that document.

This is how it works. The next example stylesheet is called `get-part-order-new.xsl`. When applied to `partners.xml`, it grabs the `Partner` node (with children) from the document `order-new.xml`:

```
<xsl:stylesheet version="1.0"
xmlns:xsl="http://www.w3.org/1999/XSL/Transform">
<xsl:output method="xml" encoding="utf-8" indent="yes"/>

<xsl:template match="Partners">
 <xsl:copy>
  <xsl:copy-of select="document('order-new.xml')//Partner"/>
 </xsl:copy>
</xsl:template>

</xsl:stylesheet>
```

The transformation gives you the following result tree:

```
<?xml version="1.0" encoding="utf-8"?>
<Partners>
 <Partner>
  <DUNS>06-853-2535</DUNS>
  <Location>
   <Address>
```

```
      <Company>Wy'east Communications</Company>
      <Mailing>P.O. Box 537</Mailing>
      <City>West Linn</City>
      <State>Oregon</State>
      <ZIPCode>97068-0537</ZIPCode>
      <Country>United States<Code>US</Code></Country>
    </Address>
  </Location>
 </Partner>
</Partners>
```

Referring to the Stylesheet with document()

With the help of XSLT base URI rules, you can even refer to the stylesheet document itself by calling the document() element with an empty string argument, that is, document(''). To demonstrate this, let's say that you just wanted to transform the current stylesheet itself, creating a result that uses the transform element instead of the stylesheet element. Given the tiny XML document transform-stylesheet.xml:

```
<xsl:transform version="1.0"
xmlns:xsl="http://www.w3.org/1999/XSL/Transform"/>
```

and the stylesheet circular.xsl:

```
<xsl:stylesheet version="1.0"
xmlns:xsl="http://www.w3.org/1999/XSL/Transform">
<xsl:output method="xml" encoding="utf-8" indent="yes"/>

<xsl:template match="xsl:transform">
 <xsl:copy>
  <xsl:copy-of select="document('')//xsl:output"/>
  <xsl:copy-of select="document('')//xsl:template"/>
 </xsl:copy>
</xsl:template>

</xsl:stylesheet>
```

you will see output like this:

```
<xsl:transform xmlns:xsl="http://www.w3.org/1999/XSL/Transform">
<xsl:output method="xml" encoding="utf-8" indent="yes"/>
<xsl:template match="xsl:transform">
 <xsl:copy>
  <xsl:copy-of select="document('')//xsl:output"/>
  <xsl:copy-of select="document('')//xsl:template"/>
 </xsl:copy>
```

```
</xsl:template>
</xsl:transform>
```

The location paths in `circular.xsl` refer to nodes within the stylesheet itself. With this transformation, the `stylesheet` element is eliminated, and it is replaced with the `transform` element in the result tree. It showed you how `document('')` refers to the current stylesheet as the document of interest. Please don't take up too much time pondering the usefulness of this rather circular stylesheet, though, unless you are an admirer of the works of M. C. Escher!

Loading a SOAP Envelope with document()

Before I go on, here is one last `document()` example that I want to show you. The example will bundle seven related order documents together into one SOAP envelope. Every immediate child of `SOAP-ENV:Body` is considered a separate entity, as long as it does not have a `SOAP-ENC:root="0"` attribute (see page 12 of Microsoft's *BizTalk Framework 2.0: Document and Message Specification*, a SOAP implementation, at www.biztalk.org).

First of all, apply the following stylesheet (`get-list-soap-order.xsl`):

```
<xsl:stylesheet version="1.0"
xmlns:xsl="http://www.w3.org/1999/XSL/Transform"
xmlns:SOAP-ENV="http://schemas.xmlsoap.org/soap/envelope/">
<xsl:output method="xml" encoding="utf-8" indent="yes"/>

<xsl:template match="SOAP-ENV:Envelope">
 <xsl:copy>
  <xsl:apply-templates select="SOAP-ENV:Body"/>
 </xsl:copy>
</xsl:template>

<xsl:template match="SOAP-ENV:Body">
<xsl:copy>
<xsl:copy-of select="document('2001-06-01-600001-order.xml')"/>
<xsl:copy-of select="document('2001-06-01-600002-order.xml')"/>
<xsl:copy-of select="document('2001-06-01-600003-order.xml')"/>
<xsl:copy-of select="document('2001-06-01-600004-order.xml')"/>
<xsl:copy-of select="document('2001-06-01-600005-order.xml')"/>
<xsl:copy-of select="document('2001-06-01-600006-order.xml')"/>
<xsl:copy-of select="document('2001-06-01-600007-order.xml')"/>
</xsl:copy>
</xsl:template>

</xsl:stylesheet>
```

to the following small document (`soap-envelope.xml`):

```
<SOAP-ENV:Envelope
xmlns:SOAP-ENV="http://schemas.xmlsoap.org/soap/envelope/" xmlns:SOAP-
ENC="http://schemas.xmlsoap.org/soap/encoding/">
 <SOAP-ENV:Body>
 </SOAP-ENV:Body>
</SOAP-ENV:Envelope>
```

The `copy` elements write the SOAP elements from `soap-envelope`
`.xml` out to the result tree. Then, in the second template, the `copy-of`
elements copy seven documents into the SOAP envelope. When `copy-of`
copies the root node of the document into the result tree, its child nodes are
copied. Element nodes take along any attribute nodes associated with it, as
well as namespace nodes, as you can see from this partial output (the first
two copied documents are shown). Each `Order` child of `SOAP-ENV:Body`
is considered a separate document:

```
<?xml version="1.0" encoding="utf-8"?>
<SOAP-ENV:Envelope
xmlns:SOAP-ENV="http://schemas.xmlsoap.org/soap/envelope/" xmlns:SOAP-
ENC="http://schemas.xmlsoap.org/soap/encoding/">
<SOAP-ENV:Body>
<Order orderID="ORD-ID-2001-06-01-60001" partner="06-853-2535">
 <Date>2001-06-01</Date>
 <Item type="ISBN">0471416207</Item>
 <Quantity>7</Quantity>
 <Comments>None.</Comments>
 <ShippingMethod>UPS</ShippingMethod>
</Order>
<Order orderID="ORD-ID-2001-06-01-60002" partner="06-853-2535">
 <Date>2001-06-01</Date>
 <Item type="ISBN">0471416207</Item>
 <Quantity>244</Quantity>
 <Comments>Apply special quantity discount.</Comments>
 <ShippingMethod class="1st">USPS</ShippingMethod>
</Order>
 . . .
```

Of course, there are many other ways you could use the `document()`
function, other than these basics, but I'm going to shift gears now. So far in
this chapter, we have discussed ways to work with multiple XML source
documents. Next I'll review how to use more than one stylesheet, first by
including stylesheets, then by importing them. Don't worry—I explain the
difference between the two soon enough.

Including Stylesheets

Speaking of SOAP, you have already seen a SOAP example that relies on an included stylesheet (way back in Chapter 4). I'll briefly review that example here.

There is an instance of the top-level element `include` in the stylesheet `order-soap-include.xsl` that may be applied against `order.xml`:

```
<xsl:stylesheet version="1.0"
xmlns:xsl="http://www.w3.org/1999/XSL/Transform">
<xsl:output method="xml" encoding="utf-8" indent="yes" />
<xsl:include href="copy-of-order-named.xsl"/>

<xsl:template match="/">
<SOAP-ENV:Envelope
xmlns:SOAP-ENV="http://schemas.xmlsoap.org/soap/envelope/">
 <SOAP-ENV:Body>
  <xsl:call-template name="copy-of-order"/>
 </SOAP-ENV:Body>
</SOAP-ENV:Envelope>
</xsl:template>

</xsl:stylesheet>
```

This element includes `copy-of-order-named.xsl` in the originating stylesheet, `order-soap-include.xsl` (both are assumed to be in the same local directory). The included stylesheet has a template named `copy-of-order`. The XSLT processor sees this named template because of the presence of `include`. Here is the included stylesheet, `copy-of-order-named.xsl`:

```
<xsl:stylesheet version="1.0"
xmlns:xsl="http://www.w3.org/1999/XSL/Transform">

<xsl:template name="copy-of-order">
 <xsl:copy-of select="Order"/>
</xsl:template>

</xsl:stylesheet>
```

More Details of include

The `href` attribute is `include`'s only attribute. It is required and always contains a URI reference for a stylesheet that is to be included in an originating or current stylesheet. The base URI rules, mentioned earlier in this chapter in relation to the `document()` function, apply here as well. The rules indicate to the processor that the following included stylesheet is in the same location relative to the current stylesheet:

```
<xsl:include href="format.xsl"/>
```

which generally means the same local or current directory as the stylesheet doing the inclusion. There is no reason why you couldn't also include a remote stylesheet, such as:

```
<xsl:include href="http://www.testb2b.org/B2B/format.xsl"/>
```

You can have as many instances of `include` in a stylesheet as you wish, as long as they are at the top level. Top-level elements must be children of `stylesheet` (or `transform`). As long as this requirement is satisfied, they can be scattered all over the stylesheet if you wish. There is no requirement that an `include` instance be the first child of `stylesheet`, only that it be a child element.

The XSLT recommendation says that when a processor encounters an instance of `include` in a stylesheet, it replaces the instance with the included stylesheet. The only thing it leaves out is the `stylesheet` element itself from the included document. This means that everything but the `stylesheet` element—template rules, top-level elements, and so forth—is included in the originating stylesheet on the XML tree level, and all items are treated just as if they were in the originating stylesheet from the beginning. No special sanctions or privileges are granted to the included template rules—they just become part of the stylesheet tree itself.

> **NOTE** When you import a stylesheet with the `import` element, special considerations do come into play, as you will soon see.

One thing you have to avoid is including a stylesheet itself either directly or indirectly. By directly, I mean that `stylesheet.xsl` must not include `stylesheet.xsl`, and by indirectly, I mean that `stylesheet.xsl` must not include another stylesheet that includes `stylesheet.xsl`, no matter how many stylesheets come between or separate them.

Another thing to watch out for is including stylesheets multiple times. Figure 8.1 shows a possible relationship that you ought to avoid.

In Figure 8.1, each box represents a stylesheet. The top stylesheet, `2001-orders.xsl`, includes two stylesheet documents, `2001-june-orders.xsl` and `2001-q2-orders.xsl`, which is all fine and good. The trouble begins when both these stylesheets include the bottom one, `2001-06-01-orders.xsl`. No, your XSLT processor won't explode, but `2001-orders.xsl` indirectly includes `2001-06-01-orders.xsl` twice, posing a subtle threat of template rule duplication and errors. With two

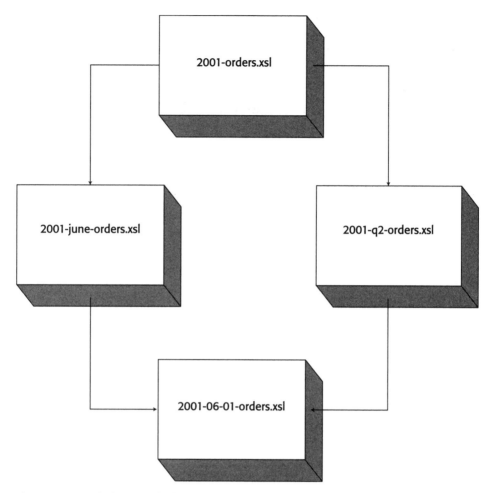

Figure 8.1 Including a stylesheet multiple times.

indirect inclusions of `2001-06-01-orders.xsl` in `2001-orders.xsl`, it may be difficult to sort out errors.

The remedy is to examine the stylesheets for duplicate template rules and then combine, eliminate, or separate those rules or the inclusions. Easier said than done, of course, but it's better than the alternative. The actual solution to the problem in Figure 8.1 is fairly complex (see the note in Section 2.6.1 of the XLST recommendation).

A Multiple Stylesheet Example

The following example uses four included stylesheets that add XSLFO formatting and properties to `order-new.xml`. These stylesheets successively transform each part of `order-new.xml`, as if the templates were all within one stylesheet. The first of these stylesheets is `format.xsl`, which follows. It includes three other stylesheets: `format-Order.xsl`, `format-Partner.xsl`, and `format-Location.xsl`.

```
<xsl:stylesheet version="1.0"
xmlns:xsl="http://www.w3.org/1999/XSL/Transform">
<xsl:output method="xml" encoding="utf-8" indent="yes"/>
<xsl:include href="format-Order.xsl"/>
<xsl:include href="format-Partner.xsl"/>
<xsl:include href="format-Location.xsl"/>

<xsl:template match="/">
<fo:root xmlns:fo="http://www.w3.org/1999/XSL/Format">
 <fo:layout-master-set>
  <fo:simple-page-master master-name="Order-US" page-height="11in" page-
     width="8.5in" margin-top="1in" margin-bottom="1in" margin-
     left="1in" margin-right="1in">
   <fo:region-body margin-top=".5in"/>
   <fo:region-before extent="1.5in"/>
   <fo:region-after extent="1.5in"/>
  </fo:simple-page-master>
 </fo:layout-master-set>
 <fo:page-sequence master-name="Order-US">
  <fo:flow flow-name="xsl-region-body">

   <xsl:apply-templates select="Order"/>

  </fo:flow>
 </fo:page-sequence>
</fo:root>
</xsl:template>

</xsl:stylesheet>
```

I won't go into the details of XSLFO here—you'll have to wait until Chapter 10, "A Simple Formatted Document," and Chapter 11, "XSLFO Tables, Lists, and More," for that—but I will mention a few highlights. This stylesheet adds a number of the preliminary XSLFO elements to the result tree by using literal result elements, including `root`, the root element of an XSLFO document. The other elements help set up a page layout, a page sequence, and a text flow. An instance of `apply-templates` selects `Order`, returning a node-set containing `Order` and its children.

The next stylesheet, `format-Order.xsl`, formats a few headings as blocks, extracting data here and there from the `orderID` attribute, `DayOrderCount`, and `Date`. It also formats `Item`, whose content is an ISBN, plus the `Quantity` ordered, and finally some shipping information (`ShippingMethod`). The `output` element is missing because `format.xsl` already has one, as well as in succeeding inclusions. (You can include more than one instance of output in more that one stylesheet without a bad consequence: Duplicate attributes and values are resolved according to rules of precedence; non-duplicated attributes and values are merged into one effective output instance.) The apply-templates element selects Partner, returning a node-set such as the following:

```
<xsl:stylesheet version="1.0"
xmlns:xsl="http://www.w3.org/1999/XSL/Transform"
xmlns:fo="http://www.w3.org/1999/XSL/Format">

<xsl:template match="Order">
<fo:block font-size="20pt" font-family="sans-serif" line-height="26pt"
     space-after.optimum="4pt" text-align="center">Order <xsl:value-of
     select="@orderID"/></fo:block>
<fo:block font-size="16pt" font-family="sans-serif" line-height="20pt"
     space-after.optimum="4pt" text-align="center">Order Number
     <xsl:value-of select="SalesYear/DayOrderCount"/></fo:block>
<fo:block font-size="16pt" font-family="sans-serif" line-height="20pt"
     space-after.optimum="4pt" text-align="center"><xsl:value-of
     select="Date"/></fo:block>
<fo:block font-size="12pt" font-family="sans-serif" line-height="16pt"
     space-after.optimum="4pt" text-align="start" padding-
     before=".5in">ISBN: <xsl:value-of select="Item"/></fo:block>
<fo:block font-size="12pt" font-family="sans-serif" line-height="16pt"
     space-after.optimum="4pt" text-align="start">Quantity: <xsl:value-
     of select="Quantity"/></fo:block>
<fo:block font-size="12pt" font-family="sans-serif" line-height="16pt"
     space-after.optimum="4pt" text-align="start">Ship by: <xsl:value-of
     select="ShippingMethod"/> (<xsl:value-of select="Shipping
Method/@class"/> class)</fo:block>

 <xsl:apply-templates select="Partner"/>

</xsl:template>

</xsl:stylesheet>
```

The next included stylesheet, format-Partner.xsl, is a short one. It formats DUNS, a child element of Partner, with a simple block and then selects Location with apply-templates:

```
<xsl:stylesheet version="1.0"
xmlns:xsl="http://www.w3.org/1999/XSL/Transform"
xmlns:fo="http://www.w3.org/1999/XSL/Format">

<xsl:template match="Partner">
<fo:block font-size="12pt" font-family="sans-serif" line-height="16pt"
     space-after.optimum="4pt" text-align="start">DUNS: <xsl:value-of
```

```
          select="DUNS"/></fo:block>

  <xsl:apply-templates select="Location"/>

</xsl:template>

</xsl:stylesheet>
```

The last stylesheet included by format.xsl is format-Location.xsl, which transforms and formats the children of Address, all descendants of Location. These children are Company, Mailing, City, State, ZIPCode, and Country. The example uses the location path Country/ text() to return the text node child of Country, which is United States. The node-test text() returns only the text child of Country rather than all the children of Country, which would include unnecessarily Code and its text node child US:

```
<xsl:stylesheet version="1.0"
xmlns:xsl="http://www.w3.org/1999/XSL/Transform"
xmlns:fo="http://www.w3.org/1999/XSL/Format">

<xsl:template match="Location/Address">
<fo:block font-size="12pt" font-family="sans-serif" line-height="16pt"
    space-after.optimum="4pt" text-align="start" padding-
before="6pt"><xsl:value-of select="Company"/></fo:block>
<fo:block font-size="12pt" font-family="sans-serif" line-height="16pt"
    space-after.optimum="4pt" text-align="start"><xsl:value-of
    select="Mailing"/></fo:block>
<fo:block font-size="12pt" font-family="sans-serif" line-height="16pt"
    space-after.optimum="4pt" text-align="start"><xsl:value-of
    select="City"/>, <xsl:value-of select="State"/><xsl:text>
</xsl:text><xsl:value-of select="ZIPCode"/></fo:block>
<fo:block font-size="12pt" font-family="sans-serif" line-height="16pt"
    space-after.optimum="4pt" text-align="start"><xsl:value-of
    select="Country/text()"/></fo:block>
</xsl:template>

</xsl:stylesheet>
```

You can apply format.xsl to order-new.xml and redirect the output to order-new.fo. Following is the beginning portion of order-new.fo:

```
<?xml version="1.0" encoding="utf-8"?>
<fo:root xmlns:fo="http://www.w3.org/1999/XSL/Format">
<fo:layout-master-set>
<fo:simple-page-master master-name="Order-US" page-height="11in" page-
    width="8.5in" margin-top="1in"
  margin-bottom="1in" margin-left="1in" margin-right="1in">
```

```
<fo:region-body margin-top=".5in"/>
<fo:region-before extent="1.5in"/>
<fo:region-after extent="1.5in"/>
</fo:simple-page-master>
</fo:layout-master-set>
<fo:page-sequence master-name="Order-US">
<fo:flow flow-name="xsl-region-body">
<fo:block font-size="20pt" font-family="sans-serif" line-height="26pt"
    space-after.optimum="4pt" text-align="center">Order ORD-ID-2001-06-
    01-600001</fo:block>
<fo:block font-size="16pt" font-family="sans-serif" line-height="20pt"
    space-after.optimum="4pt" text-align="center">Order Number
    1</fo:block>
...
```

In this form—an XSLFO file—you can further process it with Apache's Java FOP processor (http://xml.apache.org/fop/index.html), which is free, or with RenderX's XEP Rendering Engine, a commercial product (available from www.renderx.com/FO2PDF.html), which offers a downloadable evaluation version. Figure 8.2 shows what order-new.fo looks

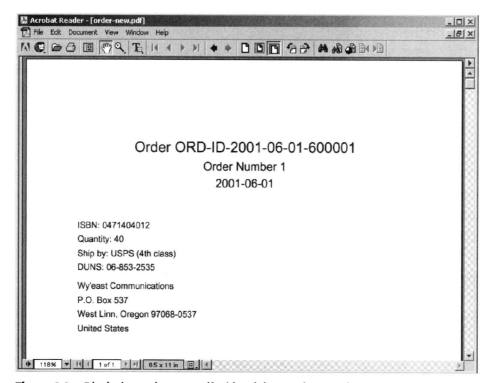

Figure 8.2   Displaying order-new.pdf with Adobe Acrobat Reader.

like when processed by FOP as a Portable Document Format (PDF) file (`order-new.pdf`.) and displayed in Adobe Acrobat Reader.

At this point, the XSLFO output is passable in appearance, but certainly it does not look as good as it could. In Part Two, I'll cover XSLFO in greater detail and you'll learn there how to make your output look even better.

Importing Stylesheets

Importing stylesheets is different from including them. The difference is that the template rules in the imported stylesheets each have a different import precedence, but included stylesheets are merged into one tree whose rules are resolved normally, just as they would for a single stylesheet (see Section 5.5 of the XSLT recommendation for nitty-gritty information on how templates are prioritized).

Imported template rules form an import tree. Any included stylesheets are resolved before an import tree is constructed. Unlike `include`, an import tree retains `stylesheet` elements (`transform`, too), apparently so that it can keep track of the order in which stylesheets are imported. As stylesheets are imported and stacked up in the import tree, each instance of stylesheet in the import tree is given a different import precedence. More on this in a minute.

The `import` element has one attribute, `href`, just like `include`. This attribute is required and should contain a URI reference for a stylesheet that is to be imported into the importing stylesheet. Base URI rules apply to `import` just as they do to `include`. These rules specify that a stylesheet imported as follows is in the same directory as the importing stylesheet:

```
<xsl:import href="report-1.xsl"/>
```

You can also import remote stylesheets, like this:

```
<xsl:import href="http://www.testb2b.org/B2B/report-1.xsl"/>
```

Like `include`, `import` is a top-level element, and you can have as many instances of `import` as you want. A difference between `include` and `import` is that `import` elements not only must be on the top level, they must also be the *immediate* children of `stylesheet` (`transform`). If you use `import` elements, it would be an error to have any other top-level element immediately following `stylesheet`.

The order in which the import elements appear affects what precedence matching templates have over one another. I'll show you how with an example.

Generating Reports

You will find in the document archive a series of report stylesheets, namely, `report-0.xsl`, `report-1.xsl`, `report-2.xsl`, `report-3.xsl`, and `report-4.xsl`. Each of these stylesheets has a single template that matches `Order`, the root element in `order-new.xml`. If all these templates (there's five of them) were in the same stylesheet, they would collide, and only the last template that occurs in the stylesheet would be instantiated. If these templates all occur in imported stylesheets, plus in the stylesheet that's doing the importing, they will collide as well, but with somewhat different consequences.

The report stylesheets can extract reports from `order-new.xml` (or documents like it). If you run them separately, of course, they won't collide because they will be instantiated independently. Here is a way you can run all of the reports at once, redirecting the result output to a single output file. Following is an example that runs on a Windows 2000 platform and uses the `for` command:

```
for %i in (report-?.xsl) do @saxon order-new.xml %i >> order-new.txt
```

The `for` command processes each file in the list `report-?.xsl` where `?` is a wildcard replacing the digit in the filename (0 through 4). Each time it processes a file in the list, it runs Saxon, applying to `order-new.xml` the stylesheet represented in the variable `%i`. With each iteration, the XML document is processed with a different stylesheet. The simple text output is appended to the file `order-new.txt`, which will look like this:

```
[Report generated by: report-0.xsl]

  152 days have elapsed since the beginning of the sales year.

[Report generated by: report-1.xsl]

  213 days remain until the end of the sales year.

[Report generated by: report-2.xsl]

  The sales year has 365 days (a non-leap year).

[Report generated by: report-3.xsl]

  The partner's DUNS number is 06-853-2535.

[Report generated by: report-4.xsl]

  The partner's company name is Wy'east Communications.
```

As the stylesheets are executed, just two lines of text are written to output, one telling where the report is coming from, the other extracting a small report from order-new.xml. I made them uncomplicated so as not to distract from the main issue in this section: importing stylesheets.

Let's have a look at all these stylesheets, in numerical order. This will lay the groundwork for understanding how import works. First, report-0.xsl:

```
<xsl:stylesheet version="1.0"
xmlns:xsl="http://www.w3.org/1999/XSL/Transform">
<xsl:import href="report-4.xsl"/>
<xsl:import href="report-3.xsl"/>
<xsl:import href="report-2.xsl"/>
<xsl:import href="report-1.xsl"/>
<xsl:output method="text" encoding="utf-8"/>

<xsl:template match="Order">
 [Report generated by: report-0.xsl]

  <xsl:value-of select="SalesYear/Days/@elapsed"/> days have elapsed
since the beginning of the sales year.
</xsl:template>

</xsl:stylesheet>
```

This stylesheet imports four other stylesheets. Its output consists of a few lines of text. The first line reports the name of the stylesheet generating the report; the second, how many days have elapsed in the sales year.

Even though this stylesheet imports several other stylesheets, it instantiates only one template. Why? Because of import precedence, the template rules in the importing or originating stylesheet have first priority. The templates in all the imported stylesheets match the same node (the root element Order), so only the template in the importing template is instantiated because it has a priority claim.

Because the templates in report-0.xsl through report-4.xsl collide—they each have only one template—you can apply them iteratively with for, as just shown. When you apply them this way, their templates won't collide because they will be instantiated separately.

Here is report-1.xsl, it reports the days remaining in the sales year:

```
<xsl:stylesheet version="1.0"
xmlns:xsl="http://www.w3.org/1999/XSL/Transform">
<xsl:output method="text" encoding="utf-8"/>

<xsl:template match="Order">
```

```
 [Report generated by: report-1.xsl]

   <xsl:value-of select="SalesYear/Days/@remaining"/> days remain until
      the end of the sales year.
 </xsl:template>

 </xsl:stylesheet>
```

Following is `report-2.xsl`. This stylesheet returns the number of days of the sales year. Using `choose`, it instantiates a different template, depending on whether the total number of days in the sales year matches leap year or not (366 for leap year, 365 for a non-leap year). If something has gone haywire in the counting, the template in `otherwise` will report the problem:

```
<xsl:stylesheet version="1.0"
xmlns:xsl="http://www.w3.org/1999/XSL/Transform">
<xsl:output method="text" encoding="utf-8"/>

<xsl:template match="Order">
 [Report generated by: report-2.xsl]
 <xsl:choose>
  <xsl:when test="SalesYear/Days/@total[.='365']">
  The sales year has <xsl:value-of select="SalesYear/Days/@total"/> days
     (a non-leap year).
  </xsl:when>
  <xsl:when test="SalesYear/Days/@total[.='366']">
  The sales year has <xsl:value-of select="SalesYear/Days/@total"/> days
     (a leap year).
  </xsl:when>
  <xsl:otherwise>
  Error in total days of sales year.
  </xsl:otherwise>
 </xsl:choose>
</xsl:template>

</xsl:stylesheet>
```

The next stylesheet, `report-3.xsl`, reports back the partner's DUNS number:

```
<xsl:stylesheet version="1.0"
xmlns:xsl="http://www.w3.org/1999/XSL/Transform">
<xsl:output method="text" encoding="utf-8"/>

<xsl:template match="Order">
 [Report generated by: report-3.xsl]

  The partner's DUNS number is <xsl:value-of select=".//DUNS"/>.
```

```
</xsl:template>

</xsl:stylesheet>
```

The final stylesheet in the series (`report-4.xsl`) extracts the company name of the partner:

```
<xsl:stylesheet version="1.0"
xmlns:xsl="http://www.w3.org/1999/XSL/Transform">
<xsl:output method="text" encoding="utf-8"/>

<xsl:template match="Order">
  [Report generated by: report-4.xsl]

  The partner's company name is <xsl:value-of select=".//Company"/>.
</xsl:template>

</xsl:stylesheet>
```

As you know, if you apply only the first stylesheet, even though it imports all the other ones, it will instantiate only the priority template, that is, the one in it. For example, if you apply `report-0.xsl` to `order-new.xml`, it yields this result:

```
[Report generated by: report-0.xsl]

152 days have elapsed since the beginning of the sales year.
```

Now for an experiment. If you comment out the template in `report-0.xsl`, which template do you think will be the next priority template? Try it and see. Hide the template in `report-0.xsl` with a comment, like this:

```
<xsl:stylesheet version="1.0"
xmlns:xsl="http://www.w3.org/1999/XSL/Transform">
<xsl:import href="report-4.xsl"/>
<xsl:import href="report-3.xsl"/>
<xsl:import href="report-2.xsl"/>
<xsl:import href="report-1.xsl"/>
<xsl:output method="text" encoding="utf-8"/>

<!--xsl:template match="Order">
  [Report generated by: report-0.xsl]

  <xsl:value-of select="SalesYear/Days/@elapsed"/> days have elapsed
      since the beginning of the sales year.
</xsl:template-->

</xsl:stylesheet>
```

Then apply the commented stylesheet to order-new.xml to produce the following output:

```
[Report generated by: report-1.xsl]

    213 days remain until the end of the sales year.
```

With the template in the importing stylesheet set aside, the next priority template is the last one imported, report-1.xsl. If you continued to comment the templates out, starting with report-0.xsl, and then each stylesheet in order (report-1.xsl, report-2.xsl, and so forth), you would see that the import precedence is based on how the import tree is created by the XSLT processor. If the templates collide, the last imported template has first priority or highest import precedence, after the one in the importing stylesheet, and the first one imported has the last priority or lowest import precedence.

In the previous examples, you saw the effects of importing documents from a single stylesheet. What if you import stylesheets that, in turn, import other stylesheets? How will this affect import precedence? Figure 8.3 shows you how.

With the number 1 being the highest precedence, Figure 8.3 shows you how to figure out which imported templates will win out over others. The templates in the importing or originating stylesheet (report-a.xsl), as you know, get first priority. Next in line are the templates from report-c.xsl, which report-a.xsl imports last, giving them second place. Following that, report-c.xsl then imports report-e.xsl, which gives report-e.xsl third priority. The stylesheet report-b.xsl comes next. Because it was imported first, it has a lower import precedence than report-c.xsl (fourth). Finally, report-d.xsl gets fifth and last billing.

> **NOTE**   Just to clarify, import precedence effectively rears its head only when templates collide. If all these stylesheets don't have any templates that collide, then importing the stylesheets isn't going to be much different from including them.

Template Priority

Another thing worth mentioning here is that, in addition to the priority of templates based on import precedence, the template element also has a priority attribute that can affect its priority. This attribute allows you to set the priority of templates based on an attribute value—the higher the

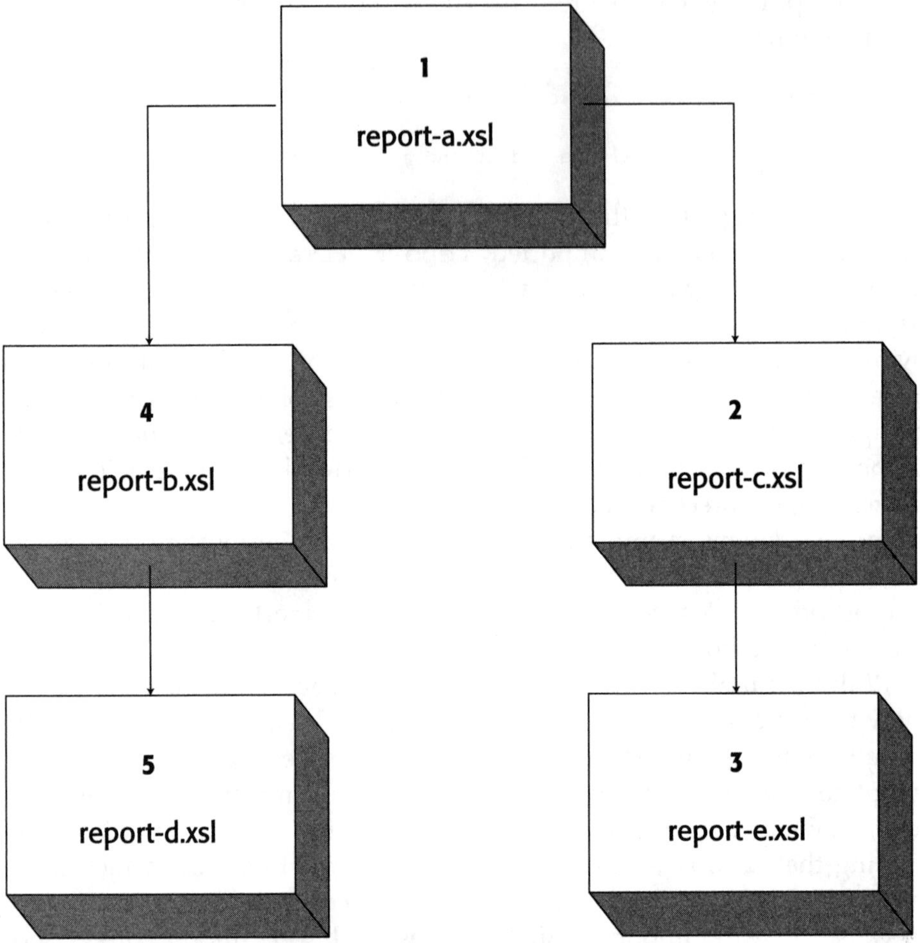

Figure 8.3 Import precedence with multiple stylesheet imports.

value, the higher the precedence. This means that a template with a `priority` attribute set to 5 (shown in bold in the following fragment) will have precedence over a template that matches the same pattern but has a `priority` of 4.

```
<xsl:template match="Order" priority="4">
 <xsl:value-of select="Item"/>
</xsl:template>

<xsl:template match="Order" priority="5">
 <xsl:value-of select="Quantity"/>
</xsl:template>
```

If you are interested in fine-tuning template priority, I would suggest you read Section 5.5 of the XSLT recommendation, which is worthy of your attention only if you plan on using templates whose patterns are liable to conflict. If you generally avoid writing templates in the same stylesheet that conflict (as I think most writers of XSLT stylesheets do), you probably needn't venture further into the details.

Now I'll turn back to imported stylesheets. When an imported template matches on the same node as a template in the importing stylesheet, it is possible to invoke the overridden rule. You can do this with apply-imports.

Using the apply-imports Element

When the stylesheet in the following example imports another stylesheet, the template in the importing stylesheet (report-0.1.xsl), which matches Order in order-new.xml, overrides the template in the imported stylesheet (report-1.1.xsl). The difference in this example, however, is that the importing stylesheet includes an instance of apply-imports. The apply-imports element invokes the template from the imported stylesheet that has been overridden by the importing stylesheet.

Following is report-0.1.xsl. It is similar to report-0.xsl, but it imports only one other stylesheet. It also uses the XML output method rather than the text method, and it instantiates a comment element and several literal result elements.

```
<xsl:stylesheet version="1.0"
xmlns:xsl="http://www.w3.org/1999/XSL/Transform">
<xsl:import href="report-1.1.xsl"/>
<xsl:output method="xml" encoding="utf-8" indent="yes"/>

<xsl:template match="Order">
<Report>
<xsl:comment>Report generated by: report-0.1.xsl</xsl:comment>
<Elapsed><xsl:value-of select="SalesYear/Days/@elapsed"/> days have
     elapsed since the beginning of the sales year.</Elapsed>
 <xsl:apply-imports/>
</Report>
</xsl:template>

</xsl:stylesheet>
```

Here is report-1.1.xsl, which report-0.1.xsl imports. It, too, uses the XML method and adds a comment element and a literal result element:

```
<xsl:stylesheet version="1.0"
xmlns:xsl="http://www.w3.org/1999/XSL/Transform">
<xsl:output method="xml" encoding="utf-8" indent="yes"/>

<xsl:template match="Order">
<xsl:comment>Report generated by: report-1.1.xsl</xsl:comment>
<Remaining><xsl:value-of select="SalesYear/Days/@remaining"/> days
remain until the end of the sales year.</Remaining>
</xsl:template>

</xsl:stylesheet>
```

When you apply `report-0.1.xsl` against `order-new.xml`, you will see this output:

```
<?xml version="1.0" encoding="utf-8"?>
<Report>
<!--Report generated by: report-0.1.xsl-->
<Elapsed>152 days have elapsed since the beginning of the sales
year.</Elapsed>
<!--Report generated by: report-1.1.xsl-->
<Remaining>213 days remain until the end of the sales year.</Remaining>
</Report>
```

As you can see, both templates are instantiated. The override doesn't trump the first priority template: It allows the other template to be instantiated as well as the first.

If you remove or comment out `apply-imports` from `report-0.1.xsl`, the overridden template in `report-1.1.xsl` is not invoked, and you get this result instead:

```
<?xml version="1.0" encoding="utf-8"?>
<Report>
<!--Report generated by: report-0.1.xsl-->
<Elapsed>152 days have elapsed since the beginning of the sales
year.</Elapsed>
</Report>
```

The `apply-imports` element allows you to get away with instantiating templates that match on the same nodes, which you normally can't do. Such templates would collide if they were in the same stylesheet.

You could turn this overriding behavior on and off by passing in a parameter. The following stylesheet (`report-0.1.1.xsl`) declares the parameter `override` with a default or initial value of 0. A `test` attribute in the `if` element checks to see if `override` is not 0. If it is not, then the template override is invoked with `apply-imports`:

```
<xsl:stylesheet version="1.0"
xmlns:xsl="http://www.w3.org/1999/XSL/Transform">
<xsl:import href="report-1.1.xsl"/>
<xsl:output method="xml" encoding="utf-8" indent="yes"/>
<xsl:param name="override" select="0"/>

<xsl:template match="Order">
<Report>
<xsl:comment>Report generated by: report-0.1.xsl</xsl:comment>
<Elapsed><xsl:value-of select="SalesYear/Days/@elapsed"/> days have
elapsed since the beginning of the sales year.</Elapsed>
<xsl:if test="$override != 0">
 <xsl:apply-imports/>
</xsl:if>
</Report>
</xsl:template>

</xsl:stylesheet>
```

So, if your command line looked like this:

```
xt order-new.xml report-0.1.1.xsl
```

you would get the following result:

```
<?xml version="1.0" encoding="utf-8"?>
<Report>
<!--Report generated by: report-0.1.xsl-->
<Elapsed>152 days have elapsed since the beginning of the sales
     year.</Elapsed>
</Report>
```

But, if the command is like this:

```
xt order-new.xml report-0.1.1.xsl override=1
```

you will get this:

```
<?xml version="1.0" encoding="utf-8"?>
<Report>
<!--Report generated by: report-0.1.xsl-->
<Elapsed>152 days have elapsed since the beginning of the sales
     year.</Elapsed>
<!--Report generated by: report-1.1.xsl-->
<Remaining>213 days remain until the end of the sales year.</Remaining>
</Report>
```

By default, only one template is invoked. If `override` equals anything except 0, both templates are invoked.

Winding Down

The XSLT part of this book is winding down. In the next chapter, I'll cover the features we haven't covered (much) in XSLT, including axes, keys, functions, and extensions. After that we'll move into Part Two, which will provide several introductory chapters on XSLFO.

More XSLT

This is the last chapter of Part One and the last to cover XSLT. In this chapter, I'll discuss how to select nodes with XPath axes. In addition, I'll explain how to define and use keys, which provide a slick way to find nodes in a document, based on their values. I'll also talk about XSLT and XPath functions that you may not have seen yet, like concat() and round(), extension elements and functions, and using namespace aliases, among other things.

I think a good place to start is with axes. By now you have learned quite a bit about using abbreviated syntax in location paths. Now I'll talk about the unabbreviated syntax.

XPath Axes

You have already seen some of the 13 XPath axes in this book, but I have not yet dealt with all of them. It's high time I covered them in more detail.

The simplest of the abbreviated location paths—which you have seen plenty of—is just the name of a node, such as Order, which addresses the root element of order.xml or order-new.xml. The node name is also known as a node test (see the section *Node Tests* later in this chapter). The unabbreviated form of this is child::Order, which refers to a child node of the current node (presumably the root node), which is named `Order`. In this context, `child::` is known as an axis specifier, with `child` as the axis name and `::` as (unofficially) the axis operator.

Axes help you hunt down and find nodes, supposedly for some kind of processing, even when they aren't children or descendents of the current node or in the current node list.

Table 9.1 lists all the axes, each with a brief description. You can read more about axes in Section 2.2 of the XPath recommendation.

Table 9.1   XPath Axes

AXIS NAME	DESCRIPTION
ancestor	Contains the ancestors of the current node, including the root node.
ancestor-or-self	Contains the ancestors of the current node, including the current node itself, plus the root node.
attribute	Contains the current node's attributes, but only if the current node is an element node (empty otherwise). Permitted in a pattern as well as an expression.
child	Contains children of the current node. Permitted in a pattern as well as an expression. (Namespace and attribute nodes are never children.)
descendant	Contains descendants of the current node. (Namespace and attribute nodes are never descendants.)
descendant-or-self	Contains descendants of the current node, including the current node itself. (Namespace and attribute nodes are never descendants.)
following	Contains nodes in the same document that follow the current node in document order, but not descendant, namespace, or attribute nodes.
following-sibling	Contains sibling nodes in the same document that follow the current node in document order, but not descendant, namespace, or attribute nodes. Siblings are on the same hierarchical level, or they share a parent.
namespace	Contains the namespace node of the current node, which must be an element node.
parent	Contains the parent of the current node. Namespace and attribute nodes have parents (always element nodes), but are never children.

Table 9.1 *(Continued)*

AXIS NAME	DESCRIPTION
preceding	Contains nodes in the same document that precede the current node in document order, but not ancestor, namespace, or attribute nodes.
preceding-sibling	Contains sibling nodes in the same document that precede the current node in document order, but not ancestor, namespace, or attribute nodes. Siblings are on the same level, or they share a parent.
self	Contains only the current node.

XPath Axes Examples

Let's talk about each of these axes, how you can use them and what you might expect from them. In the examples that follow, most of the axes are applied to order-new.xml, except where noted. All axes work in relation to the current or context node. In addition, they are always in lowercase.

The ancestor and ancestor-or-self Axes

The ancestor axis finds ancestors on the source tree. This can be a parent or an ancestor in a generation before the current node. The ancestor-or-self axis is similar but also includes the current node itself. Both ancestor axes also include the root node as well.

The following template finds an attribute node along the ancestor axis (ancestor::Order) and instantiates the attribute in the Address element:

```
<xsl:template match="child::Address">
 <xsl:copy>
  <xsl:copy-of select="ancestor::Order/attribute::orderID"/>
 </xsl:copy>
</xsl:template>
```

Output from this template looks like this:

```
<Address orderID="ORD-ID-2001-06-01-600001"/>
```

In the following, the template instantiates a copy of the Partner element using ancestor-or-self, enclosing itself in a new parent, PartnerInformation. (The self axis would work here, too.)

```
<xsl:template match="child::Partner">
  <PartnerInformation>
```

```
    <xsl:copy-of select="ancestor-or-self::Partner"/>
  </PartnerInformation>
</xsl:template>
```

The output is this:

```
<PartnerInformation>
 <Partner>
  <DUNS>06-853-2535</DUNS>
   <Location>
    <Address>
     <Company>Wy'east Communications</Company>
     <Mailing>P.O. Box 537</Mailing>
     <City>West Linn</City>
     <State>Oregon</State>
     <ZIPCode>97068-0537</ZIPCode>
     <Country>United States<Code>US</Code></Country>
    </Address>
   </Location>
  </Partner>
</PartnerInformation>
```

The attribute and child Axes

As you saw in the ancestor example, the attribute axis selects an attribute node that is associated with an element. Attribute nodes are not considered children by the XPath recommendation, but they are thought of as properties associated with an element. This template:

```
<xsl:template match="child::Order">
<ItemType><xsl:value-of
select="child::Item/attribute::type"/></ItemType>
</xsl:template>
```

produces this:

```
<ItemType>ISBN</ItemType>
```

The child axis, which is shown twice in the previous fragment, contains children of the current node. A child node is not separated by a generation from its parent. Both the child and attribute axes are acceptable in a pattern (such as in template's match attribute).

The descendant and descendant-or-self Axes

Nodes in the descendant axis can be children of the current node or descendants separated by more than one generation. This axis does not contain namespace or attribute nodes because they are not child nodes of elements. The `descendant-or-self` axis is similar to `descendant` but also includes the current node in its axis. The template:

```
<xsl:template match="child::Order">
 <USState><xsl:value-of select="descendant::State"/></USState>
</xsl:template>
```

finds a descendant (`descendant::State`) of the current node and produces this output:

```
<USState>Oregon</USState>
```

The following and preceding Axes

The `following` axis contains nodes that come after the current node in document order, but not descendant, attribute, or namespace nodes. The `preceding` axis is similar to `following` but contains nodes that come before the current node in document order, though likewise not ancestor, attribute, or namespaces nodes. Nodes in the `following` or `preceding` axes are always in the same document.

In `order-new.xml`, the `Country` element follows the `State` element, so this template:

```
<xsl:template match="child::State">
 <ShipCountry><xsl:apply-templates
select="following::Country"/></ShipCountry>
</xsl:template>
```

will yield:

```
<ShipCountry>United States</ShipCountry>
```

The following-sibling and preceding-sibling Axes

You could use the `following-sibling` axis here, too. The `following` axis is similar to the `following-sibling` axis, but the latter contains sibling nodes that follow the current node. Siblings are on the same level in an XML document, and they share the same parent. Similarly, the `preceding-sibling` axis is like the preceding axis but only for siblings. If the current node is an attribute or namespace node, the `preceding-sibling` and `following-sibling` axes are empty.

The namespace Axis

Namespace nodes are like attribute nodes in that they are never child nodes. They are considered a characteristic of an element node, but not a child of an element. A `namespace` axis will contain the namespace node of a current node if the current node is an element (empty otherwise). Here's an example applied to `order-ns.xml`:

```
<xsl:template match="child::order:Order">
 <xsl:value-of select="namespace::*"/>
</xsl:template>
```

Results may be different from what you expect, depending on the XSLT processor, but this is the general idea. When I tested it, TestXSLT, for example, returned:

```
http://www.testb2b.org/order
```

as I expected.

The parent and self Axes

The `parent` axis contains the parent of the current node. The following template returns the name of the parent of the current node, that is, `Location`:

```
<xsl:template match="child::Address">
 <xsl:value-of select="name(parent::*)"/>
</xsl:template>
```

The asterisk (`*`) will select any element. The `name()` function returns a string containing the actual name of the node.

The `self` axis is rather self-centered and is a narrow axis indeed. It points to the current node itself, and that's it. In abbreviated syntax, the `self` axis is represented by a single period (`.`), such that the following two snippets are equivalent:

```
<xsl:template match="child::Company">
 <xsl:value-of select="self::Company"/>
</xsl:template>
```

```
<xsl:template match="child::Company">
 <xsl:value-of select="."/>
</xsl:template>
```

When the template matches a child node, it can refer to itself from within the template.

Partitioning All Nodes in a Document

Taken together, the following axes contain all the nodes in a document (except namespace and attribute nodes). Also remember that these axes don't overlap and in effect partition all eligible nodes into separate axes:

- self
- ancestor
- descendant
- following
- preceding

A Commerce XML Example

Commerce XML (cXML) is an e-commerce XML vocabulary from Ariba (www.ariba.com). You can download the latest version of the vocabulary from www.cxml.org (1.2 at the time I am writing this). cXML is a fairly mature vocabulary that is intended for use by procurement and supplier applications that interface with Ariba products, though you may also use it independently. It offers markup for purchase orders, among other B2B transaction documents.

The following stylesheet is called `cxml-order.xsl`. It transforms `order-new.xml` into a new cXML order request document. Nodes are selected exclusively with unabbreviated axes syntax, as you will see highlighted in bold:

```
<xsl:stylesheet version="1.0"
xmlns:xsl="http://www.w3.org/1999/XSL/Transform">
<xsl:output method="xml" encoding="utf-8" indent="yes"/>
<xsl:output doctype-
system="http://xml.cXML.org/schemas/cXML/1.2.002/cXML.dtd"/>

<xsl:template match="/">
<xsl:param name="subOrderID" select="child::Order/attribute::orderID"/>

<cXML payloadID="{substring-after($subOrderID,'ORD-ID-')}"
      timestamp="2001-06-01T12:00:02-08:00" xml:lang="en">
<Header>
 <From>
  <Credential domain="DUNS">
   <Identity>86-757-8317</Identity>
  </Credential>
 </From>
 <To>
  <Credential domain="{name(descendant::DUNS)}">
```

```
     <Identity><xsl:value-of select="descendant::DUNS"/></Identity>
    </Credential>
  </To>
  <Sender>
   <Credential domain="{name(descendant::DUNS)}">
   <SharedSecret>4D772F82E1132500DAC007D9197B7379</SharedSecret>
     <Identity><xsl:value-of select="descendant::DUNS"/></Identity>
   </Credential>
   <UserAgent>MSIE/5.5</UserAgent>
  </Sender>
 </Header>

   <xsl:apply-templates select="child::Order"/>

</cXML>
</xsl:template>

<xsl:template match="child::Order">
<Request deploymentMode="test">
 <OrderRequest>
  <OrderRequestHeader orderID="{attribute::orderID}"
     orderDate="{child::Date}" type="new">
   <Total>
    <Money currency="USD"><xsl:value-of
select="format-number(number(22.19 * number(child::Quantity)),
     '#####.00')"/>
    </Money>
   </Total>

   <xsl:apply-templates select="child::Partner"/>

  <Payment>
   <PCard number="1234567899999999" expiration="2003-01"/>
  </Payment>
  <Comments xml:lang="en"><xsl:value-of
     select="child::Comments"/></Comments>
  </OrderRequestHeader>
  <ItemOut quantity="{child::Quantity}" requestedDeliveryDate="2001-06-
     15">
   <ItemID>
    <SupplierPartID><xsl:value-of
select="child::Item"/></SupplierPartID>
   </ItemID>
   <Shipping trackingDomain="{child::ShippingMethod}">
    <Money currency="USD">13.95</Money>
    <Description xml:lang="en-us"></Description>
   </Shipping>
   <Comments xml:lang="en-us"><xsl:value-of
     select="child::Comments"/></Comments>
  </ItemOut>
```

```
    </OrderRequest>
  </Request>
</xsl:template>

<xsl:template match="child::Partner">
 <xsl:apply-templates select="descendant::Address"/>
</xsl:template>

<xsl:template match="child::Address">
<ShipTo>
 <Address>
  <Name xml:lang="en"><xsl:value-of select="child::Company"/></Name>
  <PostalAddress name="default">
   <DeliverTo>Schlomo Schmid</DeliverTo>
   <Street><xsl:value-of select="child::Mailing"/></Street>
   <City><xsl:value-of select="child::City"/></City>
   <State><xsl:value-of select="child::State"/></State>
   <PostalCode><xsl:value-of select="child::ZIPCode"/></PostalCode>
<Country isoCountryCode="{child::Country/child::Code}"> <xsl:value-of
     select="child::Country/text()"/></Country>
  </PostalAddress>
 </Address>
</ShipTo>
<BillTo>
 <Address>
  <Name xml:lang="en"><xsl:value-of select="child::Company"/></Name>
  <PostalAddress name="default">
   <Street><xsl:value-of select="child::Mailing"/></Street>
   <City><xsl:value-of select="child::City"/></City>
   <State><xsl:value-of select="child::State"/></State>
   <PostalCode><xsl:value-of select="child::ZIPCode"/></PostalCode>
   <Country isoCountryCode="{child::Country/child::Code}"><xsl:value-of
     select="child::Country/text()"/></Country>
  </PostalAddress>
 </Address>
</BillTo>
</xsl:template>

</xsl:stylesheet>
```

You have seen most all the XSLT techniques in this stylesheet previously in the book, so I won't go over them again here. Following is the result tree from this transformation, a valid cXML order request:

```
<?xml version="1.0" encoding="utf-8"?>

<!DOCTYPE cXML
  SYSTEM "http://xml.cXML.org/schemas/cXML/1.2.002/cXML.dtd">
<cXML payloadID="2001-06-01-600001" timestamp="2001-06-01T12:00:02-
```

```
        08:00" xml:lang="en">
  <Header>
   <From>
    <Credential domain="DUNS">
     <Identity>86-757-8317</Identity>
    </Credential>
   </From>
   <To>
    <Credential domain="DUNS">
     <Identity>06-853-2535</Identity>
    </Credential>
   </To>
   <Sender>
   <Credential domain="DUNS">
<SharedSecret>4D772F82E1132500DAC007D9197B7379</SharedSecret>
    <Identity>06-853-2535</Identity>
   </Credential>
   <UserAgent>MSIE/5.5</UserAgent>
  </Sender>
 </Header>
<Request deploymentMode="test">
 <OrderRequest>
  <OrderRequestHeader orderID="ORD-ID-2001-06-01-600001"
orderDate="2001-06-01" type="new">
    <Total>
     <Money currency="USD">887.60</Money>
    </Total>
    <ShipTo>
     <Address>
      <Name xml:lang="en">Wy'east Communications</Name>
       <PostalAddress name="default">
        <DeliverTo>Schlomo Schmid</DeliverTo>
        <Street>P.O. Box 537</Street>
        <City>West Linn</City>
        <State>Oregon</State>
        <PostalCode>97068-0537</PostalCode>
        <Country isoCountryCode="US">United States</Country>
       </PostalAddress>
      </Address>
     </ShipTo>
     <BillTo>
      <Address>
       <Name xml:lang="en">Wy'east Communications</Name>
       <PostalAddress name="default">
       <Street>P.O. Box 537</Street>
       <City>West Linn</City>
       <State>Oregon</State>
       <PostalCode>97068-0537</PostalCode>
       <Country isoCountryCode="US">United States</Country>
      </PostalAddress>
     </Address>
```

```
    </BillTo>
    <Payment>
     <PCard number="1234567899999999" expiration="2003-01"/>
    </Payment>
    <Comments xml:lang="en">None.</Comments>
   </OrderRequestHeader>
   <ItemOut quantity="40" requestedDeliveryDate="2001-06-15">
    <ItemID>
     <SupplierPartID>0471416207</SupplierPartID>
    </ItemID>
    <Shipping trackingDomain="USPS">
     <Money currency="USD">13.95</Money>
     <Description xml:lang="en-us"/>
    </Shipping>
    <Comments xml:lang="en-us">None.</Comments>
   </ItemOut>
  </OrderRequest>
 </Request>
</cXML>
```

In the stylesheet `cxml-order.xsl`, you see the basic principles for converting `order-new.xml` to any vocabulary you wish. Other B2B-related vocabularies include:

- Electronic Business XML (www.ebxml.org) for OASIS-UN/CEFACT (www.oasis-open.org)

- XML Common Business Library (www.xcbl.org) from Commerce One (www.commerceone.com)

- RosettaNet Implementation Framework (www.rosettanet.org)

- BizTalk (www.biztalk.org) from Microsoft (www.microsoft.com)

Using Keys

Keys in XSLT provide an efficient way to search out, find, and even cross-reference nodes in an XML document. Keys have two main components that work together, the `key` element and the `key()` function. At first glance, keys may look somewhat complicated, but they really are not.

I will get started by presenting a single-key example that will make keys easier to understand, I hope. To get a key to work, you have to first define it with the `key` element and then, second, ring it up with the `key()` function. Here is a stylesheet called `key.xsl`:

```
<xsl:stylesheet version="1.0"
xmlns:xsl="http://www.w3.org/1999/XSL/Transform">
<xsl:output method="text" encoding="utf-8"/>
```

```
<xsl:key name="Catalog" match="Catalog/Item" use="@id"/>

<xsl:template match="/">
 <xsl:value-of select="key('Catalog','SPD-3066')/Name"/>
</xsl:template>

</xsl:stylesheet>
```

If you apply this stylesheet to `catalog.xml`, you get this result:

```
Elementary Alphabet Book
```

NOTE **The XT processor does not implement keys, and it is unlikely that it will any time soon.**

A key is also considered a generalized ID, made up of the triple values: (1) a node that has the key or node x; (2) the key name or name y; and (3) the string value of the key or value z. These triples are declared with the `key` element.

The `key` element works only at the top level. It has three attributes, and all of them are required. The `name` attribute gives the key a name that the `key()` function uses to reference it. The name of this key is `Catalog`. We will use it to access information in `catalog.xml` (or another compatible XML catalog document). The `match` attribute contains a pattern to address nodes in a document.

Here is the part of the document `catalog.xml` that this key addresses:

```
<Catalog>
 <Item id="AHA-133040">
  <Name>Pen Calligraphy Manual</Name>
  <Description>This basic calligraphy manual includes alphabets,
projects and more. For beginners of all ages.</Description>
  <Price currency="USD">19.95</Price>
 </Item>
 <Item id="SPD-3066">
  <Name>Elementary Alphabet Book</Name>
  <Description>Twenty-four page book, authored by Ross F. George,
features basic alphabets, drafting alphabets and manuscript. By
Speedball.</Description>
  <Price currency="USD">3.95</Price>
 </Item>
 <Item id="SPD-3067">
  <Name>Speedball Textbook</Name>
 . . .
```

The `match` pattern addresses all `Item` elements (children of `Catalog`) in the document. The final attribute, `use`, contains an expression that selects the `id` attribute of `Item` with `@id`.

With the `key` element defined, you can call it with the `key()` function. The function takes two arguments (both required). The first argument—a string—is the name of the key you defined earlier, that is, `Catalog`. The second argument is an object, in this case a string that is equal to the value of an `id` attribute of `Item`, namely, `SPD-3066`. When the `key()` function finds this keyed value, the `value-of` element returns the string value of the `Name` element, which is a child of `Item`. This happens because of the location path after the `key()` function, which selects the correct instance of `Name`.

That's how a simple key works. In the next example, I'll define three keys.

Defining Several Keys

Here I'll show you the stylesheet `keys.xsl`, and then I'll explain what's going on in it. The stylesheet defines three keys, each of which you may use with a different XML document. All three keys, though, work with only a single parameter (`keystring`):

```
<xsl:stylesheet version="1.0"
xmlns:xsl="http://www.w3.org/1999/XSL/Transform">
<xsl:output method="text" encoding="utf-8"/>
<xsl:param name="keystring"/>
<xsl:key name="Catalog" match="Catalog/Item" use="@id"/>
<xsl:key name="Country-code" match="country-codes/code" use="country"/>
<xsl:key name="Currency" match="currency/code" use="alphabetic"/>

<xsl:template match="/">
 <xsl:value-of select="key('Catalog',$keystring)/Name"/>
 <xsl:value-of select="key('Country-code',$keystring)/abbr"/>
 <xsl:for-each select="key('Currency',$keystring)">
  <xsl:value-of select="location-or-entity"/>
  <xsl:text>&#xa;</xsl:text>
 </xsl:for-each>
</xsl:template>

</xsl:stylesheet>
```

About the first thing this stylesheet does, after the preliminaries, is to declare the top-level `keystring` parameter, which you can use with all three keys. This parameter allows you to pass in a string that has a different meaning depending on the XML document against which the stylesheet is applied. Without the `select` attribute in its definition, the `keystring` parameter uses the empty string as its initial value.

Next, three keys are defined with three instances of the `key` element. The first key is for use with `catalog.xml` (just as in `key.xsl`), the second, for use with country-codes.xml, and the third for currency.xml. Each match attribute matches a different location path in a given document, and each use selects a different node within that document.

After the element definitions at the top of the stylesheet, the key() function is called three times from within a template. The function is called in three instances of the select attribute, as part of an expression, whether in value-of or for-each.

The function calls take names for first arguments. These names come from the top-level key definitions. For the second arguments, they all take $keystring, which references the keystring parameter definition. If you do not pass in a parameter from the processor, such as from the command line, these keys will effectively no-op.

In key.xsl, you already saw the first key work with a hard-coded string in the key() function. Now that string must come from the keystring parameter, or nothing will happen. Let's try it out a couple of ways and see what happens. The following command line:

```
saxon catalog.xml keys.xsl keystring=SPD-3066
```

has the same effect as key.xsl, giving the same result:

```
Elementary Alphabet Book
```

Of course, the difference is that you passed in the value for keystring at runtime. Because you can choose this value at runtime, your options have expanded considerably. You can search for a different Item ID from the catalog:

```
msxsl catalog.xml keys.xsl keystring=SPD-3092
```

which gives you this result:

```
Abe Lincoln Italic Workbook
```

You can also use another key to find nodes in another document. For example, you can search for a country name using a key:

```
testxslt -q -in country-codes.xml -xsl keys.xsl -param keystring 'India'
```

and get a country code in response:

```
IN
```

Or you could input an alphabetic currency code:

```
saxon currency.xml keys.xsl keystring=CHF
```

and get back a list of countries that use that currency:

```
Liechtenstein
Switzerland
```

The key named `Currency` in `keys.xsl` is a little different because the template uses a `for-each` element. It is possible to get multiple values in return, and `for-each` will process each one, whereas `value-of` will return only the string value of the first node in the node-set, truncating the expected result.

Using Keys as Cross-References

Keys allow you to cross-reference nodes in a document while processing another node. Of course, you could do this in countless ways, but I'll just show you only one example to give you an idea. The stylesheet is `key-xref.xsl`:

```
<xsl:stylesheet version="1.0"
xmlns:xsl="http://www.w3.org/1999/XSL/Transform">
<xsl:output method="text" encoding="utf-8"/>
<xsl:key name="Currency" match="currency/code" use="location-or-entity"/>

<xsl:template match="/">
 <xsl:apply-templates select="country-codes/code/country"/>
</xsl:template>

<xsl:template match="country-codes/code/country">
<xsl:variable name="keyxref" select="."/>

 Country code: <xsl:value-of select="preceding-sibling::abbr"/>
 <xsl:for-each select="document('currency.xml')">
 Currency symbol: <xsl:value-of select="key('Currency',
     $keyxref)/alphabetic"/>
 </xsl:for-each>
</xsl:template>

</xsl:stylesheet>
```

When you apply this stylesheet against `country-codes.xml`, you get the following output (this is only the first 20 lines of the result):

```
Country code: AD
Currency symbol: ESP

Country code: AE
Currency symbol: AED
```

```
Country code: AF
Currency symbol: AFA

Country code: AG
Currency symbol: XCD

Country code: AI
Currency symbol: XCD

Country code: AL
Currency symbol: ALL

Country code: AM
Currency symbol: AMD
```

The key named `Currency` is defined with a `key` element, just as in `keys.xsl`, but with a different value for `use`. As the template matches on nodes in the node-set `country-codes/code/country`, it squirrels away the name of a country (from the location path `country-codes/code/country`) into the variable `keyxref`. Then it writes the string value of the `abbr` element that it found on the preceding-sibling axis. Then country names in `country-codes.xml` are matched with those in `currency.xml` by using the `$keyxref` reference as a value of the `key()` function. This sort of cross-referencing helps produce output that brings together country codes and currency symbols for the same countries.

NOTE The stylesheet does not always produce perfect output because the names of countries are not identical in both files—most are, however.

XSLT Functions

XSLT furnishes a group of nine functions. You have used four of them already in this book (`current()`, `document()`, `format-number()`, and `key()`). This section will review the functions you have already seen and explore how to use the others. Table 9.2 lists all XSLT functions and provides a description for each one.

Brief XSLT Function Examples

In the following subsections, I'll provide short examples for all the functions, starting with `current()`. These examples offer brief illustrations of how the functions work. Functions are always used within expressions.

Table 9.2 XSLT Functions

FUNCTION	DESCRIPTION
`current()`	Returns the current node. You can also use a single period (.).
`document(object, node-set)`	Returns the nodes of the document specified in the argument. May reference the current stylesheet with `document('')` or the current document with `document(.)`.
`element-available(string)`	Checks to see if an element is available. Used for extension elements.
`format-number(number, string, string)`	Formats a number.
`function-available(string)`	Checks to see if a function is available. Used for extension functions.
`generate-id(node-set)`	Generates a unique ID.
`key(sting, object)`	Applies a named key.
`system-property(string)`	Returns a system property.
`unparsed-entity-uri(string)`	Returns a URI for an unparsed entity (such as a JPEG image).

The current() Function

The `current()` function returns the current node. The following templates will all produce the same result (the string value of `Date`), though the `select` value is different in each instance:

```
<xsl:template match="Date">
 <xsl:value-of select="current()"/>
</xsl:template>

<xsl:template match="Date">
 <xsl:value-of select="."/>
</xsl:template>

<xsl:template match="Date">
 <xsl:value-of select="self::Date"/>
</xsl:template>
```

The document() Function

Chapter 8, "Multiple Documents," covered the `document()` function, and you saw an example of it in the previous section (in `key-xref.xsl`). Here is another short example:

```
<xsl:template match="Date">
<OrderDate><xsl:value-of select="."/></OrderDate>
<OrderDays><xsl:value-of select="document('order-
    new.xml')/Order/SalesYear/Days/@elapsed"/></OrderDays>
</xsl:template>
```

which produces:

```
<OrderDate>2001-06-01</OrderDate>
<OrderDays>152</OrderDays>
```

The element-available() and function-available() Functions

The `element-available()` and `function-available()` functions test to see if an extension element or function, that is, one that is not available from the XSLT namespace, is available. I will discuss these functions in the section titled *Extension Elements and Functions* a little later in this chapter, but here are a few brief samples:

```
<xsl:if test="element-available('saxon:assign')">
 <xsl:text>The element saxon:assign exists!</xsl:text>
</xsl:if>
```

```
<xsl:if test="function-available('saxon:if')">
 <xsl:text>The element saxon:if exists!</xsl:text>
</xsl:if>
```

These few lines test to see if the stylesheet and XSLT processor (presumably Saxon) recognize the `assign` element and `if` function from the saxon namespace (`http://icl.com/saxon`). If either `saxon:assign` or `saxon:if` is recognized, the `if` element from XSLT returns true and executes its content.

The format-number() Function

The `format-number()` function was explained in detail in Chapter 5, "Sorting and Numbering Lists." The following fragment shows how to place a grouping separator (a comma) after the thousands place in an integer:

```
<xsl:value-of select="format-number(1000,'#,###')"/>
```

This will generate `1,000` as output.

The generate-id() Function

The generate-id() function generates a unique ID for an object so that you can refer to that object elsewhere specifically. The IDs generated by generate-id() are alphanumeric and are limited to the US-ASCII character set. These IDs also must start with a letter, so they are legal as names in XML (see www.w3.org/tr/rec-xml.html#sec-common-syn for a definition).

An XSLT processor is permitted to generate this identifier any way it wants as long as it always generates the same unique ID for the same node. The processor, though, is not obligated to generate the same IDs each time it transforms a document, which would probably require some sort of messy persistent storage scheme. Be cautioned that the IDs created by generate-id() may not be distinct from the IDs in a source document— there is no easy way to guarantee this.

For example, if you were outputting HTML and you wanted to create a unique fragment identifier (preceded by #) for an anchor (a) element, you could do something like this:

```
<xsl:template match="Item">
<xsl:variable name="gid" select="generate-id()"/>
 <a href="#{$gid}">Go!</a>
 ...
 <a name="{$gid}"><xsl:value-of select="."/></a>
</xsl:template>
```

By using the variable gid, you can insert the unique ID value in several places, so that an HTML link based on a fragment ID will work. The result of this template will appear as follows:

```
<a href="#d1e6">Go!</a>
 ...
<a name="d1e6">0471416207</a>
```

The link will work in a browser, just as you would suspect. This is just the start of what you could do with generate-id(). Here is just one more example of what generate-id() can accomplish. Because an ID must be unique for a given node, a test such as the following is possible:

```
<xsl:if test="$gid != generate-id(.)">
 <xsl:text>Oops! Something's not right.</xsl:text>
</xsl:if>
```

If the current node (.) is the same node for which gid was created, this test will return true.

The key() Function

Earlier in this chapter, in the section titled *Using Keys*, I discussed how to use key elements and key() functions together. For example, in the following piece:

```
<xsl:key name="Catalog" match="Catalog/Item" use="@id"/>

<xsl:template match="/">
 <xsl:value-of select="key('Catalog','SPD-3066')/Name"/>
</xsl:template>
```

the key() function invokes a key named Catalog, returning the string value of a Name element whose Item parent has an id attribute equal to SPD-3066.

The system-property() Function

With the system-property() function, you can examine the values of system properties. The XSLT recommendation specifies three properties that a processor must produce when requested. They are the name of the vendor that created the processor (xsl:vendor), the URL for the vendor's Web site (xsl:vendor-url), and the XSLT version number (xsl:version) indicating what XSLT is supported. If the following line were processed by XT:

```
<xsl:value-of select="system-property('xsl:vendor')"/>
```

XT would report back:

```
Vendor: James Clark
```

The unparsed-entity-uri() Function

The unparsed-entity-uri() function returns a URI for an unparsed entity that is declared properly in a DTD. An unparsed entity in XML is an object that is not parsed by an XML processor. An unparsed entity might be some non-XML text, an image in JPEG format, a PDF file, or what have you. The following template:

```
<xsl:template match="PDFVersion">
 <xsl:value-of select="unparsed-entity-uri('order-pdf')"/>
</xsl:template>
```

would return the following output:

```
http://www.testb2b.org/B2B/order-unparsed-entity.pdf
```

provided that an XML document (`order-unparsed-entity.xml`) contains the line:

```
<PDFVersion file="order-pdf"/>
```

and that the DTD (`<!DOCTYPE Order SYSTEM "order-unparsed-entity.dtd">` declared in `order-unparsed-entity.xml`) contains the following ENTITY declaration:

```
<!ENTITY order-pdf SYSTEM "http://www.testb2b.org/B2B/order-unparsed-entity.pdf" NDATA PDF>
```

You can find out more about declaring entities, unparsed and otherwise, in Section 4 of the XML recommendation, available at www.w3.org/tr/rec-xml.html#sec-physical-struct.

XPath Functions

XPath also provides a large number of functions. Table 9.3 lists all 27 of these functions in alphabetical order and gives a short description of each one. XPath functions are categorized into four basic types: (1) node-set; (2) string; (3) Boolean; and (4) number. As you can guess, functions in a given category work with data of their given type.

Table 9.3 XPath Functions

FUNCTION	TYPE	DESCRIPTION
`boolean(object)`	Boolean	Returns true or false based on the object in the argument.
`ceiling(number)`	Number	Returns the smallest possible integer.
`concat(string, string,string*)`	String	Concatenates two or more strings.
`contains(string, string)`	String	Returns true if the first string contains the second.
`count(node-set)`	Node-set	Counts the number values of the content of the given nodes.
`false()`	Boolean	Returns false.

continues

Table 9.3   XPath Functions (*Continued*)

FUNCTION	TYPE	DESCRIPTION
floor(number)	Number	Returns the largest possible integer.
id(object)	Node-set	Selects a node based on its unique ID.
lang(string)	Boolean	Returns true or false based on xml:lang.
last()	Node-set	Returns the number of the last node in the node-set (equals context size).
local-name (node-set?)	Node-set	Returns the local name of the expanded name of a node.
name(node-set?)	Node-set	Returns a qualified name (QName).
namespace-uri (node-set?)	Node-set	Returns the namespace URI of the expanded name of a node.
normalize-space (string?)	String	Strips extra whitespace from a string.
not(boolean)	Boolean	Returns true if the argument is false, false otherwise.
number(object)	Number	Returns the number value of an object.
position()	Node-set	Returns the position of the current node (said of the context position).
round(number)	Number	Converts the argument to its closest integer.
starts-with (string,string)	String	Returns true if the string in the first argument starts with the string in the second.
string(object?)	String	Converts an object to a string.
string-length (string?)	String	Returns the length of a string in characters.
substring(string, number,number?)	String	Returns a substring of the first argument based on a starting position (second argument) and length (third argument).
substring-after (string,string)	String	Returns a substring of the first argument after the string in the second argument.
substring-before (string,string)	String	Returns a substring of the first argument before the string in the second argument.
sum(node-set)	Number	Adds the number values of the content of the given nodes.
translate(string, string,string)	String	Translates the string in the first argument with characters from the string in the second argument converted to those of the third.
true()	Boolean	Returns true.

Brief XPath Function Examples

The following subsections present examples of all XPath functions. Each subsection tackles the functions of a basic type. The examples only briefly illustrate how these functions work. Often I will use examples that you have seen earlier in the book. As with XSLT functions, XPath functions are always used in expressions.

Node-Set Functions

There are seven node-set functions, and I'll cover each briefly in the following subsections.

The id() Function

The id() function selects nodes based on an id attribute that is of type ID in XML. It can't just have the name *id*; it must also be of type ID, which must be declared in a DTD. The document catalog-id.xml adds a document type declaration for a DTD that declares the id attribute to be of type ID. Given that declaration, the following template, when applied to catalog-id.xml:

```
<xsl:template match="id('SPD-3092')">
 <xsl:copy-of select="Price"/>
</xsl:template>
```

yields this result:

```
<Price currency="USD">14.50</Price>
```

The count() Function

The count() function returns an integer representing the number of nodes in a given node-set. For example, in counter.xsl, which is applied to counter.xml, is the following attribute value template ({ }):

```
<Sum day="{count(Count)}"><xsl:value-of select="$sumit"/></Sum>
```

The count() function counts the number of Count elements in the current node-set. This line in the stylesheet returns:

```
<Sum day="7">56</Sum>
```

The number 7 is the value returned by count().

The position() and last() Functions

For every node-set there is a context size and position. Both are positive integers representing the number of nodes in the set (context size) and a number that indicates the current position in the context (context position). You can access these numbers with the position() and last() functions.

Assuming that space is stripped in Order with strip-space (removing text nodes that contain whitespace only), the following template:

```
<xsl:strip-space elements="Order"/>
...
<xsl:template match="Order/*">
Position: <xsl:value-of select="position()"/> Node: <xsl:copy-of
     select="."/>
</xsl:template>
```

renders this result:

```
Position: 1 Node: <Date>2001-06-01</Date>
Position: 2 Node: <Item type="ISBN">0471416207</Item>
Position: 3 Node: <Quantity>40</Quantity>
Position: 4 Node: <Comments>None.</Comments>
Position: 5 Node: <ShippingMethod class="4th">USPS</ShippingMethod>
```

To determine the number of code elements in currency.xml, you can apply this template (space in currency is stripped):

```
<xsl:template match="currency/code">
 <xsl:if test="position()=last()">
  <ContextSize><xsl:value-of select="last()"/></ContextSize>
 </xsl:if>
</xsl:template>
```

The result is:

```
<ContextSize>266</ContextSize>
```

The name() Function

In the cXML example shown a few pages ago, I used the name() function several times, such as in this line:

```
<Credential domain="{name(descendant::DUNS)}">
```

The name() function returns the name of the element that is addressed, namely, DUNS. This function actually returns a qualified name (QName), which means that if the element name were qualified with a namespace prefix, name() would return that, too. It can have a single node-set argument; if not, it assumes the current node. In either case, it processes the first node of a node-set (in document order).

The local-name() Function

An expanded name is represented internally by an XSLT processor. An expanded name consists of a local-part or local-name and a namespace URI. The namespace URI may be null. Like name(), local-name() uses a single node-set argument, but if an argument is not present, it assumes the current node. It also processes the first node of a node-set (in document order). When applied to order-ns.xml, the following template:

```
<xsl:template match="order:Order">
 <ThisElement local-name="{local-name()}"/>
</xsl:template>
```

effects this result:

```
<ThisElement local-name="Order"/>
```

The namespace-uri() Function

To retrieve a namespace URI that is part of an expanded name, you can use the namespace-uri() function. An expanded name is an internal representation of a namespace prefix as a namespace URI.

This function has an optional node-set argument, but it assumes the current node if no argument is present. It likewise processes the first node of a node-set (in document order). If the namespace URI is null, namespace-uri() returns an empty string.

If you apply the following to order-ns.xml:

```
<xsl:template match="order:order">
 <xsl:value-of select="namespace-uri()"/>
</xsl:template>
```

you get:

```
http://www.testb2b.org/order
```

String Functions

XPath has 10 string functions. These functions convert and manipulate strings to get them to do what you want them to do.

The string() Function

The string() function converts an object into a string. The object may be a node-set, a number, or even a Boolean. If no argument is given, the current node is assumed to be the argument.

If the argument is a node-set, it processes the first node of a node-set (in document order). If the node-set is empty, `string()` returns an empty string. If the argument is a number, a variety of constraints take effect. If the argument is not a number, the string NaN is returned. Positive and negative zero are both returned as 0. Positive infinity is returned as Infinity and negative infinity as -Infinity. Integers drop leading zeros and have no decimal point if converted to a string. A minus sign is used on negative numbers. Non-integers may have a decimal point. The Boolean values are converted to the strings true or false.

The following snippet converts an integer into a string:

```
<xsl:value-of select="string(000001)"/>
```

The result is 1.

The stylesheet `string.xsl` uses the `string()` function in several places to manipulate values for output:

```
<xsl:stylesheet version="1.0"
xmlns:xsl="http://www.w3.org/1999/XSL/Transform">
<xsl:output method="text" encoding="utf-8"/>

<xsl:template match="Catalog">
 <xsl:for-each select="Item/Price">
  <xsl:choose>
   <xsl:when test="number() &lt; 10.00">
    <xsl:value-of select="concat('Price: $  ', string(),
     ' ID: ', string(parent::Item/attribute::id), '&#xa;')"/>
   </xsl:when>
   <xsl:otherwise>
    <xsl:value-of select="concat('Price: $ ', string(),
     ' ID: ', string(parent::Item/attribute::id), '&#xa;')"/>
   </xsl:otherwise>
  </xsl:choose>
 </xsl:for-each>
</xsl:template>
```

When applied to `catalog.xml`, the result tree from this stylesheet is as follows:

```
Price: $ 19.95 ID: AHA-133040
Price: $  3.95 ID: SPD-3066
Price: $  8.95 ID: SPD-3067
Price: $ 14.50 ID: SPD-3092
Price: $  5.99 ID: TAP-081182
```

This stylesheet also uses the `concat()` function to concatenate or join strings.

The concat() Function

The `concat()` function accepts two or more strings as arguments and then concatenates them for output. This is a great convenience, and as you get familiar with it, you'll find it showing up in your stylesheets more often. As you will see in the following example, you can used variables, whitespace, and character references in the string arguments of `concat()`.

The `concat.xsl` stylesheet that follows may be applied to `currency.xml`:

```
<xsl:stylesheet version="1.0"
xmlns:xsl="http://www.w3.org/1999/XSL/Transform">
<xsl:output method="xml" encoding="utf-8" omit-xml-declaration="yes"/>
<xsl:param name="lt"/>

<xsl:template match="/">
 <xsl:apply-templates select="currency/code"/>
</xsl:template>

<xsl:template match="currency/code">
<xsl:variable name="cn" select="location-or-entity"/>
<xsl:variable name="a" select="alphabetic"/>

 <xsl:for-each select="location-or-entity[starts-with(.,$lt)]">
  <xsl:value-of select="concat($a, '      ', $cn, '&#xa;')"/>
 </xsl:for-each>

</xsl:template>

</xsl:stylesheet>
```

If you pass in the letter *D* like this:

```
xt currency.xml concat.xsl lt=D
```

you would get output as follows:

```
DKK     Denmark
DJF     Djibouti
XCD     Dominica
DOP     Dominican Republic
```

The contains() Function

The `contains()` function returns a Boolean indicating whether the string in the first argument contains the string in the second. For example, if you applied the following template against `catalog.xml`, you would test whether a `Description` element contains the word *Uncial*. If it does, the template in the `if` element is instantiated, that is, the matching string is written to output.

```
<xsl:template match="Catalog/Item">
<xsl:variable name="desc" select="Description"/>

 <xsl:if test="contains($desc,'Uncial')">
  <xsl:apply-templates select="$desc"/>
 </xsl:if>

</xsl:template>
```

Here is the output:

```
Presents 26 alphabets and variations from the basic Roman capital
through Uncial, Gothic, Batarde and Italic hands with explanations of
their appropriate applications. By Parkwest Publishing.
```

The starts-with() Function

The `starts-with()` function also returns a Boolean. It checks to see whether the string in the first argument starts with the string in the second. In the following template, the first argument interprets the node's content as a string.

```
<xsl:template match="currency">
 <xsl:apply-templates select="code[starts-with(location-or-entity,
     'A')]"/>
</xsl:template>
```

When this template is applied to `currency.xml`, it writes to output the content of all `code` elements whose child element `location-or-entity` starts with the letter *A*.

The substring() Function

The `substring()` function takes three arguments. The first is a string from which you want to pull out a substring. The second argument counts characters from the beginning of the string in the first argument to the position where the substring begins. The third argument counts from the position in the second out to where the substring ends. Given the following string:

```
<Order orderID="ORD-ID-2001-06-01-600001">
```

if a stylesheet applies the following template to a document containing this string:

```
<xsl:template match="Order">
<xsl:variable name="s" select="attribute::orderID"/>

<DerivedDate><xsl:value-of select="substring($s,8,10)"/></DerivedDate>

</xsl:template>
```

it will write this to output:

```
<DerivedDate>2001-06-01</DerivedDate>
```

The substring-after() Function

The function `substring-after()` returns a substring based on two arguments. The first argument is a string from which you want to derive a substring. The second argument is a substring from the first argument string that says, in effect, "return a substring that starts after me." In the stylesheet `cxml-order.xsl`, `substring-after()` is called in an attribute value template, as shown, to derive a substring from an attribute in `order-new.xml`:

```
<cXML payloadID="{substring-after($subOrderID,'ORD-ID-')}"
    timestamp="2001-06-01T12:00:02-08:00" xml:lang="en">
```

This gives you:

```
<cXML payloadID="2001-06-01-600001" timestamp="2001-06-01T12:00:02-
    08:00" xml:lang="en">
```

The substring-before() Function

The `substring-before()` function returns a substring also based on two arguments. The first argument is a string from which you want to derive a substring. The second argument indicates where you want the string to stop with everything before going into the substring. The following template may also be applied to `order-new.xml`:

```
<xsl:template match="Order">
<xsl:variable name="s" select="attribute::orderID"/>

<DerivedOrderPrefix><xsl:value-of select="substring-before($s,'-6')"/></
    DerivedOrderPrefix>

</xsl:template>
```

which would yield the following result:

```
<DerivedOrderPrefix>ORD-ID-2001-06-01</DerivedOrderPrefix>
```

The string-length() function

A string length returns the length of a string. It has one argument—a string whose length you want to determine. If you skip the argument, the current node—whose content is converted to a string—is assumed. Here is the stylesheet `string-length.xsl`:

```
<xsl:stylesheet version="1.0"
xmlns:xsl="http://www.w3.org/1999/XSL/Transform">
<xsl:output method="xml" encoding="utf-8" omit-xml-declaration="yes"/>

<xsl:template match="Catalog/Item">
<xsl:variable name="desc" select="Description"/>

 <xsl:for-each select="$desc">
String length for <xsl:value-of select="name()"/> of <xsl:value-of
     select="parent::Item/attribute::id"/>: <xsl:value-of
     select="string-length($desc)"/>
 </xsl:for-each>

</xsl:template>

</xsl:stylesheet>
```

When applied to `catalog.xml`, this is the expected output:

```
String length for Description of AHA-133040: 95

String length for Description of SPD-3066: 125

String length for Description of SPD-3067: 228

String length for Description of SPD-3092: 130

String length for Description of TAP-081182: 191
```

The normalize-space() Function

To understand how `normalize-space()` works, take a look at the Comments element in `order-normalize.xml`:

```
<?xml version="1.0" encoding="utf-8" ?>

<Order partner="06-853-2535">
 <Date>2001-06-01</Date>
 <Item type="ISBN">0471416207</Item>
 <Quantity>40</Quantity>
 <Comments>   And now just                what happened to
          my last order?</Comments>
```

```
<ShippingMethod class="4th">USPS</ShippingMethod>
</Order>
```

`Comments` content has a lot of extra whitespace, both leading and inter-word space. When applied to such content, which is converted to a string when processed, the `normalize-space()` function removes leading and trailing space, plus reduces a sequence of more than one whitespace character to a single space. The function takes a string argument or, if not present, assumes the converted-to-a-string current node.

To see how it works, apply `normalize.xsl` to `order-normalize.xml` and watch what happens:

```
<xsl:stylesheet version="1.0"
xmlns:xsl="http://www.w3.org/1999/XSL/Transform">
<xsl:output method="xml" encoding="utf-8" indent="yes"/>

<xsl:template match="Order">
 <xsl:copy>
 <xsl:copy-of select="Date|Item|Quantity"/>
 <Comments><xsl:value-of select="normalize-space(Comments)"/></Comments>
 <xsl:copy-of select="ShippingMethod"/>
 </xsl:copy>
</xsl:template>

</xsl:stylesheet>
```

Here's the output:

```
<?xml version="1.0" encoding="utf-8"?>
 <Order>
 <Date>2001-06-01</Date>
 <Item type="ISBN">0471416207</Item>
 <Quantity>40</Quantity>
 <Comments>And now just what happened to my last order?</Comments>
 <ShippingMethod class="4th">USPS</ShippingMethod>
 </Order>
```

You can see that the function has space-normalized the contents of `Comments`.

The translate() Function

The `translate()` function translates given characters in a string to different characters. It has three arguments, all strings. The first is the string that you want to translate, or at least a portion of it. The second argument represents characters in the first string that you want to translate into the characters of the last. It sounded confusing to me at first, too; if you look at the following example, you'll see that it isn't all that tough. Given the following element node:

```
<lowercase>xml</lowercase>
```

the following template uses an instance of translate():

```
<xsl:template match="lowercase">
<xsl:variable name="t" select="."/>
<uppercase>
 <xsl:value-of select="translate($t,'xml', 'XML')"/>
</uppercase>
</xsl:template>
```

to convert the lowercase characters *xml* to uppercase characters *XML* in the output, as shown:

```
<uppercase>XML</uppercase>
```

One thing to watch out for: If your string has more than one occurrence of a character that you want to translate, all the matching characters will be translated, sometimes creating odd results. Improvements to this function are planned for the next release of XPath.

Boolean Functions

XPath has five Boolean functions, all of which return true or false.

The boolean() Function

In the stylesheet boolean.xsl, which you saw in an earlier chapter (Chapter 7, "Variables and Parameters"), the following instance of when occurs:

```
<xsl:when test="boolean($okay)">
```

In the test attribute is the boolean() function with the parameter reference $okay as an argument. This parameter, a string, is defined as an empty string. Because it is empty, the test returns false. If the string has a length greater than zero, however, the test will return true. It would also return true if the parameter were a node-set and were non-empty, or if it were a number if the number were not zero (either positive or negative) or not NaN.

The not() Function

In the order-param-var.xsl stylesheet is the following occurrence of not() in the test attribute of when:

```
<xsl:when test="not($dayOrderCount = 0 or $monthCount = 0)">
```

If the expression or other object inside not() were true, not() returns false; if the expression or object were false, not() returns true.

The true() and false() Functions

The true() and false() functions simply return true or false, as their names indicate. They do not take an argument. The following would return true and instantiate the template in if:

```
<xsl:if test="true()">
```

But the following would return false:

```
<xsl:if test="false()">
```

You could turn templates on or off with these attribute values, but because of the way Booleans resolve, you can't pass in these functions as parameters. You can, however, turn templates on and off by editing the stylesheet and using the appropriate function.

The lang() Function

The lang() function returns true if its argument contains a language that is declared in an xml:lang attribute belonging to the current node or one of its ancestors. Let's say that you have this node in your source file:

```
<Comments xml:lang="de">Wo ist unser letzter Auftrag?</Comments>
```

If the following template were applied:

```
<xsl:template match="Comments">

<xsl:if test="lang('de')">
Auf Deutsch
</xsl:if>
...
</xsl:template>
```

the test would return true and the string *Auf Deutsch* would be written to the result tree. Sublanguages should work as well. For example, lang('en') should resolve for both xml:lang="en" or xml:lang="en-US", according to the recommendation.

Number Functions

Number functions return values of the basic type number. XPath has five number functions.

The number() Function

The `number()` function converts its argument to a number, just as `string()` converts its argument to a string. If no argument is present, then the current node is used.

The `number()` function even converts Booleans to numbers. The following instance returns 1:

```
<xsl:value-of select="number(true())"/>
```

and the next instance returns 0:

```
<xsl:value-of select="number(false())"/>
```

The node `DayCount` has the content of 1, which is converted to a number in a variable declaration.

```
<?xml version="1.0" encoding="utf-8"?>
<DayCounter>
 <DayCount>1</DayCount>
</DayCounter>
```

Here is that declaration:

```
<xsl:variable name="dayCount"
select="number(document('daycounter.xml'))"/>
...
<xsl:value-of select="$dayCount"/>
```

The recommendation counsels against converting a string from an element whose semantics do not indicate its content is a number (see Section 4.4 of XPath).

The sum() Function

The `sum()` function adds the number values of a node-set. As you see in the following variable declaration:

```
<xsl:variable name="sumit" select="sum(Counter/Count)"/>
```

```
<Sum day="{count(Count)}"><xsl:value-of select="$sumit"/></Sum>
```

the content of the `Count` children of `Counter` (`counter.xml`) are added up, producing the sum of:

```
<Sum day="7">56</Sum>
```

The string values of the content of summed nodes are first converted to numbers, and these numbers are added together to come up with a sum.

The floor() and ceiling() Functions

The `floor()` function converts a number to an integer that is the largest number that is not equal to the argument. The `ceiling()` function likewise converts a number to an integer, the smallest number that is closest to the number. Both `floor()` and `ceiling()` take numbers as arguments.

The following:

```
<xsl:value-of select="floor(4.593)"/>
<xsl:value-of select="ceiling(99.9928)"/>
```

produce the values 4 and 100, respectively.

The round() Function

The `round()` function rounds a number argument to its nearest integer value. For example, this instruction:

```
<xsl:value-of select="round(3.43)"/>
```

would return 3, and the following would return 4:

```
<xsl:value-of select="round(3.53)"/>
```

This function returns NaN for a NaN argument, positive infinity or zero for positive infinity or zero, negative infinity or zero for negative infinity or zero. If the number is less than zero but greater than or equal to -0.5, `round()` returns negative zero.

Node Tests

Part of a location path is a node test, such as `child::Order`, where `Order` is the node test and `child::` is the axis name and specifier. You are already quite familiar with node tests, perhaps without knowing the term well; however, I will offer some terminology and features worthy of explanation here. (I'd suggest you cross-reference Section 2.3 of the XPath recommendation.)

A node test describes the name and type of node in the location path. You have been using node tests all through this book, mostly by specifying a node name, with or without an axis name and specifier. These node tests are more precisely known as name tests. The name test takes three forms. I describe them here with informal names, for as far as I can determine, the XPath recommendation does not formally name them:

The select all test (*). The select all node test will, like a wildcard, select any node of the principal node type. The principal node type is determined by the context. For example, `child::*` selects all children of the current node, which excludes attribute and namespace nodes.

The prefix test (prefix:*). This node test takes the form of an NCName followed by a colon (`:`) followed by an asterisk (`*`), where the NCName (non-colonized name) is a namespace prefix. This prefix is expanded by the XSLT processor so that it is associated with a namespace, which means that the prefix must be declared somewhere in scope. The prefix node test finds any node that has the same namespace URI, no matter what the local name (or part) is. (I don't see this test used often.) For example, `order:*` selects all child nodes of the current node that are in namespace `http://www.testb2b.org/order`, which is declared with the `order:` prefix.

The name test (QName). The node test checks a node name, with or without a prefix and colon. A qualified name or QName is expanded internally so that a prefix is associated with a namespace URI. Examples include `Order` or `order:Order` or `child::Order`.

Additional Node Tests

There are a few other node tests that appear to be function calls, but they're not. They are `node()`, `text()`, `comment()`, and `processing-instruction()`.

The node() Node Test

The `node()` test returns true if it finds any of the seven types of nodes in a location path. For example, the identity transform (Section 7.5 of XSLT) uses this test to address all nodes in a document:

```
<xsl:template match="@*|node()">
  <xsl:copy>
    <xsl:apply-templates select="@*|node()"/>
  </xsl:copy>
</xsl:template>
```

The additional `@*` axis specifier is used to find all attribute nodes. Joined by the union operator `|`, these two tests find all nodes in a document.

The text(), comment(), and processing-instruction() Node Tests

The `text()` node test returns true if it encounters a text node. For example, you saw this test applied earlier in this chapter in the `cxml-order.xsl` stylesheet:

```
<Country isoCountryCode="{child::Country/child::Code}"> <xsl:value-of
select="child::Country/text()"/></Country>
```

This location path selects the text child node of Country, thus not picking up the element child node of Country (Code). Similarly to text(), the comment() node test tests to see if a node is of the comment node type, as in child::comment(), and the processing-instruction() node test checks for a PI node, as in descendant::processing-instruction().

Operators and Specifiers

You have seen operators and other specifiers used throughout this book. Table 9.4 collects all these in one place and provides a description of each one.

Table 9.4   XSLT Operators and Specifiers

OPERATOR OR SPECIFIER	DESCRIPTION
.	An abbreviated location step specifying the node itself. It is the same as self::node(). The current() function is a synonym. In an expression, you can combine . with // like this .//Date, which indicates all Date descendants of the current node.
..	An abbreviated location step specifying the parent node. It is the same as parent::node(). For example, name(..) returns the name of the parent node. Another example, ../Item, is the same as the unabbreviated form parent::node()/child::Item. This location path selects the Item child elements of the current node's parent.
:	Part of a location step that separates a namespace prefix with a local name or part, or a prefix with the select all specifier (*). For example, order:Order or order:*.
::	The axis specifier that connects axis names with node names or tests. For example, in following-sibling::Quantity, following-sibling is the axis name, :: is the axis specifier, and Quantity is the node name.
*	The select all specifier or wildcard. This specifier matches any node of the principal type, as in Order/*, which selects all element children of Order.

continues

Table 9.4   XSLT Operators and Specifiers (*Continued*)

OPERATOR OR SPECIFIER	DESCRIPTION
/	A location step separator or operator. It separates location steps, as in `Order/Date`, indicating a relative location path. It can also indicate the document root, as in `/Order`.
//	A location step separator or operator. It separates location steps where the second step in the path is a child or descendant of the first step. For example, `Order//Address` for `Address` descendants of `Order`, `//Address` for `Address` elements anywhere in the document.
|	The union operator computes the union of node-sets, as in `Date | Item | Quantity | Comments | ShippingMethod`. In an expression, this would select all these elements in union.
@	The abbreviated syntax specifier used exclusively with attributes, as in `@*` for selecting all attributes or `@id` for selecting attributes named `id`.
$	In expressions or predicates, a variable reference specifier, as in `$letter`.
+	In expressions or predicates, the addition operator adds two values, as in `$num + 3`.
-	In expressions or predicates, the subtraction operator subtracts the right operand from the left, as in `12 - 6`. Also the unary operator, indicating a negative number, as in `-42`.
*	In expressions or predicates, the multiplication operator multiplies two operands, as in `$factor * 5`. When the asterisk (*) is used for multiplication rather than select all (wildcard), it must have at least one space on either side.
div	In expressions or predicates, the division operator, as in `144 div 12`.
mod	In expressions or predicates, the mod operator, which returns the remainder from a division operation, as in `5 mod 2` returns `1`.
or	In expressions or predicates, the `or` Boolean operator returns true if either of its operands are true, as in `$dayOrderCount = 0 or $monthCount = 0`. (Not limited to two operands.)
and	In expressions or predicates, the `and` Boolean operator returns true if both of its operands are true, as in `$dayOrderCount = 0 and $monthCount = 0`. (Not limited to two operands.)
=	In expressions or predicates, the equality operator tests if two objects are equivalent, as in `$flag = 1`.
!=	In expressions or predicates, the inequality operator tests if two objects are not equivalent, as in `$flag != 2`.

Table 9.4 (*Continued*)

OPERATOR OR SPECIFIER	DESCRIPTION
<= (<=)	In expressions or predicates, the less-than or equal-to operator tests to see if the left operand is less than or equal to the right operand, as in $orders <= 34. Because expressions and predicates are always in attribute values, you must use the entity reference form to express this operator because the less-than symbol is not allowed in attribute values in XML.
< (<)	In expressions or predicates, the less-than operator tests to see if the left operand is less than the right operand, as in $orders < 27. Because expressions and predicates are always in attribute values, you must use the entity reference form to express this operator because the less-than symbol is not allowed in attribute values in XML.
>=	In expressions or predicates, the greater-than or equal-to operator tests to see if the left operand is greater than or equal to right operand, as in 72 >= $sales. You can use the greater-than symbol in an attribute value. The entity reference form is also permitted.
>	In expressions or predicates, the greater-than operator tests to see if the left operand is greater than the right operand, as in 98 > $sales. You can use the greater-than symbol in an attribute value. The entity reference form is also permitted.
()	The grouping operators (parentheses) allow you to group arithmetic operations, as in (3 + 4) * 70. The XPath recommendation does not specify whether grouped equations have higher precedence over those not grouped.
[]	The predicate or filter operators enclose expressions or filter nodes. Predicates are permitted in patterns as well as in expressions. For example, Item[2] indicates the second Item element in a node-set or Date[.='2001-06-01'] tests to see whether the current node (Date) has content that matches the string 2001-06-01.

Following is the order of precedence for logical, equality, and relational operators (highest precedence first). Expressions using these operators evaluate from left to right:

1. <= (<=), < (<), >= (>=), > (>)
2. =, !=
3. and
4. or

Extension Elements and Functions

XSLT allows you to extend the language with additional elements, attributes, and functions. You can use the extensions offered by existing XSLT processors, or you can create functionality yourself, which will have an effect only if the processing software knows what to do with such extensions.

> **NOTE** Rather than explore the wide variety of extensions available from Saxon, Xalan, or MSXSL and their implications, I will cover only how XSLT handles extensions. I suggest exploring your favorite processor's documentation (usually available locally after you download an XSLT package) for information on how to use and add extension. I believe this is an advisable approach given the variety of solutions that are possible and the likelihood that the next version of XSLT will offer an across-the-board solution.

Declaring a Namespace for Extensions

You must declare a namespace for the extensions. XSLT also relies on the `extension-element-prefixes` attribute of the `stylesheet` or `transform` element to distinguish elements that are from an extension namespace. For example, if you wanted to use the extension elements from the Saxon distribution (see http://users.iclway.co.uk/mhkay/saxon), you would add a namespace declaration and an `extension-element-prefixes` attribute to the `stylesheet` element as follows:

```
<xsl:stylesheet version="1.0"
 xmlns:xsl="http://www.w3.org/1999/XSL/Transform"
 xmlns:saxon="http://icl.com/saxon"
 extension-element-prefixes="saxon">
```

After declaring the namespace, the `saxon` prefix appears as an attribute value of `extension-element-prefixes`. XSLT will now recognize elements and attributes with the `saxon` prefix. The `extension-element-prefixes` attribute will stop the processor for outputting the extension prefix in any of its results.

Extension Elements

The section in the XSLT recommendation on extension elements (Section 14.1) says that it does not deal with top-level extension elements, but only elements within templates or instructions. Processors like Saxon, however, implement top-level elements with little apparent trouble.

How the processor supports or interprets these instructions is up to the implementation. Likewise, Saxon extension elements are not supported by other XSLT processors such as Xalan, nor are other processors obligated to support Saxon extensions. These same rules apply to any XSLT processor.

Rather than using the extension elements offered by an XSLT implementation (such as Saxon), you could even add your own extension elements by declaring a namespace and prefix, but unless you plan to write an XSLT processor to recognize them, or do some kind of pre- or post-process that will recognize your special elements, your extensions won't do you much good. Fortunately, there is a way to do this without writing an entire processor yourself.

Xalan-J (Java), for one, advances a method for adding scripts or Java classes to your stylesheets with the `script` element. For the whole story, see http://xml.apache.org/xalan-j/extensions.html. The Saxon function element also allows you to access external code within XSLT (see extensions.html#saxon:function in the downloaded doc directory). The Microsoft solution is the `msxsl:script` function, which is documented online at http://msdn.microsoft.com/library/psdk/xmlsdk/xslr4s50.htm.

In the current release—6.3 at the time of this writing—Saxon, for example, offers a dozen extension elements (see extensions.html in the doc directory under the main directory where you installed Saxon). An example that follows (see the section *Fallback and Messages* later in this chapter) uses a Saxon extension element, `saxon:assign`.

> **NOTE** There is no mention of attributes in the extension section of the XSLT recommendation (Section 14), but you can use them anyway, as you will see in `fallback.xsl`.

Extension Functions

You can also add extension functions. An XSLT processor recognizes extension functions by the presence of a declared namespace prefix. Like elements, what those functions actually do is up to the implementation. A given implementation, such as Microsoft's MSXSL, can't force its functions on Saxon, nor can Saxon force its private functions on Xalan.

In the absence of new functions from W3C and XSLT, Exslt (www.exslt.org) is working to unify extension efforts so that stylesheets are more transportable between implementations. They offer a number of downloadable modules, including math and set manipulation.

One of the most common extension functions you see is the `node-set()` function. This extension function, available from Exslt, Saxon,

MSXSL, XT, and Xalan, can convert a result tree fragment into a node-set so that you can then navigate it with XPath. The next release of XSLT will undoubtedly support this function natively, rather than depending on fragmented implementations of the same function in different name-spaces.

Here is how the `node-set()` function works. Say that you have a variable that defines a result tree fragment as follows (`node-set.xsl`):

```
<xsl:stylesheet version="1.0"
xmlns:xsl="http://www.w3.org/1999/XSL/Transform"
xmlns:msxsl="urn:schemas-microsoft-com:xslt"
extension-element-prefixes="msxsl">
<xsl:output method="xml" encoding="utf-8" indent="yes"/>
<xsl:variable name="newDate">
<Date>
 <Year>2001</Year>
 <Month>06</Month>
 <Day>01</Day>
</Date>
</xsl:variable>

<xsl:template match="/Order">

 <xsl:copy>
  <Month><xsl:value-of select="msxsl:node-
     set($newDate)/Date/Month"/></Month>
  <xsl:copy-of select="child::* "/>
 </xsl:copy>

</xsl:template>

</xsl:stylesheet>
```

You must use the MSXSL processor with this example. The MSXSL function `node-set()` evaluates the variable `newDate` as a node-set and outputs the correct value. Here is the output when this stylesheet is applied to `order.xml`:

```
<?xml version="1.0" encoding="utf-8"?>
<Order>
<Month>06</Month>
<Date>2001-06-01</Date>
<Item type="ISBN">0471416207</Item>
<Quantity>40</Quantity>
<Comments>First order this month.</Comments>
<ShippingMethod class="4th">USPS</ShippingMethod>
</Order>
```

If you write a stylesheet that uses extensions and then process the stylesheet with a processor that does not support the extension, what recourse do you have? This is where the `fallback` element comes in handy.

Fallback and Messages

As I mentioned in an earlier chapter, XSLT does not offer a mechanism for an incremented loop. Saxon attempts to remedy this situation with its extension elements, `saxon:while` and `saxon:assign`, and the attribute `saxon:assignable`. The following stylesheet (`fallback.xsl`) uses these extensions:

```
<xsl:stylesheet version="1.0"
 xmlns:xsl="http://www.w3.org/1999/XSL/Transform"
 xmlns:saxon="http://icl.com/saxon"
 extension-element-prefixes="saxon">
<xsl:output method="xml" encoding="utf-8"/>
<xsl:output omit-xml-declaration="yes" indent="yes"/>
<xsl:variable name="i" select="40" saxon:assignable="yes"/>
<xsl:attribute-set name="order.atts">
 <xsl:attribute name="partner">06-835-2535</xsl:attribute>
</xsl:attribute-set>

<xsl:template match="Order">
 <saxon:while test="$i &lt; 44">
  <xsl:copy use-attribute-sets="order.atts">
   <xsl:copy-of select="Date|Item"/>
   <Quantity><xsl:value-of select="$i"/></Quantity>
   <xsl:copy-of select="Comments|ShippingMethod"/>
  </xsl:copy>
  <saxon:assign name="i" select="$i+1"/>
  <xsl:fallback>
   <xsl:message terminate="yes">
    Stylesheet failed; must use Saxon XSLT processor.
   </xsl:message>
  </xsl:fallback>
 </saxon:while>
</xsl:template>

</xsl:stylesheet>
```

Here is the output you can expect if you process the stylesheet with Saxon:

```
<Order partner="06-835-2535">
 <Date>2001-06-01</Date>
```

```
<Item type="ISBN">0471416207</Item>
<Quantity>40</Quantity>
<Comments>None.</Comments>
<ShippingMethod class="4th">USPS</ShippingMethod>
</Order>
<Order partner="06-835-2535">
<Date>2001-06-01</Date>
<Item type="ISBN">0471416207</Item>
<Quantity>41</Quantity>
<Comments>None.</Comments>
<ShippingMethod class="4th">USPS</ShippingMethod>
</Order>
<Order partner="06-835-2535">
<Date>2001-06-01</Date>
<Item type="ISBN">0471416207</Item>
<Quantity>42</Quantity>
<Comments>None.</Comments>
<ShippingMethod class="4th">USPS</ShippingMethod>
</Order>
<Order partner="06-835-2535">
<Date>2001-06-01</Date>
<Item type="ISBN">0471416207</Item>
<Quantity>43</Quantity>
<Comments>None.</Comments>
<ShippingMethod class="4th">USPS</ShippingMethod>
</Order>
```

Saxon, of course, has no problem recognizing these extensions. But because Xalan's TestXSLT processor does not recognize these extensions, it falls back on the template in the `fallback` element and writes a message to standard output with the `message` element. The `terminate="yes"` attribute/value pair terminates the transformation explicitly. Here is the message it writes, the bold text is from the content of `message` in `fall-back.xsl`:

```
XSLException Type is : ElemMessageTerminateException
Message is :
    Stylesheet failed; must use Saxon XSLT processor.
```

Checking the Availability of Extensions

The `element-available()` and `function-available()` functions can test to see if an element or function is available to a processor. The `available.xsl` stylesheet shows you how:

```
<xsl:stylesheet version="1.0"
xmlns:xsl="http://www.w3.org/1999/XSL/Transform"
```

```
xmlns:saxon="http://icl.com/saxon"
xmlns:msxsl="urn:schemas-microsoft-com:xslt"
extension-element-prefixes="saxon msxsl">
<xsl:output method="text" encoding="utf-8"/>
<xsl:param name="een" select="'no-op'"/>
<xsl:param name="efn" select="'no-op'"/>

<xsl:template match="/">
<xsl:choose>
 <xsl:when test="element-available($een)">
  The element <xsl:value-of select="$een"/> exists!
 </xsl:when>
 <xsl:when test="function-available($efn)">
  The function <xsl:value-of select="$efn"/> exists!
 </xsl:when>
 <xsl:otherwise>
  The element or function is not available.
 </xsl:otherwise>
</xsl:choose>

</xsl:template>

</xsl:stylesheet>
```

Let's say that you wanted to find out if the `node-set()` function from Microsoft is available. You could apply this stylesheet:

```
msxsl order.xml available.xsl efn=msxsl:node-set
```

and get this output in response:

```
The function msxsl:node-set exists!
```

If you tried to check the availability of this function on Saxon, you are going to get a disappointment:

```
saxon order.xml available.xsl efn=msxsl:node-set
```

This command produces the following:

```
The element or function is not available.
```

Aliasing Namespace Prefixes

If you would like to create an XSLT stylesheet as a result tree from a transformation, you have a bit of a problem. The problem lies in the namespace declaration and prefix. If you want to output elements with the `xsl` prefix, an XSLT processor will have a tough time sorting out which element is an XSLT instruction and which is a literal result element that needs to be written to the result tree.

XSLT manages this problem with its top-level element `namespace-alias`. This element allows you to specify a temporary namespace and prefix in the stylesheet that will change to another namespace and prefix in the result tree.

The following example is called `namespace-alias.xsl`:

```
<xsl:stylesheet version="1.0"
xmlns:xsl="http://www.w3.org/1999/XSL/Transform"
xmlns:temp="http://www.testb2b.org/temp">
<xsl:output method="xml" encoding="utf-8" indent="yes"/>
<xsl:namespace-alias stylesheet-prefix="temp" result-prefix="xsl"/>

<xsl:template match="/">
<temp:transform version="1.0">
 <xsl:apply-templates/>
</temp:transform>
</xsl:template>

<xsl:template match="Order">
<temp:template match="{name(.)}">
 <NewOrder partner="{@partner}">
  <temp:apply-templates/>
 </NewOrder>
</temp:template>
 <xsl:apply-templates/>
</xsl:template>

<xsl:template match="Date">
<temp:template match="{name(.)}">
 <NewDate><temp:value-of select="."/></NewDate>
</temp:template>
</xsl:template>

<xsl:template match="Item">
<temp:template match="{name(.)}">
 <NewItem type="{@type}"><temp:value-of select="."/></NewItem>
</temp:template>
</xsl:template>

<xsl:template match="Quantity">
<temp:template match="{name(.)}">
 <NewQuantity><temp:value-of select="."/></NewQuantity>
</temp:template>
</xsl:template>

<xsl:template match="Comments">
```

```
<temp:template match="{name(.)}">
 <NewComments><temp:value-of select="."/></NewComments>
</temp:template>
</xsl:template>

<xsl:template match="ShippingMethod">
<temp:template match="{name(.)}">
 <NewShippingMethod class="{@class}"><temp:value-of
select="."/></NewShippingMethod>
</temp:template>
</xsl:template>


</xsl:stylesheet>
```

You can apply this stylesheet and redirect the result to a file, like this:

```
msxsl -o nsa.xsl order.xml namespace-alias.xsl
```

which will then give you this output—a new stylesheet:

```
<?xml version="1.0" encoding="utf-8"?>
<xsl:transform version="1.0"
xmlns:xsl="http://www.w3.org/1999/XSL/Transform">
<xsl:template match="Order">
<NewOrder partner="06-853-2535">
<xsl:apply-templates />
</NewOrder>
</xsl:template>
<xsl:template match="Date">
<NewDate><xsl:value-of select="." /></NewDate>
</xsl:template>
<xsl:template match="Item">
<NewItem type="ISBN"><xsl:value-of select="." /></NewItem>
</xsl:template>
 <xsl:template match="Quantity">
<NewQuantity><xsl:value-of select="." /></NewQuantity>
</xsl:template>
 <xsl:template match="Comments">
<NewComments><xsl:value-of select="." /></NewComments>
</xsl:template>
 <xsl:template match="ShippingMethod">
<NewShippingMethod class="4th"><xsl:value-of select="." />
     </NewShippingMethod>
</xsl:template>
</xsl:transform>
```

Now you can apply this new stylesheet to the original document for a different result. For good measure, let's use a different processor, like XT:

```
xt order.xml nsa.xsl
```

This command will yield:

```
<?xml version="1.0" encoding="utf-8"?>
<NewOrder partner="06-853-2535">
 <NewDate>2001-06-01</NewDate>
 <NewItem type="ISBN">0471416207</NewItem>
 <NewQuantity>40</NewQuantity>
 <NewComments>None.</NewComments>
 <NewShippingMethod class="4th">USPS</NewShippingMethod>
</NewOrder>
```

Forwards Compatibility

XSLT supports forwards-compatible processing, which makes provision for future developments in XSLT. The behavior is triggered by a `version` attribute from the XSLT namespace whose number is not equal to 1.0. Certain rules of behavior are prescribed should a higher number appear, either in the `stylesheet` or `transform` element or in a literal result element, even behavior in expressions.

Basically, a compliant XSLT processor must not signal an error if it encounters such elements, along with their attributes and even expressions. It must ignore such elements if they appear at the top level, and if these elements are instantiated in a template, the processor must perform some sort of fallback (see the previous section, *Fallback and Messages*). If these non-1.0 elements have attributes, the attributes are ignored. Expressions must be offered a wide berth if they appear in attributes that fall into this category. (See Section 2.5 of the XSLT recommendation if you want more details.)

Java XSLT Processors

Up until now, when I've processed stylesheets in examples, I've done it with processors that have command-line executable interfaces. MSXSL (`msxsl.exe`) and TestXSLT (`testXSLT.exe`) are both written in C++, and XT and Saxon are written in Java. XT and Saxon both have Windows executable versions available that are also built as console applications (`xt.exe` and `saxon.exe`).

Those of you who are Java programmers, and perhaps others, may prefer to use a straight Java interface. I will demonstrate how to do this with Saxon 6.3 (the latest version, no doubt slightly behind the times by the time this book is in your hands). These examples assume that the Java interpreter is in the execution path (with the path environment variable) and that the Java classes can be found in the classpath. If you don't understand what path and classpath mean, just hang tough for a minute and I'll explain them.

Using the Saxon Full Java Version

You can download the latest version of the full Saxon Java package from http://users.iclway.co.uk/mhkay/saxon. (The Instant Saxon version is the command-line executable version—saxon.exe. You want the version labeled *Full Saxon* for this example.) After you extract the archive, provided that all files are in their expected locations, you can enter the following at the command line:

```
java -cp saxon.jar com.icl.saxon.StyleSheet order-new.xml order-fo.xsl
```

This command uses the archived Java classes in saxon.jar so that it can execute the class com.icl.saxon.Stylesheet with the source file order-new.xml and the stylesheet order-fo.xsl.

The classpath lets the Java interpreter know where the class files are. The class files (compiled Java) are what the interpreter executes. The -cp option or switch means that saxon.jar should be in the classpath. To set the classpath on Windows, your command line could look something like the following:

```
set classpath .;c:\saxon-6.3
```

where the single period (.) represents the current directory and the directory following the semi-colon (;) is the path for the saxon.jar file.

In a Unix environment, you might type in this:

```
setenv CLASSPATH .:/usr/local
```

You can find out more about setting the classpath in the Windows environment at http://java.sun.com/j2se/1.3/docs/tooldocs/win32/classpath .html or, in a Unix environment, at http://java.sun.com/products/jdk/ 1.2/docs/tooldocs/solaris/classpath.html.

When the Java interpreter is in the path, it means that the path environment variable has been set. In Windows, you can set this in a variety of ways. One way is to set the path variable in the autoexec.bat file like this:

```
set path c:\jdk1.3\bin;%path%
```

This line places the directory c:\jdk1.3\bin, where java.exe lives, in the path and appends the current path environment after it.

On a Unix machine, this command might look as follows in a C shell script (such as in `.cshrc`):

```
set path=(/usr/local/jdk1.2.2/bin $path)
```

You can read more about the path environment variable on Windows at http://java.sun.com/j2se/1.3/install-windows.html#Environment or on Unix at http://java.sun.com/products/jdk/1.2/install-solaris.html# Environment.

If you enter the command without arguments:

```
java -cp saxon.jar com.icl.saxon.StyleSheet
```

you will get the following options list:

```
SAXON 6.3 from Michael Kay
Usage:  java com.icl.saxon.StyleSheet [options] source-doc style-doc
{param=value}..
Options:
  -a              Use xml-stylesheet PI, not style-doc argument
  -ds             Use standard tree data structure
  -dt             Use tinytree data structure (default)
  -o filename     Send output to named file or directory
  -m classname    Use specified Emitter class for xsl:message output
  -r classname    Use specified URIResolver class
  -t              Display version and timing information
  -T              Set standard TraceListener
  -TL classname   Set a specific TraceListener
  -u              Names are URLs not filenames
  -w0             Recover silently from recoverable errors
  -w1             Report recoverable errors and continue (default)
  -w2             Treat recoverable errors as fatal
  -x classname    Use specified SAX parser for source file
  -y classname    Use specified SAX parser for stylesheet

  -?              Display this message
```

You can read more about how to use Saxon from the instructions in using-xsl.html under the doc directory from the Saxon download.

On to Part Two

This concludes Part One of this book, which covered transforming XML documents with XSLT. The next few chapters in Part Two will provide you with a hands-on overview of formatting XML documents with XSLFO.

PART

Two

Formatting XML Documents

Part Two explains how to format XML documents using W3C's Extensible Stylesheet Language formatting objects or XSLFO. Chapter 10, "A Simple Formatted Document," lays out the necessary steps for creating a minimal XSLFO document, setting up page masters, defining formatting objects such as blocks for headings and paragraphs, basic formatting properties, and then generating Portable Data Format (PDF) output, among other formats, with Apache's FOP engine. Chapter 11, "XSLFO Tables, Lists, and More," shows you how to create tables and lists and provides summaries of formatting objects and properties, the area model, expressions, and functions. Finally, Chapter 12, "XSL Technology Review," recaps XSL's features and terminology with a brisk review of the language.

A Simple Formatted Document

In this chapter, a tour of XSL formatting objects and properties, or XSLFO, begins. Originally, XSLT and XSLFO were together in one W3C working document. Work on XSLT progressed reasonably well and was split into its own domain, but the remaining part, XSLFO, as it is called informally, seemed to get left behind.

The first working draft of XSL appeared in August of 1998 (www.w3 .org/tr/1998/wd-xsl-19980818), about six months after XML was approved as a recommendation. The first XSL draft was about 140 pages long and had two editors, James Clark and Stephen Deach. In April 1999, the single XSL draft broke into two parts with Clark as the editor of XSLT (just over 80 pages) and Deach as the editor of XSL or what is now commonly called XSLFO (about 260 pages). When XSLT finally became a recommendation in November of 1999 (www.w3.org/tr/xslt), it topped out at less than 100 pages. The XSLFO document, a candidate recommendation since November 2000, is now over 400 pages long and has 10 authors and contributors, Stephen Deach still among them.

If you haven't already picked this up from our conversation, XSLFO is ponderous. It takes nearly a ream of paper to print it out single-sided. To some, a mere glance at the draft strikes fear into the heart because it is, indeed, nothing less than daunting.

But don't get worried. I'm not going to cover the whole enchilada here in this book. I am going to cover the essential stuff, the things that will get you producing attractive, formatted output worthy of the nearest 1200-dpi laser printer. I'm going to review the best parts of XSLFO, in my estimation, and leave the rest until the recommendation reaches final approval.

Revisiting an Earlier XSLFO Example

Back in Chapter 8, "Multiple Documents," I showed you an XSLFO example that was broken into several documents in order to demonstrate how to include multiple stylesheet documents. That example is repeated here, but the templates have been combined into a single stylesheet called format-fo.xsl (it is somewhat long, but you'll be hard pressed to find an XSLFO document that isn't):

```
<xsl:stylesheet version="1.0"
xmlns:xsl="http://www.w3.org/1999/XSL/Transform"
xmlns:fo="http://www.w3.org/1999/XSL/Format">
<xsl:output method="xml" encoding="utf-8" indent="yes"/>

<xsl:template match="/">
<fo:root>
 <fo:layout-master-set>
  <fo:simple-page-master master-name="Order-US"
    page-height="11in" page-width="8.5in" margin-top="1in"
    margin-bottom="1in" margin-left="1in" margin-right="1in">
   <fo:region-body margin-top=".5in"/>
   <fo:region-before extent="1.5in"/>
   <fo:region-after extent="1.5in"/>
  </fo:simple-page-master>
 </fo:layout-master-set>
 <fo:page-sequence master-name="Order-US">
  <fo:flow flow-name="xsl-region-body">
   <xsl:apply-templates select="Order"/>
  </fo:flow>
 </fo:page-sequence>
</fo:root>
</xsl:template>

<xsl:template match="Order">
<fo:block font-size="20pt" font-family="sans-serif"
 line-height="26pt" space-after.optimum="4pt"
 text-align="center">Order <xsl:value-of select="@orderID"/></fo:block>

<fo:block font-size="16pt" font-family="sans-serif"
 line-height="20pt" space-after.optimum="4pt"
 text-align="center">Order Number <xsl:value-of
```

```
select="SalesYear/DayOrderCount"/></fo:block>

<fo:block font-size="16pt" font-family="sans-serif"
 line-height="20pt" space-after.optimum="4pt"
 text-align="center"><xsl:value-of select="Date"/></fo:block>

<fo:block font-size="12pt" font-family="sans-serif"
line-height="16pt" space-after.optimum="4pt" text-align="start" padding-
     before=".5in">ISBN: <xsl:value-of select="Item"/></fo:block>

<fo:block font-size="12pt" font-family="sans-serif"
 line-height="16pt" space-after.optimum="4pt"
 text-align="start">Quantity: <xsl:value-of
     select="Quantity"/></fo:block>

<fo:block font-size="12pt" font-family="sans-serif"
 line-height="16pt" space-after.optimum="4pt"
 text-align="start">Ship by: <xsl:value-of select="ShippingMethod"/>
     (<xsl:value-of select="ShippingMethod/@class"/> class)</fo:block>
 <xsl:apply-templates select="Partner"/>
</xsl:template>

<xsl:template match="Partner">
<fo:block font-size="12pt" font-family="sans-serif"
 line-height="16pt" space-after.optimum="4pt"
 text-align="start">DUNS: <xsl:value-of select="DUNS"/></fo:block>
 <xsl:apply-templates select="Location"/>
</xsl:template>

<xsl:template match="Location/Address">
<fo:block font-size="12pt" font-family="sans-serif"
 line-height="16pt" space-after.optimum="4pt"
 text-align="start" padding-before="6pt"><xsl:value-of
     select="Company"/></fo:block>

<fo:block font-size="12pt" font-family="sans-serif"
 line-height="16pt" space-after.optimum="4pt"
 text-align="start"><xsl:value-of select="Mailing"/></fo:block>

<fo:block font-size="12pt" font-family="sans-serif"
 line-height="16pt" space-after.optimum="4pt"
 text-align="start"><xsl:value-of select="City"/>, <xsl:value-of
     select="State"/><xsl:text> </xsl:text><xsl:value-of
     select="ZIPCode"/></fo:block>

<fo:block font-size="12pt" font-family="sans-serif"
 line-height="16pt" space-after.optimum="4pt"
 text-align="start"><xsl:value-of select="Country/text()"/></fo:block>
</xsl:template>

</xsl:stylesheet>
```

This stylesheet, when applied to `order-new.xml`, produces the document `order-new.fo`:

```xml
<?xml version="1.0" encoding="utf-8"?>

<fo:root xmlns:fo="http://www.w3.org/1999/XSL/Format">
 <fo:layout-master-set>
  <fo:simple-page-master master-name="Order-US"
    page- height="11in" page-width="8.5in" margin-top="1in"
    margin-bottom="1in" margin-left="1in" margin-right="1in">
   <fo:region-body margin-top=".5in" />
   <fo:region-before extent="1.5in" />
   <fo:region-after extent="1.5in" />
  </fo:simple-page-master>
 </fo:layout-master-set>
 <fo:page-sequence master-name="Order-US">
  <fo:flow flow-name="xsl-region-body">

   <fo:block font-size="20pt" font-family="sans-serif" line-
     height="26pt" space-after.optimum="4pt" text-align="center">Order
     ORD-ID-2001-06-01-600001</fo:block>

<fo:block font-size="16pt" font-family="sans-serif" line-height="20pt"
    space-after.optimum="4pt" text-align="center">Order Number
    1</fo:block>

<fo:block font-size="16pt" font-family="sans-serif" line-height="20pt"
    space-after.optimum="4pt" text-align="center">2001-06-01</fo:block>

<fo:block font-size="12pt" font-family="sans-serif" line-height="16pt"
    space-after.optimum="4pt" text-align="start" padding-
    before=".5in">ISBN: 0471416207</fo:block>

<fo:block font-size="12pt" font-family="sans-serif" line-height="16pt"
    space-after.optimum="4pt" text-align="start">Quantity:
    40</fo:block>

<fo:block font-size="12pt" font-family="sans-serif" line-height="16pt"
    space-after.optimum="4pt" text-align="start">Ship by: USPS (4th
    class)</fo:block>

<fo:block font-size="12pt" font-family="sans-serif" line-height="16pt"
    space-after.optimum="4pt" text-align="start">DUNS: 06-853-
    2535</fo:block>

<fo:block font-size="12pt" font-family="sans-serif" line-height="16pt"
    space-after.optimum="4pt" text-align="start" padding-
    before="6pt">Wy'east Communications</fo:block>

<fo:block font-size="12pt" font-family="sans-serif" line-height="16pt"
```

```
        space-after.optimum="4pt" text-align="start">P.O. Box
        537</fo:block>

 <fo:block font-size="12pt" font-family="sans-serif" line-height="16pt"
        space-after.optimum="4pt" text-align="start">West Linn, Oregon
        97068-0537</fo:block>

 <fo:block font-size="12pt" font-family="sans-serif" line-height="16pt"
        space-after.optimum="4pt" text-align="start">United
        States</fo:block>

   </fo:flow>
  </fo:page-sequence>
 </fo:root>
```

This document can now be processed further to produce a final document such as one formatted in Portable Document Format (PDF) or with Java Abstract Window Toolkit (AWT) classes. AWT classes are part of Java Foundation Classes (JFC), which is Sun's standard API for creating graphical user interfaces (GUIs). You can anticipate mainstream Web browser support—by mainstream I mean Microsoft and Netscape browsers—in the future, but it isn't there yet. One tool that you can use right now for this final processing is Apache Foundation's FOP—not an overdressed, sniffling courtier, but a free, open source Java package for exercising XSLFO's formatting objects and properties developed by James Tauber (www.jtauber.com).

Getting Started with FOP

There is a small but growing list of XSLFO processors (see the heading about XSLFO processors at www.w3.org/Style/XSL/#software), but when time and space are limited, you have to be selective. For the purposes of this book, I think the best bet is FOP.

You can read more about the package at http://xml.apache.org/fop/index.html and download the latest TAR or ZIP archive from http://xml.apache.org/dist/fop/ (currently 0.18.1). You will also need the latest version of Java from Sun (1.3.0_02 at the time of this writing), available at http://java.sun.com/products/?frontpage-main. After you have downloaded it and extracted the files from the archive, you, of course, have to set your path and classpath environment variables (for information on setting these variables, see the section titled *Using the Saxon Full Java Version* in Chapter 9, "More XSLT").

When these variables are in order, you should be ready to run FOP from the command line.

> **NOTE** The versions of Java and FOP that I am using are the latest versions available at the time of writing. It is likely that before this book hits the shelves, those versions will increment upward and things may not work exactly as described here. This is part of the adventure, but it can get a little frustrating at times. If you wind up using more recent versions of Java or FOP than are described in this chapter, you may have to review the product documentation to get it to work properly. Feel free to submit any problems as errata on the book's companion Web site at www.wiley.com/compbooks/fitzgerald.

The FOP command line looks similar to those you may have used with XSLT processors. For example, to convert `order-new.fo` to `order-new.pdf`, you could use the following:

```
java -cp fop.jar;\lib\w3c.jar;\lib\xalan-2.0.0.jar;\lib\xerces-
1.2.3.jar;\lib\jimi-1.0.jar org.apache.fop.apps.Fop order-new.fo order-
new.pdf
```

This command assumes that the path variable includes the location of the Java executable (such as c:\jdk1.3\bin or /usr/local/bin) and that the classpath is set so that it can find the proper Java class archives, such as `fop.jar` or, in a subdirectory, `w3c.jar` (for example, in c:\fop\ and c:\fop\lib or in /usr/local/fop and /usr/local/fop/lib). You can see that this command gives you access to the Xalan XSLT transform engine (`xalan-2.0.0.jar`) and the Xerces XML parser (`xerces-1.2.3.jar`).

The `w3c.jar` archive contains classes for rendering with W3C's Scalable Vector Graphics or SVG (www.w3.org/Graphics/SVG/Overview.htm8) and W3C's Synchronized Multimedia Integration Language or SMIL (see http://www.w3.org/AudioVideo/). The JIMI class library from Sun—originally from Activated Intelligence—helps manage graphical images (see http://java.sun.com/products/jimi/).

> **NOTE** If you have other questions about FOP, you can find the FOP FAQ at www.owal.co.uk:8090/asf/servlet/asf/screen/MainMenu/action/SetAll/screen/DisplayTopics/faq_id/276/.

When all is working correctly, the FOP processor will report how well it is getting along by writing a few messages to standard output, like the following:

```
FOP 0.18.1-DEV
using SAX parser org.apache.xerces.parsers.SAXParser
building formatting object tree
setting up fonts
```

```
formatting FOs into areas
 [1]
rendering areas to PDF
writing out PDF
```

Figure 10.1 shows `order-new.pdf` displayed in Adobe Acrobat Reader.

Using fop.bat or fop.sh

The FOP project also provides the `fop.bat` batch file (for Windows) and the `fop.sh` shell script (for Unix) to reduce typing and make running FOP a little easier. This is the batch file:

```
java -cp fop.jar;lib\w3c.jar;xalan-2.0.0.jar;lib\xerces-
1.2.3.jar;lib\jimi-1.0.jar org.apache.fop.apps.Fop %1 %2 %3 %4 %5 %6 %7 %8
```

The batch file uses variables to handle command-line options, sources, and other input. Here is `fop.sh`:

```
#!/bin/sh
java -cp fop.jar:lib/w3c.jar:lib/xalan-2.0.0.jar:lib/xerces-
    1.2.3.jar:lib/jimi-1.0.jar org.apache.fop.apps.Fop "$@"
```

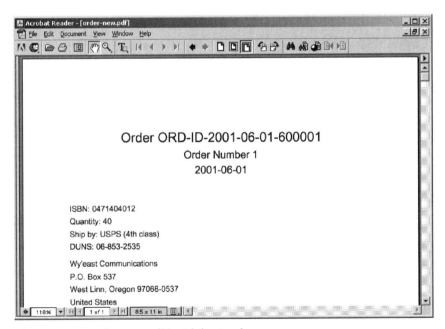

Figure 10.1 order-new.pdf in Adobe Acrobat.

The Unix shell script needs only a single variable ($@) to handle other input. I will be using this batch/script syntax from now on. The following will work on either Windows or Unix:

```
fop order-new.fo order-new.pdf
```

This command produces the same results as those shown earlier in Figure 10.1.

Processing Files with Java AWT

The following directive produces similar results but uses the Java AWT for output (see Figure 10.2):

```
fop order-new.fo -awt
```

You can zoom in or out on the document image and even print it from the File menu. To close the AWT window, you can choose Exit from the File menu.

Processing Files as MIF Files

If you use Adobe FrameMaker, you will be happy to know that FOP has an option for writing output to Maker Interchange Format (MIF) files, the

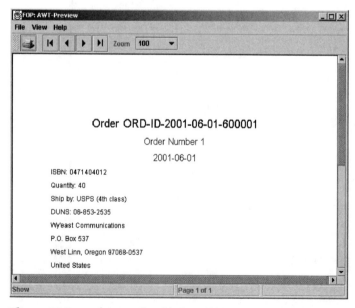

Figure 10.2 order-new.fo with Java AWT.

native text version for FrameMaker files. To output an MIF version of `order-new.fo`, use this command:

```
fop order-new.fo -mif order-new.mif
```

Figure 10.3 shows this MIF file after it has been opened by FrameMaker. As you can see, it has lost some of its formatting in the process, but now you can edit and format the file with FrameMaker and save it as a FrameMaker file (`order-new.fm`) or even in the Microsoft Word or Corel WordPerfect formats.

Transforming and Formatting Files at the Same Time

Another way you can process files with FOP is by transforming them with XSLT at the same time that you format them with FOP. If you enter the following on the command line:

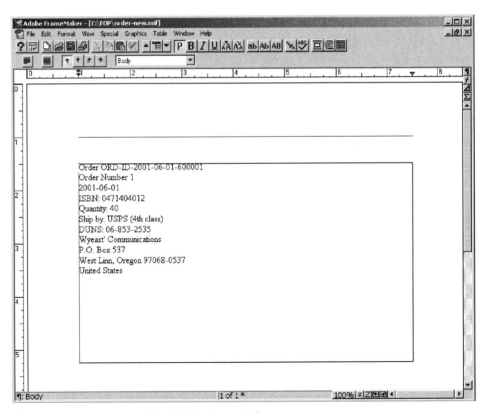

Figure 10.3   order-new.fo in Adobe FrameMaker.

```
fop -xml order-new.xml -xsl format-fo.xsl -pdf order-new.pdf
```

the XSLT transformation takes place first. The result tree from the transformation is not saved in an intermediate file like `order-new.fo`; it is passed on for XSLFO processing and then saved as a PDF file. Just as for PDF output, you can also use this syntax to produce AWT or MIF files:

```
fop -xml order-new.xml -xsl format-fo.xsl -awt
```

```
fop -xml order-new.xml -xsl format-fo.xsl -mif order-new.mif
```

The XSLFO Basics

Now it's time to take a close look at the fundamental parts of an XSLFO document. I am going to focus on the essentials of what it takes to get XSLFO working for you, but I am not going to get overwrought about the details. I'll refer you to a section number in parentheses in the XSLFO specification—such as (6.4.2)—where you can track down all of the details, but for the most part, I'll be hitting just the basics.

As you already have a pretty solid background with transforming documents (if you've read Part One), I won't spend time dealing with the transformation of XSLFO files (as in `format-fo.xsl`): I'll deal first with formatting objects and then with formatting properties.

Namespace and Root

The namespace URI for XSLFO is `http://www.w3.org/1999/XSL/Format`, which is similar to its companion, `http://www.w3.org/1999/XSL/Transform`. The conventional namespace prefix is `fo`. You are not forced to use this prefix, but this is what people use commonly, and it is what I'll use.

The root element for this formatting namespace or dialect is `root`. This must be the first or top element for any XSLFO document and the place where the namespace is declared, as shown here:

```
<fo:root xmlns:fo="http://www.w3.org/1999/XSL/Format">
...
</fo:root>
```

The first child of `root` must be a `layout-master-set` formatting element (6.4.6). This element may be followed by zero or one `declarations` element (6.4.3), then one or more `page-sequence` elements (6.4.5).

NOTE Support for the `declarations` element is not yet implemented in FOP. As specified, this element can have one or more `color-profile` children (6.4.4), which declare an International Color Consortium (ICC) Color Profile for the stylesheet. Support for `color-profile` is also not implemented yet in FOP.

The building blocks of `layout-master-set` and `page-sequence` each have `master-name` properties (7.24.8), both containing the name `Order-US`. This name identifies an order document for partners trading in the United States. This name is not chiseled in stone. You can certainly choose another name if you wish.

What we normally call elements in XML are transformed into formatting objects in XSLFO. Likewise, attributes in XML are considered formatting properties, and as the document processing progresses, these properties are refined into document formatting traits. By the end of the chapter, you will understand why and how this happens. To keep things simple, for the purposes of discussion, I will generally refer to elements as objects and attributes as properties from now until the end of the next chapter of the book.

Page Masters

The `layout-master-set` object must contain one or more of either a `simple-page-master` object (6.4.12) or a `page-sequence-master` object (6.4.7). I'll use only `simple-page-master` in the examples that follow. The `page-master-sequence` object is, as you can guess, more complicated than `simple-page-master` and is more suitable to longer documents that contain a variety of page formats.

A `page-master-sequence` can have one or more `single-page-master-reference` (6.4.8), `repeatable-page-master-reference` (6.4.9), or `repeatable-page-master-alternatives` (6.4.10) as children. If you find that the `simple-page-master` object limits what you can do with your document, you can step up to the `page-master-sequence` model later.

A `simple-page-master` must have a `master-name` property. The value of this property will match the value in the `master-name` property of `page-sequence`, a mandatory sibling of `simple-page-master`.

Defining the Geometry of a Page

The `simple-page-master` in essence defines a page based on regions. It must have at least one `region-body` child object (6.4.13). This defines the middle part of the page where the body text usually goes. This and other regions are part of XSLFO's area model. You will learn more about the area model in Chapter 11, "XSLFO Tables, Lists, and More."

There are four other regions that you can define:

- The `region-before` object (6.4.14) defines a region that corresponds to the top margin of a page, where a header may go.

- The `region-after` object (6.4.15) defines a corresponding bottom margin or footer region.

- The `region-start` object (6.4.16) deals with what is normally the left margin (that is, in left-right, top-bottom writing systems).

- The `region-end` object (6.4.17) deals with the right margin region.

Figure 10.4 shows you where these basic regions lie on the page.

The `region-body` object is required; the other four are optional. All region elements are empty. The `region-body` object has a default `region-name` (7.24.16), that is, `xsl-region-body`. This region name must match the value of `flow-name` (7.24.5) in `flow` (6.4.18). The `flow` object is the required child of `page-sequence`. A flow channels a stream of text, so to speak, cascading from page to page.

A `page-sequence` may also have an optional `title` object (6.4.20), which has a similar role as title in HTML. (The `title` object is currently not implemented in FOP.) A `page-sequence` may also contain a `static-content` object (6.4.19), which is used for producing repeated content such as running headers and footers.

Now you know enough about XSLFO to be dangerous. If you process the following XSLFO document (`minimal.fo`) with FOP, it will work, but it will give you only a blank, 8.5- × 11-inch page:

```
<fo:root xmlns:fo="http://www.w3.org/1999/XSL/Format">
 <fo:layout-master-set>
  <fo:simple-page-master master-name="Order-US">
   <fo:region-body region-name="xsl-region-body"/>
  </fo:simple-page-master>
 </fo:layout-master-set>
 <fo:page-sequence master-name="Order-US">
  <fo:flow flow-name="xsl-region-body">
   <fo:block/>
  </fo:flow>
 </fo:page-sequence>
</fo:root>
```

With a minimal document in place, you build it up to produce something more elaborate and attractive.

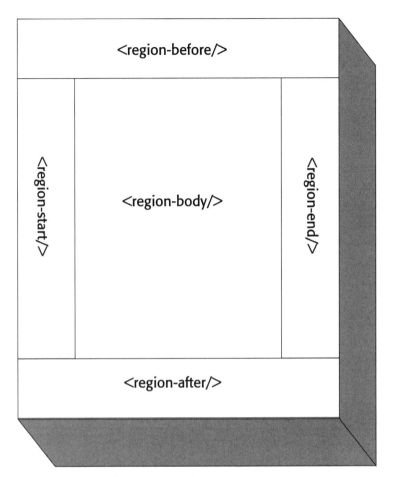

Figure 10.4 The basic regions of a page.

Defining the Page

The simple-page-master object may have several properties in addition to master-name. For example, you can define a page's width and height with page-width (7.24.14) and page-height (7.24.12). These objects are automatically set to the size of the user agent window, such as an Acrobat or AWT window. That failing, the setting falls back to 8.26 inches × 11 inches, which fits into both 8.5 × 11 and A4 page sizes.

The simple-page-master object also lets you use common margin properties (7.9), such as margin-top (7.9.1), margin-bottom (7.9.2), margin-left (7.9.3), margin-right (7.9.4), space-before (7.9.5), space-after (7.9.6), start-indent (7.9.7), and end-indent (7.9.8).

If you are familiar with W3C's Cascading Style Sheets (CSS), the properties margin-top, margin-bottom, margin-left, and margin-right will also be familiar to you. Where possible, XSLFO has attempted to adopt the names of CSS/2 properties, which is probably a good, if not essential, approach. XSLFO, which is more elaborate, expands on the CSS/2 list. It will be interesting to see if CSS/3 adopts all the XSLFO properties!

You can rotate the region area 90, 180, and 270 degrees (or in reverse, -90, -180, -270) with reference-orientation (7.19.3). You can also set the writing direction of text content with writing-mode (7.26.7). The initial or default writing mode is left-right/top-bottom (lr-tb), the common writing direction for English and other European languages, but this is not suitable to all languages. Modes such as right-left/top-bottom (rl-tb) and top-bottom/right-left (tb-rl) are also available.

Here is an example of simple-page-master with a few additional properties:

```
<fo:simple-page-master master-name="Order-US" page-width="8.5in" page-
height="11in" margin-top=".5in" margin-bottom=".5in" margin-left=".5in"
margin-right=".5in">
```

The region-body Object

Like simple-page-master, you can apply all the seven common margin properties (7.9). You can also use 38 border, padding, and background properties (7.6). Border properties include border-left-color (7.6.25) and border-left-style (7.6.26), which allow you to set the color and style of the left border. The padding-top object (7.6.35) adds padding to the top of the region, and padding-bottom (7.6.36) adds padding to the bottom. The background properties include background-color (7.6.2), which allows you to set a background color for the region, and background-image (7.6.3), which allows you to use an image in the background.

Columns are possible within region-body. The properties column-count (7.24.2) and column-gap (7.24.3) allow you to set the number of columns and the gap between columns, respectively. Only region-body can have columns—they are not permitted in other regions.

The display-align property (7.12.4) affects the alignment of child areas such as an external-graphic (6.6.5). The clip property (7.19.1) works together with the overflow property (7.19.2) to determine (basically) if element content that flows outside the box is visible. Finally, you can use `reference-orientation` and `write-mode` for `region-body` just as you can for `simple-page-master`.

The Other Page Regions

In `minimal.fo`, only the `region-body` object is defined. You can also explicitly define other regions. Similarly to `region-body`, `region-before`, `region-after`, `region-start`, and `region-end` can all have region names and can use border, padding, and background properties, as well as `clip`, `overflow`, `display-align`, `reference-orientation`, and `writing-mode`. In addition, these regions can have a `precedence` property (7.24.15) that allows them to have precedence over simple page masters for the regions of the page they cover.

Other than `region-body`, the region objects can have an `extent` property that determines the height or width of the region, either as a percentage of the height or width in relation to the page or as a measurement given in inches (`in`), centimeters (`cm`), millimeters (`mm`), points (`pt`), picas (`pc`), pixels (`px`), or a size relative to the current size (`em`).

This fragment defines all the possible regions in `simple-page-master`, all with their default region names and extents.

```
<fo:region-before region-name="xsl-region-before" extent="1in"/>
<fo:region-after region-name="xsl-region-after" extent="1in"/>
<fo:region-start region-name="xsl-region-start" extent="1in"/>
<fo:region-end region-name="xsl-region-end" extent="1in"/>
```

Inserting Static Content

The following `static-content` formatting object, which goes inside a `page-sequence`, places a centered page number at the bottom of the page:

```
<fo:static-content flow-name="xsl-region-after">
 <fo:block space-before=".75in" text-align="center">
 <fo:page-number/></fo:block>
</fo:static-content>
```

The `block` in the `static-content` object will be repeated on each page of the resulting document in the `region-after` area (bottom of the page), which is identified in the `flow-name`. Three-quarters of an inch of space will go above the `page-number` (6.6.10), as specified by `space-before` (7.9.5), and the page number will be centered with `text-align` (7.14.9).

Block Formatting Objects

The `minimal.fo` document contains one empty block formatting object, which acted as a dummy placeholder just to get the formatter to work. Blocks are used for formatting for paragraphs, headings, captions, and so forth. They represent distinct blocks of text in a text flow. You can add all sorts of properties to blocks to control the appearance of text and other things that they contain. The `block` formatting object (6.5.2) can have a very large variety of properties, only a few of which I'll demonstrate.

Blocks really represent a class of objects. Beyond the `block` object, there are block containers, tables, and lists as well. The `block-container` object (6.5.3) holds blocks that usually use a different writing mode. I won't be using a different writing mode than lr-tb in my examples, so I won't show you how to use `block-container`, which is a good thing because it isn't implemented by FOP yet.

Other block objects include `table` (6.7.3), `table-and-caption` (6.7.2)—which is not implemented currently by FOP—and `list-block` (6.8.2). I will show you how to use tables and lists in Chapter 11, "XSLFO Tables, Lists, and More."

I'll start demonstrating the properties of `block` by formatting a heading. Some of this will look familiar to you if you recall Chapter 8. Following is a fragment showing the heading of an order document.

```
<fo:block font-family="sans-serif" font-size="24pt"
font-weight="bold" text-align="center" space-after="10pt" background-
color="lightgray">Order ORD-ID-2001-06-01-60001</fo:block>
```

This `block` object uses three font properties (7.7), which all resemble CSS/2 properties of the same names. The `font-family` property (7.7.2) specifies a generic font family. The `sans-serif` keyword just identifies a sans-serif font without being particular about what is supplied by the system. Other generic fonts include `serif`, `cursive`, `fantasy`, and `mono-space`. You can also, as with CSS/2, submit a prioritized series of font family names, as in `font-family="Tahoma, Verdana, Helvetica, Arial, Geneva,"` which instructs the formatter to select the first font family in the list that it finds on the system. Whitespaces are optional. (FOP does not support this too well at the moment.)

The `font-size` property (7.7.4) lets you choose a font size for the text child of `block`. Using a size such as 24 points (`24pt`) is fine-grained. Other options are available, such as relative sizes `smaller` or `larger`, absolute sizes such as `small`, `medium`, and `large`, and percentages (`90%`) based on the parent element's font size. The `font-weight` property (7.7.9) indicates the font weight as in `normal` (default), `bold`, `bolder`, `lighter`, or `100` through `900`. Other font properties (not shown) are `font-selection-strategy` (7.7.3), `font-stretch` (7.7.5), `font-size-adjust` (7.7.6) for bicameral scripts, `font-style` (7.7.7), and `font-variant` (7.7.8).

The `text-align` property centers the heading, and `space-after` (7.9.6) adds 10 points of space after the heading. You could specify this value as `space-after.optimum="10pt"` or `space-after.minimum="10pt"` as well. The `background-color` property gives the block a light gray backdrop.

Following the main heading, we can add a few more blocks for subheadings. These subheadings identify the order number and the date of the order:

```
<fo:block font-family="sans-serif" font-size="16pt"
font-weight="bold" text-align="center" space-after="6pt">
Order Number 1 (600001)</fo:block>

<fo:block font-family="sans-serif" font-size="16pt"
font-weight="bold" text-align="center" space-after="18pt">
2001-06-01</fo:block>
```

The font size for both blocks has been reduced by six points and the space after has been both reduced and increased. The background color has been dropped.

The Inline Formatting Object

The `inline` formatting object (6.6.7) allows you to format inline text within blocks. For example, the following four blocks each contain an `inline` object that applies bold and the color blue to some text:

```
<fo:block font-size="14pt" font-family="sans-serif"
line-height="18pt" text-align="start" padding-before=".5in">
<fo:inline color="blue" font-weight="bold">ISBN:</fo:inline> 0471416207
    </fo:block>
<fo:block font-size="14pt" font-family="sans-serif"
line-height="18pt" text-align="start"><fo:inline color="blue" font-
    weight="bold">Quantity:</fo:inline> 40</fo:block>
<fo:block font-size="14pt" font-family="sans-serif"
line-height="18pt" text-align="start"><fo:inline color="blue" font-
```

```
      weight="bold">Ship by:</fo:inline> USPS (4th class)</fo:block>
<fo:block font-size="14pt" font-family="sans-serif"
line-height="18pt" text-align="start"><fo:inline color="blue" font-
      weight="bold">DUNS:</fo:inline> 06-853-2535</fo:block>
```

A few other possible properties for `inline` are border, background, padding, margin, and font properties, plus `text-decoration` (7.15.4), such as `underline`, `overline`, `line-through`, and `blink`, and `visibility` (7.27.8), as in `visible` (default), `hidden`, and `collapse`.

The blocks also add the `line-height` property (7.14.4). This property sets the height of the line and should be a reasonable value in relation to the font size. Other possible values include `normal` (default) and `120%`. The `text-align` property is set to `start`, which is equivalent to left in lr-tb writing mode. Using `start` is good because it indicates that XSLFO is not mired in Western European writing systems.

Enhancing the Appearance of the Order

The next blocks format the shipping address nicely, using properties that you have already seen:

```
<fo:block space-before="26pt" space-after="4pt"
font-weight="bold" color="blue" font-size="14pt">Shipping
      Address</fo:block>
<fo:block font-size="12pt" font-family="sans-serif"
line-height="16pt" space-after.optimum="4pt"
text-align="start">Wy'east Communications</fo:block>
<fo:block font-size="12pt" font-family="sans-serif"
line-height="16pt" space-after.optimum="4pt"
text-align="start">P.O. Box 537</fo:block>
<fo:block font-size="12pt" font-family="sans-serif"
line-height="16pt" space-after.optimum="4pt"
text-align="start">West Linn, Oregon 97068-0537</fo:block>
<fo:block font-size="12pt" font-family="sans-serif"
line-height="16pt" space-after.optimum="4pt"
text-align="start">United States</fo:block>
```

As you have moved through this chapter, you have watched the document `minimal.fo` become `order-enhanced.fo`. The full listing for this formatted document follows:

```
<fo:root xmlns:fo="http://www.w3.org/1999/XSL/Format">
 <fo:layout-master-set>
  <fo:simple-page-master master-name="Order-US"
page-width="8.5in" page-height="11in" margin-top=".5in"
margin-bottom=".5in" margin-left=".5in" margin-right=".5in">
    <fo:region-body region-name="xsl-region-body"/>
```

```
    <fo:region-before region-name="xsl-region-before" extent="1in"/>
    <fo:region-after region-name="xsl-region-after" extent="1in"/>
    <fo:region-start region-name="xsl-region-start" extent="1in"/>
    <fo:region-end region-name="xsl-region-end" extent="1in"/>
   </fo:simple-page-master>
  </fo:layout-master-set>
  <fo:page-sequence master-name="Order-US">
   <fo:static-content flow-name="xsl-region-after">
    <fo:block space-before=".75in" text-align="center">
     <fo:page-number/></fo:block>
   </fo:static-content>
   <fo:flow flow-name="xsl-region-body">
    <fo:block font-family="sans-serif" font-size="24pt"
font-weight="bold" text-align="center" space-after="10pt" background-
     color="lightgray">Order ORD-ID-2001-06-01-60001</fo:block>
    <fo:block font-family="sans-serif" font-size="16pt"
font-weight="bold" text-align="center" space-after="6pt">Order Number 1
     (600001)</fo:block>
    <fo:block font-family="sans-serif" font-size="16pt"
font-weight="bold" text-align="center" space-after="18pt">2001-06-
     01</fo:block>
    <fo:block font-size="14pt" font-family="sans-serif"
line-height="18pt" text-align="start" padding-before=".5in"><fo:inline
     color="blue" font-weight="bold">ISBN:</fo:inline> 0471416207
     </fo:block>
    <fo:block font-size="14pt" font-family="sans-serif"
 line-height="18pt" text-align="start"><fo:inline color="blue" font-
     weight="bold">Quantity:</fo:inline> 40</fo:block>
    <fo:block font-size="14pt" font-family="sans-serif"
 line-height="18pt" text-align="start"><fo:inline color="blue" font-
     weight="bold">Ship by:</fo:inline> USPS (4th class)</fo:block>
    <fo:block font-size="14pt" font-family="sans-serif"
 line-height="18pt" text-align="start"><fo:inline color="blue" font-
weight="bold">DUNS:</fo:inline> 06-853-2535</fo:block>
    <fo:block space-before="26pt" space-after="4pt"
font-weight="bold" color="blue" font-size="14pt">Shipping
     Address</fo:block>
    <fo:block font-size="12pt" font-family="sans-serif"
line-height="16pt" space-after.optimum="4pt" text-align="start">Wy'east
     Communications</fo:block>
    <fo:block font-size="12pt" font-family="sans-serif"
line-height="16pt" space-after.optimum="4pt" text-align="start">P.O. Box
     537</fo:block>
    <fo:block font-size="12pt" font-family="sans-serif"
line-height="16pt" space-after.optimum="4pt" text-align="start">West
     Linn, Oregon 97068-0537</fo:block>
    <fo:block font-size="12pt" font-family="sans-serif"
line-height="16pt" space-after.optimum="4pt" text-align="start">United
     States</fo:block>
   </fo:flow>
  </fo:page-sequence>
 </fo:root>
```

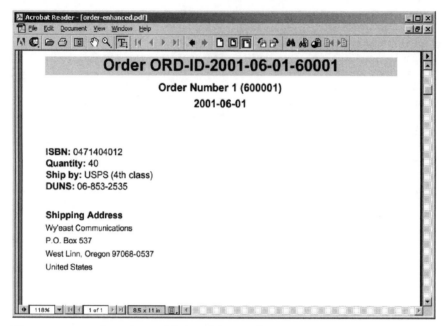

Figure 10.5 order-enhanced.fo in Adobe Acrobat.

Using FOP, you could convert this formatting object document into a PDF document, as shown in Figure 10.5.

XSLFO Tables and Lists

This chapter has covered a number of the XSLFO basics, at least enough for you to build your own documents. You have seen how to build one from a minimal document to one containing a variety of formatting objects. In the next chapter, I'll discuss how to use tables and lists in XSLFO.

CHAPTER 11

XSLFO Tables, Lists, and More

In Chapter 10, "A Simple Formatted Document," you learned about some basic formatting objects and properties for creating documents formatted with XSLFO. This chapter will explain how to create tables and lists. It will also broaden Part Two's coverage of objects, properties, and the area model.

If you are familiar with HTML tables, you are likely to come up to speed on XSLFO tables in a hurry. I'll illustrate XSLFO tables by first comparing them with HTML tables; I hope this will help most readers. Let's get started.

Formatting Tables

I hope most of you have seen HTML 4.01 tables. If so, it will make the leap over the chasm to XSLFO tables a bit shorter. Following is an HTML table giving the quantity of orders in the first seven days of June 2001 (`2001-06-counter-table.html`). Figure 11.1 shows what this table looks like rendered by Netscape Navigator 6:

```
<table align="center" width="250" style="font-family:sans-serif">
<thead style="font-size:16pt" align="center">
```

```
<td colspan="2">Orders for June 2001</td>
</thead>
<tfoot>
<td colspan="2"><b>Note:</b> So far, this represents only the first
    seven days of the month.</td>
</tfoot>
<tbody align="center">
<tr><th>Day</th><th>Quantity<th></tr>
<tr><td>1</td><td>7</td></tr>
<tr bgcolor="d3d3d3"><td>2</td><td>0</td></tr>
<tr><td>3</td><td>0</td></tr>
<tr bgcolor="d3d3d3"><td>4</td><td>11</td></tr>
<tr><td>5</td><td>9</td></tr>
<tr bgcolor="d3d3d3"><td>6</td><td>21</td></tr>
<tr><td>7</td><td>8</td></tr>
</tbody>
</table>
```

If the markup in this example isn't very familiar to you, don't worry: I'll explain what's going on.

The `table` element is the containing element for structured tables in HTML. The `table` element has a number of attributes, but I mention only three here: `align`, `width`, and `style`. The `align` attribute with a value of `center` centers the table on the user agent canvas (the Netscape window in the case of Figure 11.1). The `width` attribute value sets the table width to 250 pixels. The `style` attribute uses CSS-like syntax to set the font to a generic (first available) family, `sans-serif`.

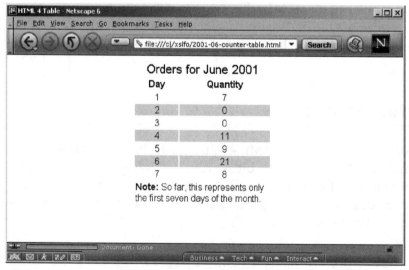

Figure 11.1 HTML 4 table in Netscape Navigator 6.

The next element, thead, sets a heading for the entire table. The style attribute enlarges the font size to 16 points, and align centers the heading above the table. The td element holds table cell data. The colspan attribute with a value of 2 spans the heading across two columns.

The tfoot element defines a footer for the table, a bit of relative information that goes just below the table. This information also spans across two columns (colspan). The word *Note* is made bold with the inline b element.

The tbody element (table body) holds all the table row and cell information in a single container, allowing it to be formatted as a unit, such as centering it with align. Immediately following that is a table row (tr) holding two table header (th) cells, one for Day and another for Quantity. Following that are seven more table rows, each one holding two cells (td elements). The first one displays the day of the month; the second, the number of orders received on that day. Alternating table rows have a light gray background color (bgcolor). The color is represented by a hexadecimal RGB (red/green/blue) triple. As d3 in hexadecimal is equivalent to 211 in decimal, d3d3d3 is equivalent to an RGB value of 211,211,211.

XSLFO Table Formatting Objects

With the foundation of that HTML table under us, I'll translate that table into an XSLFO table. It'll take more markup, but with more markup, you also get the potential for more accuracy and power.

Following is a portion of order-table.fo that defines a table similar to the previous HTML table. This table is displayed in Figure 11.2, which shows the table rendered in AWT:

```
<fo:block space-before="26pt" space-after="4pt" font-weight="bold"
    color="blue" font-size="14pt">Orders for June 2001</fo:block>

<fo:table width="2.5in">
 <fo:table-column column-number="1" column-width="1in"/>
 <fo:table-column column-number="2" column-width="1in"/>
 <fo:table-footer>
  <fo:table-row>
  <fo:table-cell column-number="1">
  <fo:block font-size="9pt"><fo:inline font-weight="bold">Note:
</fo:inline> So far, this represents only the first seven days of the
    month.</fo:block>
   </fo:table-cell>
   <fo:table-cell column-number="2"/>
  </fo:table-row>
 </fo:table-footer>
 <fo:table-header>
```

```
<fo:table-row>
<fo:table-cell column-number="1"><fo:block font-weight="bold" text-
    align="center">Day</fo:block></fo:table-cell>
<fo:table-cell column-number="2"><fo:block font-weight="bold" text-
    align="center">Quantity</fo:block></fo:table-cell>
</fo:table-row>
</fo:table-header>
<fo:table-body>
<fo:table-row><fo:table-cell column-number="1"><fo:block text-
    align="center">1</fo:block></fo:table-cell>
<fo:table-cell column-number="2"><fo:block text-
    align="center">7</fo:block></fo:table-cell></fo:table-row>
</fo:table-body>
<fo:table-body background-color="#d3d3d3">
<fo:table-row><fo:table-cell column-number="1"><fo:block text-
    align="center">2</fo:block></fo:table-cell>
<fo:table-cell column-number="2"><fo:block text-
    align="center">0</fo:block></fo:table-cell></fo:table-row>
</fo:table-body>
<fo:table-body>
<fo:table-row><fo:table-cell column-number="1"><fo:block text-
    align="center">3</fo:block></fo:table-cell>
<fo:table-cell column-number="2"><fo:block text-
    align="center">0</fo:block></fo:table-cell></fo:table-row>
</fo:table-body>
<fo:table-body background-color="#d3d3d3">
<fo:table-row><fo:table-cell column-number="1"><fo:block text-
    align="center">4</fo:block></fo:table-cell>
<fo:table-cell column-number="2"><fo:block text-
    align="center">11</fo:block></fo:table-cell></fo:table-row>
</fo:table-body>
<fo:table-body>
<fo:table-row><fo:table-cell column-number="1"><fo:block text-
    align="center">5</fo:block></fo:table-cell>
<fo:table-cell column-number="2"><fo:block text-
    align="center">9</fo:block></fo:table-cell></fo:table-row>
</fo:table-body>
<fo:table-body background-color="#d3d3d3">
<fo:table-row><fo:table-cell column-number="1"><fo:block text-
align="center">6</fo:block></fo:table-cell>
<fo:table-cell column-number="2"><fo:block text-
    align="center">21</fo:block></fo:table-cell></fo:table-row>
</fo:table-body>
<fo:table-body>
<fo:table-row><fo:table-cell column-number="1"><fo:block text-
    align="center">7</fo:block></fo:table-cell>
<fo:table-cell column-number="2"><fo:block text-
    align="center">7</fo:block></fo:table-cell></fo:table-row>
</fo:table-body>
</fo:table>
```

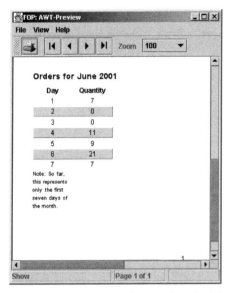

Figure 11.2 XSLFO table rendered with AWT.

Because all the formatting objects for tables are not implemented in FOP yet—and probably won't be until after XSLFO reaches W3C recommendation status—there are some limitations to what you can do with XSLFO tables right now. I believe that these limitations and obstacles will be removed in due time, so there is no reason not to learn the proposed features of tables in XSLFO as well as what works today.

The `table` formatting object in XSLFO (6.7.3) corresponds to the `table` element in HTML. Many formatting properties may be applied to tables (those in 7.25 among others), but only a minority of them are implemented in FOP. Among those put into service are the border, background, and padding properties (7.6), margin properties (7.9), `width` (7.13.12), `height` (7.13.4), `break-after` (7.18.1), `break-before` (7.18.2), `table-omit-header-at-break` (7.25.18), and `table-omit-footer-at-break` (7.25.17). In the example, the `table` object has a `width` property with a value of 2.5 inches (`2.5in`). Beside those mentioned, no other properties are implemented. Properties that could center the table easily, as `align="center"` does in XHTML, are not yet available.

The current FOP version forces you to explicitly state column widths, so there is an artificial dependency now because the `table` object permits you to define tables without using `table-column`. Among other properties, you can give a column a number identifier with `column-number` (7.25.8) and a width with `column-width` (7.25.9). You can hide columns with `visibility` (7.27.8) and apply background properties and border properties, under certain conditions. The `number-columns-repeated` property (7.25.12) will, once implemented, allow you to repeat column definitions; `number-columns-spanned` (7.25.13) specifies the number of columns spanned by the `table-cell` property that accesses properties from a `table-column` object by using the `from-table-column()` function.

The `table-footer` object, like `tfoot` in HTML, defines a footer for the table, and the `table-header` object, like `thead` in HTML, defines a header. The footer in the XSLFO table spans only a single column in the example, but probably when all span-related properties are implemented, you will be able to improve the appearance of the footer by making columns span properly. Border, padding, background, and relative position (7.11) properties apply. The header in XSLFO affects columns or cells, not the overall table as does `thead` in HTML. The objects `table-and-caption` (6.7.2) and `table-caption` (6.7.5) used together distinguish a table with caption information, but both are not yet supported in FOP.

As specified, a `table-body` object (6.7.8) can contain either one or more `table-row` objects (6.7.9) or one or more `table-cell` objects (6.7.10). As now implemented by FOP, you have `table-row` objects (`tr` in HTML) containing `table-cell` objects (`td` in HTML), which contain `block` objects, as you can see in the example.

I admit, the syntax is a little up-in-the-air as it stands. As the XSLFO candidate draft progresses toward recommendation status, I fully expect these discontinuities to smooth out.

Formatting Lists

To help explain how lists work in XSLFO, I'll turn back to HTML again. Here is a short list from `2001-q2-list.html`. Figure 11.3 shows how the following list looks when rendered in a Microsoft Internet Explorer browser:

```
<h4>Summary for Second Quarter 2001</h4>
<p>Following is a summary of the second quarter's order activity:</p>

<ul>
<li style="padding-top:4pt">April 2001 order total: 221</li>
<li style="padding-top:4pt">May 2001 order total: 281</li>
<li style="padding-top:4pt">June 2001 order total (first 7 days only) :
55</li>
<li style="padding-top:4pt">Second Quarter 2001 order total: 557</li>
</ul>
```

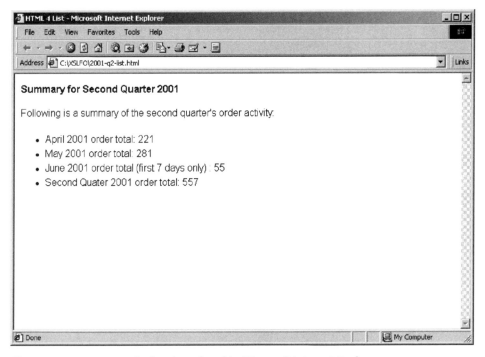

Figure 11.3 2001-q2-list.html rendered in Microsoft Internet Explorer.

Though not shown, the `body` element has a `style` attribute that sets the CSS `font-family` property to `sans-serif`. The `h4` (heading level 4) element and a `p` (paragraph) element introduce the list. The `ul` element encloses an unordered list block, which, by default, is presented as a bulleted list. Each `li` (list item) element adds a little padding above it for readability and contains text for the list. When rendered, such items are automatically preceded by bullets.

As you know, HTML does not cleanly separate content from presentation. CSS helps give developers more independent control over presentation, but browsers give you a lot of presentation properties by means of default, internal stylesheets. CSS properties such as `list-style-type`, `list-style-image`, `list-style-position`, and `list-style` (www.w3.org/tr/css2/generate.html#lists) can give you more control over the presentation of lists if you choose to use them.

Compare how lists are generated in XSLFO. Here is part of `order-table-list.fo`, which formats a list (near the end of the document). Again, it takes more markup than HTML, but ultimately it can give you more power and flexibility. Figure 11.4 shows how this list looks as a PDF displayed in Adobe Acrobat:

```
<fo:block break-before="page" space-before="12pt" space-after="12pt"
    font-weight="bold" color="blue" font-size="14pt">Summary for Second
    Quarter 2001</fo:block>
<fo:block font-size="12pt">Following is a summary of the second
    quarter's order activity:</fo:block>

<fo:list-block space-before="10pt">
 <fo:list-item start-indent=".5in">
  <fo:list-item-label start-indent=".25in" space-before="4pt">
   <fo:block>&#x2022;</fo:block>
  </fo:list-item-label>
  <fo:list-item-body>
   <fo:block>April 2001 order total: 221</fo:block>
  </fo:list-item-body>
 </fo:list-item>
 <fo:list-item start-indent=".5in" space-before="4pt">
  <fo:list-item-label start-indent=".25in">
   <fo:block>&#x2022;</fo:block>
  </fo:list-item-label>
  <fo:list-item-body>
   <fo:block>May 2001 order total: 281</fo:block>
  </fo:list-item-body>
 </fo:list-item>
 <fo:list-item start-indent=".5in" space-before="4pt">
  <fo:list-item-label start-indent=".25in">
   <fo:block>&#x2022;</fo:block>
  </fo:list-item-label>
  <fo:list-item-body>
   <fo:block>June 2001 order total (first 7 days only): 55</fo:block>
  </fo:list-item-body>
 </fo:list-item>
 <fo:list-item start-indent=".5in" space-before="4pt">
  <fo:list-item-label start-indent=".25in">
   <fo:block>&#x2022;</fo:block>
  </fo:list-item-label>
  <fo:list-item-body>
   <fo:block>Second Quarter 2001 order total: 557</fo:block>
  </fo:list-item-body>
 </fo:list-item>
 </fo:list-block>
```

This is what's going on in the markup. Before the list, two `block` objects provide a heading and a paragraph that introduce the list. The first block has a `break-before` property (7.18.2) that, in effect, introduces a hard page break just before the block, placing the list on the second page of the document.

The `list-block` object (6.8.2) is the overall container for a list in XSLFO. It is analogous to HTML elements `ul` (unordered or bulleted list) or `ol` (ordered or numbered list). A `list-block` contains one or more

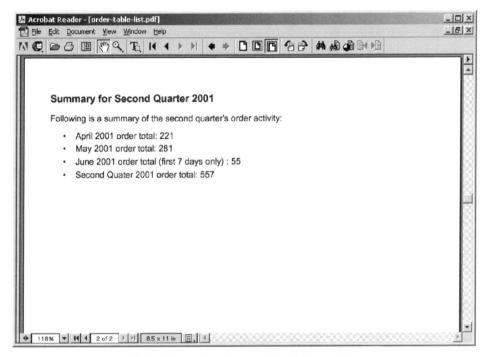

Figure 11.4   order-table-list.fo rendered as PDF in Adobe Acrobat.

list-item objects (6.8.3). A list-item, in turn, contains a single instance of list-item-label (6.8.5), followed by a single instance of list-item-body (6.8.4), in that order. Both list-item-label and list-item-body contain blocks.

Notice how the list-item starts its indentation deeper (.5in) than the list-item-label (.25in). This places the label a quarter of an inch before the list text. The label is defined by a Unicode character reference to a bullet character (•). You can use any legal XML character as a label, such as 1, a, i, or with references to more exotic characters. When processing XSLFO with XSLT, you can use the number element to insert a formatted number as a label (see 6.8.1.1.1 for an example).

Beside the common border, padding, margin, and background properties, list-block and list-item objects can have placement properties such as break-after (7.18.1) and break-before (7.18.2), plus keep-together (7.18.3), keep-with-next (7.18.4), and keep-with-previous (7.18.5). Of these, list-item-label and list-item-body support only keep-together.

NOTE To generate lists that resemble HTML dl (definition list) lists, see section 6.8.1.1.2 of the XML draft specification.

Other Formatting Objects

XSLFO also has a variety of other formatting objects that I will touch only lightly because current support is lacking, the object is obscure, or it's just plain impractical to cover them in depth at this point in the development of the language.

You have already seen inline formatting objects (6.6) `inline` and `page-number`. Another inline object includes `bidi-override` (6.6.2), which allows a string to be written in a different direction, such as text from a language written in a direction other that the default direction. The object `character` (6.6.3) lets you present a glyph character as an atomic unit. The `external-graphic` object (6.6.5) displays graphics from outside the document, and the `initial-property-set` (6.6.4) object specifies special formatting for the first line of a block. It is similar to the CSS `first-line` pseudo-element (see www.w3.org/tr/css2/selector.html#first-line- pseudo).

A handful of dynamic-effect objects allow you to add a native, single-directional links with `basic-link` (6.9.2) or expand and collapse table of contests with `multi-switch` (6.9.3) and `multi-case` (6.9.4). Other interactive objects, `multi-toggle` (6.9.5) and `multi-properties` (6.9.6), contain one or more `multi-property-sets` (6.9.7), and a `wrapper` object (6.11.2) carries properties so that they can be inherited by other objects.

The three out-of-line (as opposed to inline) objects are `float` (6.10.2), `footnote` (6.10.3), and `footnote-body` (6.10.4). The `float` object allows you to add non-obtrusive areas to a page. Such areas may contain text or what have you. The object `footnote` lets you cite footnotes from body text and generate the actual footnote; `footnote-body` holds the footnote content.

The objects `marker` (6.11.3) and `retrieve-marker` (6.11.4) are used to produce running feet and headers. Marker properties (7.22) help you have finer control over these.

Additional Formatting Properties

I'll give you a quick tour of the formatting properties that I have not discussed up to this point, but that will be available in a full-blown XSLFO processor. There are approximately 250 properties, and many of them may apply to many formatting objects. The effect is one of overwhelming complexity or power, depending on how you look at it. Personally, I don't get uptight about complexity: I just use what I need to use and leave the rest of it alone. You don't have to use everything in the language to make it work, just what's important to you and your project.

The source-document (7.3.1) property provides a pointer to a URI of an XML document used to create the current tree. Such a reference follows the Dublin Core definition of a *source* (http://purl.org/dc/documents/rec-dces-19990702.htm.). It may be useful to renderers such as aural readers if the structure of the current tree is not appropriate for the renderer. The role (7.3.2) property can be a simple string indicating semantics or a URI to a Resource Description Framework (RDF) document that helps decipher the role of the object.

Absolute position properties (7.4), that is, absolute-position, top, right, bottom, and left, can place a box containing block and other formatting information in an absolution position in regard to its underlying area (see the next section, *The Area Model*). Aural properties (7.5) may be used to style audio content. These include volume (7.5.18), speech-rate (7.5.15), and play-during (7.5.9). Hyphenation properties (7.8) help control word hyphenation characteristics, which may have roots in country (7.8.1) or language (7.8.2). In addition to common margin properties, several inline margin properties are available, namely, space-end (7.10.1) and space-start (7.10.2).

Area alignment (7.12) and dimension (7.13) properties help control area sizes and the relative placement of other objects within areas. Of these you have already seen width (7.13.12) and height (7.13.4). Earlier you saw some properties related to blocks and lines (7.14), such as text-align (7.14.9) and line-height (7.14.4). Two others are text-indent (7.14.11) and white-space-collapse (7.14.12).

Character properties (7.15) control things like letter-spacing (7.15.2), word-spacing (7.15.8), and text-shadow (7.15.6). You can set a color with the color property (7.16.1), call up a color profile with color-profile-name (7.16.2), and indicate a CMYK rendering-intent (7.16.3). Set a box's float characteristics with float (7.12.2) and clear (7.17.1). Keep and break properties (7.18) include break-before (7.18.2) and keep-with-next (7.18.4), plus orphans (7.18.6) and widows (7.18.7).

Layout properties (7.19) like clip (7.19.1) and overflow (7.19.2) determine what is or isn't visible under given circumstances. With leader properties (7.20), you can control leaders such as those used between a title and a page number in a table of contents. Dynamic effects properties (7.21) set states that direct how these effects behave. For example, active-state (7.21.1) can control the appearance of links with values such as visited, active, and hover.

Four properties are available to help with number-to-string conversion (7.23). Pagination and layout properties (7.24) handle such characteristics as page-height (7.24.12) and page-width (7.24.14), and they even can force the desired number of pages with force-page-count (7.24.6).

Because writing systems may go in any possible direction and may have a wide variety of characters, writing-mode properties (7.26) are available to set things like text-altitude (7.26.4) and direction (7.26.1). In Section 7.27, a variety of general or miscellaneous properties are offered. Among them are id (7.27.2), which applies to all formatting objects and allows you to associate an ID with any formatting object as an aid to finding and processing objects. Others include content-type (7.27.1) for setting a content or MIME type for an external object (in the form content-type="content-type:xml/svg") and src (7.27.7) for specifying the URI of an external graphic.

Finally, you can use shorthand properties to combine several of one kind of property into a single specification. For example, the font property allows you to specify font-style, font-variant, font-weight, font-size, line-height, and font-family, at one time, in one fell swoop. Other shorthand properties include background (7.28.1), border (7.28.3), and margin (7.28.14).

That wraps up our brief fly-by over formatting properties. The next section will help you get a grip on the area model.

The Area Model

This chapter and the last hint at the area model used by XSLFO. In a nutshell, the area model is an abstract way of looking at how a formatter lays out, in a precise, geometric manner, what a page is and where things like text blocks will go on it. Section 4 of the XSLFO draft recommendation (www.w3.org/tr/xsl) gives a complete, if not verbose, explanation of the area model that I will try to pare down to a few essentials. If you will be building an XSLFO processor/formatter, you can't really avoid reading Section 4; if you are just throwing text and graphics on a page, you can learn a lot by trial. I hope that this brief review of the area model will reduce your trial period.

CSS, which came before XSLFO, has a box model that is similar to XSLFO's area model. Because XSLFO extended its reach with added control over spacing in blocks, lines, and regions, among other things, it also had to extend the CSS box model. When XSLFO formats its input and sends the result to a destination output, such as PDF, it is output to areas. Before areas are generated, the XSLFO processor/formatter refines its properties into traits. These traits are output to areas. Traits have the same relationship to areas as formatting properties have to formatting objects and as attributes have to XML elements.

An area is made up of subareas or rectangles, each with its own place and purpose. Figure 11.5 shows and labels these rectangles.

The allocation rectangle is the entire, allocated area, which may include a whole page or just part of it, such as block or inline areas. An innermost

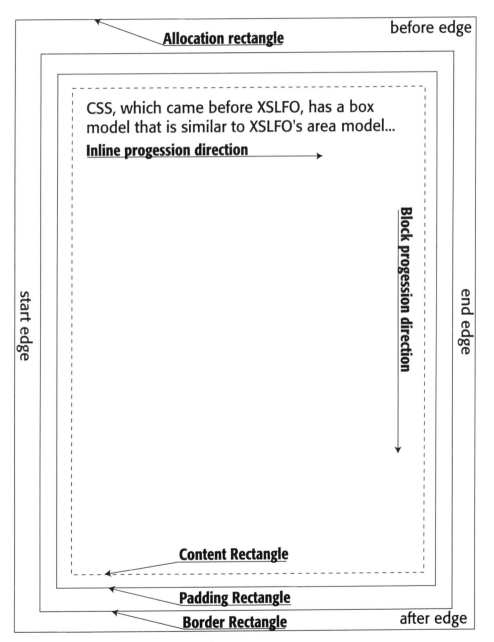

Figure 11.5   The general area model.

content rectangle holds content, such as text. Content such as text has both inline and block progression directions, which are related to writing mode properties (7.26). Text content in the English language, for example, moves from left to right (inline direction) and from top to bottom (block direction).

Optionally, a content rectangle may be surrounded by padding and border rectangles. In some instances (not shown), a border rectangle can extend to an allocation rectangle. The extent of these rectangles may be controlled by padding and border properties (7.6).

Rectangles have start-end and before-after edges. The start and end edges correspond with the inline progression direction, and the before and after edges correspond to the block progression direction. Because text or characters of various languages may go in different directions, XSLFO makes it possible for any side of a rectangle to represent any edge.

Areas also have viewports. One way to think of a viewport is as a clear pane of glass set in the center of an opaque frame. If you lay it on a surface, the pane of glass may reveal the entire surface or just a portion of it, depending on the size of the surface or the pane. A viewport may reveal an entire area or just a desired portion of that area. Viewports may be scrolled (see layout properties in 7.19).

When areas are rendered, they are usually stacked and have a stacking relation of some sort with other areas. This means that one rectangle may have a hierarchical relation to another—parent-child, for example. For an in-depth review of these relations, see 4.2.5.

XSLFO Expressions and Functions

Like XSLT, XSLFO equips you with the power of expressions and functions (5.9). Any property values can be calculated as expressions, just as with the `select` attribute in XSLT. These expressions can contain numerics, operators (such as +, -, *, `div`, and `mod`), and even keywords (such as `inherit`). The following example adds 12 points to a variable to arrive at a font size:

```
<fo:block font-size="$fs + 12pt"/>
```

Here is an example of a function call that assigns an RGB color value to `color` property:

```
<fo:block font-family="Helvetica" color="rgb(211,211,211)">
```

Table 11.1 alphabetically lists the currently proposed core functions for XSLFO, each with its type and a brief description.

Table 11.1   XSLFO Core Functions

FUNCTION	TYPE	DESCRIPTION
`abs(numeric)`	Numeric	Returns the absolute value of the argument
`body-start()`	Numeric	Returns a calculated body start value for lists
`ceiling(numeric)`	Numeric	Returns the smallest integer that is not less than the argument
`floor(numeric)`	Numeric	Returns the highest integer that is not greater than the argument
`from-parent(NCName)`	Object	Returns a computed property value from a parent
`from-nearest-specified-value(NCName?)`	Object	Returns a computed property value from the nearest ancestor
`from-table-column (NCName?)`	Object	Returns a computed property value from a matching table column
`icc-color(numeric, numeric, numeric,NCName, numeric,numeric)`	Color	Returns a color from an ICC profile.
`inherited-property-value (NCName)`	Object	Returns a computed property value inherited from a parent or ancestor
`label-end()`	Numeric	Returns a calculated label end value for lists
`max(numeric,numeric)`	Numeric	Returns the maximum of two arguments of the same unit power
`merge-property-values (NCName?)`	Object	Returns a value that matches one in the last `m-property-set`
`min(numeric,numeric)`	Numeric	Returns the minimum of two arguments of the same unit power
`proportional-column-width(numeric)`	Numeric	Returns a column width in units based on the argument
`rgb(numeric,numeric, numeric)`	Color	Returns an RGB color

continues

Table 11.1   XSLFO Core Functions (*Continued*)

FUNCTION	TYPE	DESCRIPTION
`round (numeric)`	Numeric	Returns an integer value closest to the argument
`system-color(NCName)`	Color	Returns a system color
`system-font(NCName, NCName?)`	Font	Returns a characteristic of a system font

Last Words

The XSLFO recommendation is not complete or approved, but it surely will be before too long. I have attempted to give you a tour of the language, with examples emphasizing what works right now (at least in FOP). In the future, it is likely that all this XSLFO syntax will be hidden from the eyes of the user by an attractive interface. For those of us too impatient to wait for the future to arrive, it's sensible to have a good look anyway, even though the vehicle is still on the assembly line.

There's one chapter left, if you can hang on for a few more pages. The next, and final, chapter caps off the book with a technology and terminology review of XSL.

XSL Technology Review

This book has introduced you to XSL, but my main goal has been to teach you how to use it. If you have read the entire book and tried out the examples for yourself, congratulations: You probably have a pretty good handle on the language. You know by now how to transform an XML document with XSLT into text, HTML, XML, or XHTML, and you also know how to format an XML document for presentation or print with XSLFO.

This final chapter is a brief reexamination of XSL, its features and terminology (in **bold**). If you feel that you're already an expert in XSL, you may be ready to close the covers of this book now. But maybe in the future, when you feel that you need a quick language refresher, I suggest you return to this chapter for a brisk review.

The Seven Nodes Types

When an XSLT processor looks at an XML **source tree** or document, it does so with the help of an XML parser. The parser, usually with either a DOM or SAX engine, sorts through this source tree to find up to seven kinds of **nodes**. These nodes are defined by the XPath data model, and they consist of the **root node**, **element nodes** (including a root or document element),

attribute nodes, text nodes, namespace nodes, comment nodes, and processing-instruction nodes.

A View of the Tree

One way that you can look at the nodes of a document is a US-ASCII tree
view stylesheet that is available at http://skew.org/xml/stylesheets/
ascii-treeview/ascii-treeview.xsl. When this stylesheet, developed by Jeni
Tennison and Mike Brown, is applied to order.xml:

```
<?xml version="1.0" encoding="utf-8" ?>

<Order partner="06-853-2535">
 <Date>2001-06-01</Date>
 <Item type="ISBN">0471416207</Item>
 <Quantity>40</Quantity>
 <Comments>First order this month.</Comments>
 <ShippingMethod class="4th">USPS</ShippingMethod>
</Order>
```

such as by the command line:

```
saxon order.xml http://skew.org/xml/stylesheets/ascii-treeview/ascii-
    treeview.xsl
```

it produces the following output:

```
root
   |___element 'Order'
         |  \___attribute 'partner' = '06-853-2535'
         |___text '\n '
         |___element 'Date'
         |     |___text '2001-06-01'
         |___text '\n '
         |___element 'Item'
         |     |  \___attribute 'type' = 'ISBN'
         |     |___text '0471404012'
         |___text '\n '
         |___element 'Quantity'
         |     |___text '40'
         |___text '\n '
         |___element 'Comments'
         |     |___text 'None.'
         |___text '\n '
         |___element 'ShippingMethod'
         |     |  \___attribute 'class' = '4th'
         |     |___text 'USPS'
         |___text '\n'
```

The stylesheet identifies in its **result tree** every node in the source tree. This simple output can help you see the relationships and presence of nodes that may be invisible at first glance. For example, this output shows you that the root node has only one child, the root element `Order`. `Order` has five element node children and six text node children. These text children, all whitespace, are not immediately apparent when looking at the document, but the `ascii-treeview.xsl` stylesheet digs them out. The contents of the five sibling elements are all text nodes in XSLT. An XML parser, if validating the same document against a DTD (`order.dtd`), would see this text as `#PCDATA`.

The elements `Order`, `Item`, and `ShippingMethod` each have an associated attribute node. Attributes, again, are not children of element nodes, but are only associated with them. (The same is true of namespace nodes.) This is most likely because attributes and namespaces are thought to be properties or characteristics of an element node and so have a unique relationship to them. In addition, attribute values are not text node children of attributes, only associated values. Though attributes are not children of their coupled elements, these elements are parents to the attributes (always single parents, by the way).

The Tree Data Model

The XPath data model is based on the tree data model that comes to us from computer science (see a representation of the traditional tree model in Figure 12.1). In this tree model, data are represented as nodes on a tree, with each node connected to another.

In Figure 12.1, each circle represents a node. These nodes are all interconnected, and you can follow paths along the edges (the lines connecting the nodes), tree walking or ascending and descending the tree. The first or top node is known as the **root** (A), and terminal nodes (D, E, G, H, I, and J), which do not have children, are known as **leaves**. In the traditional tree model, all nodes have some sort of **parent-child**, **sibling**, or **ancestor-descendant** relationship with other nodes.

For example, there is a parent-child relationship between parent C and children E, F, and G. (The tree data model calls any node with one or more children an **interior node**.) A sibling relationship exists between D, E, F, and G, as well as H, I, and J. Children are also considered descendants of their parents, and parents are considered ancestors. J is called a **proper descendant** of C because it is removed by more than one node or generation. Likewise, C is a proper ancestor of J for the same reason.

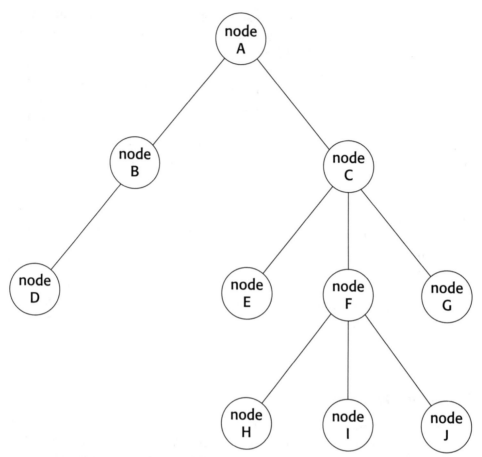

Figure 12.1 The tree data model.

Processing Stylesheets

With the source tree parsed, each node in the XML document can be handled, extracted, or set aside depending on what the XSLT stylesheet contains. Stylesheets can be independent documents or even included in the XML source document itself (as **literal result element stylesheets**). You can also **include** one or more stylesheets in the current stylesheet, which has the effect of merging the stylesheets on the XML tree level. Importing a stylesheet gives each **imported stylesheet**, and the templates it contains, an ordered **import precedence**, starting with the importing stylesheet and then moving through succeeding stylesheets, with the last stylesheet imported having the highest import precedence.

Templates

The root element of a stylesheet is either `stylesheet` or `transform`. Stylesheets contain **top-level elements**, such as `import` and `template`, and **instruction elements** such as `apply-templates` and `value-of`. Some elements work as both top-level and instruction elements (`variable`, for example), depending on how they are used. Instruction elements are always contained within templates. A **template** may simply be a `template` element, but other elements may contain additional templates, such as `copy` and `for-each`. Any element that contains a template must be contained in a `template` element itself. Instructions in templates are called **template rules**. As a template rule is being processed, it is considered the **current template rule**.

Most likely, a stylesheet contains one or more templates. Each of these templates specifies a **pattern** (patterns are subsets of expressions), which should match one or more nodes in the source tree. It selects nodes by using either abbreviated or unabbreviated **location paths**. The **abbreviated path** uses location paths such as `Order` or `@orderID`; the **unabbreviated path** includes **axes specifiers** like `child::Order` and `attribute::orderID`.

As the XSLT processor processes the stylesheet, when it finds a matching node, it returns that node and its children as an unordered **node-set** or **current node-list** to the processor. Then, depending on the template, the processor processes that node and all its children. In absence of a template that matches any nodes in the source document, the XSLT processor has **built-in templates** that will process all the nodes in the tree by default, in spite of the stylesheet's lack of a matching pattern. Templates that match identical nodes may be prioritized with the `template` element's `priority` attribute—the higher the number, the higher the priority.

The `template` element may also be a **named template**. When a `template` element has a `name` attribute, a `call-template` element instance can call that template by name. In addition, templates may have a **mode**. When this `mode` attribute matches a `mode` attribute on an `apply-templates` instruction, a node may be processed more than once, each time in a different mode and with a different result.

As each node is being processed, it takes on the role of **current node** or **context node**. The current node is a member of the **current node-list**. Each node in a list or set has its own **context position** within the list. The list also has a **context size**, with the last node's position representing also the size of the context or list.

Expressions and Patterns

When a template contains an `apply-templates` instruction, for example, its `select` attribute can contain an **expression**, which may refine its selection of a node, perform arithmetic, call a function, and more.

Expressions differ from patterns. A **pattern**, which is a subset of an expression, may match nodes, use `child` and `attribute` XPath axes, use the union operator (|), and use predicates or filters (using []). Expressions may use all XPath axes, arithmetic, variables, predicates, and functions.

An expression can return one of **four basic types**: (1) a node-set; (2) a string; (3) a number; or (4) a Boolean. If defined in a variable, an expression can also return an additional type known as a **result tree fragment**. A result tree fragment can contain text and even markup characters, which normally require special handling.

Expressions may call XPath **functions**, such as functions returning numbers like `sum()` and `round()`, or Boolean functions like `boolean()`, `true()`, and `false()`. Node-set functions, of course, work on node-sets—`position()` and `last()` are a few. String functions include `substring()` and `string-length()`, to name a couple. XSLT functions like `document()` and `generate-id()` extend the set of XPath functions. In addition, **keys** may be defined with the `key` element and `key()` function working together to create a special method for identifying, selecting, and cross-referencing nodes.

Node-sets are generally **unordered**, but in some circumstances, the **document order** of the nodes is taken into consideration. For example, when you use the `select` attribute with `apply-templates`, an expression in `select` must evaluate to a node-set and the nodes in such a set are evaluated in document order. Document order refers to the order of start-tags in the source document. In addition, you can **sort** elements with a **sort key** using the `sort` element and output **formatted numbers** with the `number` element, together with the `decimal-format` element and the `format-number()` function.

When you select a node-set with the `value-of` instruction, it returns the string value of the text child of the first node in the current node list. The `for-each` instruction, on the other hand, processes every node, in document order, in the current list with a template.

The `if` and `choose` elements (with `choose`'s children when and `otherwise`) select a node based on **conditional processing**, that is, whether the `test` attribute (which contains an expression) returns true. **Logical operators** such as and and or are useful in selecting on multiple criteria.

Variables and Parameters

XSLT also lets you define **variables**, either at the top level or in templates, and then reference them later in the stylesheet. This is done with the `variable` instruction. **Parameters** may also be defined with `param`. Parameters allow you to pass in values at runtime, such as from the command line. You can also pass parameters between templates using the `with-param` element. Variables, once set, are pretty much constant values—you can't change them dynamically. XSLT processors, however, will allow you to redefine variables when processing nodes in a list. Variables may be defined as any of the allowed types, namely, node-sets, strings, numbers, Booleans, or result tree fragments.

Working with Namespaces

As stated earlier, XPath makes provision for **namespace** nodes that are associated with element nodes. A namespace may be associated with an element by declaring it with `xmlns`. A **prefix** may be associated with a namespace. When a prefix is attached to a **local part** or element or attribute **local name** (also called an **NCName** or non-colonized name), the combined name is called a **QName**. When QNames internally become **expanded names**, the prefix is replaced with the full **namespace URI**. The `namespace-alias` element lets you use a temporary namespace and prefix in a stylesheet that will be replaced with another namespace and prefix in the result tree. You can declare extension element prefixes or exclude prefixes from a result tree with attributes of the `stylesheet` or `transform` element.

Extensions

XSLT provides a mechanism for using **extension elements** and **functions**. You can define and add you own namespace for qualifying extended element and function names and then bind those extensions with your own code, or you can simple use extensions provided with a processor, such as Saxon or Xalan. The `fallback` element can provide an escape hatch if your processor does not recognize an extension in your stylesheet. In such a case, it is good practice to use the `message` element to write an error or distress **message** to standard output and to use `message`'s `terminate` attribute with a value of `yes`.

The Result Tree

The output element helps you determine the form and shape of your **result tree**, whether it contains XML, XHTML, HTML, or plain text, including particulars like **encoding**, **document type declarations**, even media or **content types**. Further, templates create output that is written to result trees. You can use **literal result elements** and other literal text, including **attribute value templates**, which use braces ({ }) to derive attribute values from an expression.

You can use instructions that are intended to create specific output, such as the element and attribute instructions. You can create reusable sets of attributes with attribute-set, as well as comments with comment, and processing instructions with the processing-instruction instruction. You may output text with the text element and even output literal characters, normally forbidden, by **disabling output escaping** with the disable-output-escaping attribute.

You can **copy nodes** to the result tree, too. The copy instruction copies a current node along with any namespace nodes attached to it, but it does not copy attributes or child nodes. The copy-of instruction, however, copies child nodes, attributes, namespace nodes, the works. This element may also be used to insert result tree fragments' variable values into a result tree.

Whitespace Handling

You can control how **whitespace characters**—spaces, tabs, linefeeds, and carriage returns—are handled in the output in a number of ways. The strip-space and preserve-space elements can eliminate or preserve whitespace-only text nodes in specified elements. The indent attribute on the output element can, depending on the processor, indent elements in the result tree. The normalize-space() function collapses whitespace in selected text node children. You can also add whitespace with the format attribute of the number instruction. As a last resort, adding xml:space="preserve" to literal result elements or with the attribute element will preserve whitespace in output.

Formatting

XSLFO, XSLT's companion specification, provides **formatting objects** and **formatting properties** to prepare XML documents for presentation.

XSLFO has an **area model** that allows a formatter to output text and other objects precisely on a page. The area model defines **regions** containing **content rectangles** (and other rectangles) that can hold body text, headings, paragraphs, tables, lists, headers, footers, graphics—whatever you can imagine being printed on a page—in a variety of languages. Language support includes directionality constraints and, by virtue of XML, thousands of Unicode characters that can represent the languages of the world.

Each document is laid out using mandatory **page masters**. These page masters determine what goes into **page sequences**. Page sequences contain text flows that hold formatting objects. Formatting objects, such as the objects `block` or `inline`, provide containers for creating and writing text and other objects to areas. A formatting object can have formatting properties, such as properties for fonts, margins, page breaks, and so forth. All properties can contain expressions in their values, just as `select` attributes in XSLT elements; XSLFO also has its own set of functions, such as `min()`, `system-color()`, and `from-parent()`, that may be used in expressions.

When created on the document level, formatting objects are first XML elements and formatting properties are XML attributes. As the document moves from a markup stage to a formatting stage, the elements and attributes are considered objects and properties. Further, properties are refined into traits before they finally output to an electronic representation of the page.

At the beginning stages, documents formatted with XSLFO may be transformed using XSLT. XSLFO processors or formatters, such as Apache's FOP (http://xml.apache.org/fop/), allow you a variety of output options, such as PDF, Java AWT, and Adobe FrameMaker MIF. Browser support is slow in coming, but it will no doubt be in place in due time.

Though complex (and not yet recommended fully by W3C), XSLFO is an extremely powerful and versatile language for expressing formatted documents in nearly all of the world's languages.

A Look Ahead

The XSL Working Group (WG) at W3C has published several documents relative to future releases of XSLT and XPath. The WG published a list of requirements for XSLT 1.1 (www.w3.org/tr/xslt11req) in August 2000, and a working draft of 1.1 in December 2000 (www.w3.org/tr/xslt11/).

The latest word is that work on 1.1 is on hold and that the focus of the WG is now on XSLT 2.0 (www.w3.org/tr/xslt20req) and XPath 2.0

(www.w3.org/tr/xpath20req), though we could assume that the work proposed for version 1.1 will find its way into 2.0. Another believable report is that it will be quite some time before 2.0 is available. Nonetheless, I think it is worthwhile to anticipate what's ahead for XSLT and XPath, even if completion is a year or two out.

> **NOTE** By the way, the current version of Saxon (6.3 at the moment) has implemented some 1.1 functionality. See http://users.iclway.co.uk/mhkay/saxon/ for details.

Some interesting requirements proposed for 1.1 include requirements for portable extension functions, multiple output documents, and result tree fragment operations.

Extension functions. New extension functions will be required to work like built-in or native XSLT functions, and they must provide Java and ECMAScript bindings, though support for other languages must be possible, too (Section 3 of the 1.1 requirements document).

Multiple outputs. Currently, an XSLT stylesheet can have only one output stream. Under 1.1 (and beyond), you should be able to send output to more than one URI (Section 4 of the 1.1 requirements document).

Result tree fragments. XSLT 1.0 supports only a subset of node-set operations on result tree fragments (for example, use of the operators /, //, and [] is forbidden). To compensate for this, a number of XSLT processors have provided a `node-set` extension function that can convert result tree fragments to node-sets, so all node-set operations are permitted. In the future, it is proposed that result tree fragments be treated just the same as node-sets (Section 5 of the 1.1 requirements document).

Proposed requirements for XSLT and XPath version 2.0 include those that must be implemented, those that should be implemented, and those that could be implemented. I highlight here a few proposed items of interest:

Null (Nil) values. As XSLT 2.0 must support other XML standards (1 in XSLT 2.0 requirements), XSLT 2.0 must be able to match elements and attributes with null (nil) content or values. I mention nil because XML Schema now uses the term *nil* rather than null in its handling of null (nil) values (1.2 of XSLT 2.0 requirements).

XHTML. It is possible that 2.0 will add `xhtml` to its output methods. Currently, output methods are `xml`, `html`, and `text` (1.8 of XSLT 2.0 requirements).

Unparsed text. Under 2.0, you should be able to insert unparsed text, such as a Java source file, in XSLT output (2.5 of XSLT 2.0 requirements).

Casting a datatype to type node-set. Currently, you can't coerce, cast, or convert data of another type into type node-set. Version 2.0 may permit you to do this (2.18 of XSLT 2.0 requirements).

Scientific notation. Under 2.0, it is proposed that `format-number()` will be able to output numbers in scientific notation (3.3 of XSLT 2.0 requirements).

Grouping. XSLT 1.0 does not directly support grouping. Grouping refers to the ability to arrange elements into groups, such as grouping by content or grouping by node position. Some good solutions for grouping are available now—such as those offered by Jeni Tennison at www.jenitennison.com/xslt/grouping/index.html—but version 2.0 of XSLT plans to offer simplified grouping based on string values, names, or other expressions. The requirements document provides 13 potential use cases (see 4 in XSLT 2.0 requirements).

Added functions. XPath 2.0 will probably add `min()` and `max()` functions (like those available from XSLFO), plus intersection and difference functions. An intersect function would likely retrieve members that belong to two or more sets, and a difference function would produce members that are in one set but not in another (1.4 and 1.6 of XPath 2.0 requirements). Other function changes will most likely include enhancements to `translate()` (2.4.1 of XPath 2.0 requirements) and the addition of a string padding function (2.4.2 of XPath 2.0 requirements).

Regular expression syntax. XPath 2.0 is on a mission to support regular expressions (see 3 in XPath 2.0 requirements). Regular expressions provide a powerful and precise way to describe exact or variable strings patterns. For example, a regular expression that matches a DUNS number could be defined as `\d{2}-\d{3}-\d{4}`, that is, a pattern matching any two digits followed by a hyphen and any three digits followed by a hyphen and then any four digits.

XML schema support. XPath 2.0 intends to support XML Schema's primitive datatypes, such as `int`, `float`, and `double`, as well as its own basic datatypes string, number, Boolean, and node-set. (See Section 4 of the XPath 2.0 requirements document.) Also, support for XML Schema structures, such as derivation by restriction and extension (see 5 in XPath 2.0 requirements), is planned. This derivation scheme lets you derive new types by restricting an existing type (such as a complex type containing a number of elements and attributes) by removing elements or attributes from consideration and also by extending or adding to types by adding elements or attributes to an existing type.

Those aren't all the potential additions to XSLT and XPath planned for 2.0, but they are among the more interesting and important ones.

On the Shoulders of Giants

XML and XSL are exciting technologies that are well suited for document storage, transformation, and formatting. They were built on the earlier successes (and failures) of SGML, HTML, and DSSSL, but they have refined and improved on their predecessors. Originally designed with documents in mind, these tools are also sensible solutions for the exchange of data between incompatible systems.

Neither approach—be it processing documents or data—would be so compelling if it were not for the success of the Web, which only a decade ago opened up a new universe of communication, collaboration, and commerce to the world. It isn't the technology alone that is significant, though, but the people who invented and developed the technology that have made a difference in the way our online world turns today, people such as James Clark and Michael Kay. XML and XSL are supported on the shoulders of these giants, and they will be with us for years to come.

Index

Page references followed by italic *t* indicate material in tables.

CUSTOMER NOTE: IF THIS BOOK IS ACCOMPANIED BY SOFTWARE, PLEASE READ THE FOLLOWING BEFORE OPENING THE PACKAGE.

This software contains files to help you utilize the models described in the accompanying book. By opening the package, you are agreeing to be bound by the following agreement:

This software product is protected by copyright and all rights are reserved by the author, John Wiley & Sons, Inc., or their licensors. You are licensed to use this software as described in the software and the accompanying book. Copying the software for any other purpose may be a violation of the U.S. Copyright Law.

This software product is sold as is without warranty of any kind, either express or implied, including but not limited to the implied warranty of merchantability and fitness for a particular purpose. Neither Wiley nor its dealers or distributors assumes any liability for any alleged or actual damages arising from the use of or the inability to use this software. (Some states do not allow the exclusion of implied warranties, so the exclusion may not apply to you.)

To use this CD-ROM, your system must meet the following requirements:

IBM-compatible with Pentium I or greater processor running Windows 98/Me/2000.

128 Mb of RAM or greater recommended.

At least 25 Mb of hard disk space.